Operating Law in a Global Context

Operating Law in a Global Context

Comparing, Combining and Prioritising

Jean-Sylvestre Bergé

Professor, University of Lyon, Fellow of the University Institute of France, France

Geneviève Helleringer

Professor, ESSEC Business School and Fellow of the Institute of European and Comparative Law, Oxford, UK

Edward Elgar PUBLISHING

Cheltenham, UK • Northampton, MA, USA

Published by
Edward Elgar Publishing Limited
The Lypiatts
15 Lansdown Road
Cheltenham
Glos GL50 2JA
UK

Edward Elgar Publishing, Inc.
William Pratt House
9 Dewey Court
Northampton
Massachusetts 01060
USA

A catalogue record for this book
is available from the British Library

Library of Congress Control Number: 2016962574

This book is available electronically in the **Elgar**online
Law subject collection
DOI 10.4337/9781785367335

FSC www.fsc.org MIX Paper from responsible sources FSC® C013056

ISBN 978 1 78536 732 8 (cased)
ISBN 978 1 78536 733 5 (eBook)

Typeset by Columns Design XML Ltd, Reading
Printed and bound in Great Britain by TJ International Ltd, Padstow

Contents

Preface

Lawyers have to adapt their reasoning to the increasingly global nature of the situations with which they deal. Often, rules formulated in a national, international or European environment have all to be jointly applied to a given case. In a single situation, several laws must be mobilised, alternatively, cumulatively, at the same time or at different moments, in or on one or several spaces or levels, by one or by multiple actors. The book seeks to make explicit the analysis the lawyer engages in every time he is confronted by the operation of several laws in different contexts.

The subject matter of the book is not the definition or description of a so-called 'global law'. The book focuses on the needs of a global lawyer who is required to reach conclusions in a pluralistic context. It makes explicit the required global reasoning. Readers are presented with concrete cases involving more than one legal rule and different levels as well as a *modus operandi* that the authors found to be invariant in global contexts. Legal reasoning in a global context has to be organised according to a basic three-step approach, consisting of the comparison (Part I), then the combination (Part II) and, finally, the ordering or 'prioritisation' (Part III) of the methods and solutions of national, international and European law to be used to solve the case. The book conveys in detail how the law is operated through a wide range of situations and concrete examples cutting across domains, including criminal law, contract law, fundamental rights, internal market, international trade, procedure.

The book is aimed at an international audience. Illustrations of how lawyers have to combine different contexts are taken in various domestic case law including the UK, Germany, Belgium, Italy, Spain, the US, as well as France. The book is adapted from an analytical framework that was developed in a book written in French by Jean-Sylvestre Bergé, *L'application du droit national, international et européen*, Paris: Dalloz, Méthodes du droit, 2013.

Academic lawyers as well as practitioners often realise that some cases trigger uncertainty as to the applicable legal reasoning. For example, in cases presented before an international court, lawyers may wonder whether the effects produced by a law applied at a national or European level may be considered. In a European context, lawyers need to be able to determine precisely whether the methods and solutions that have been developed over the last 60 years substitute or add to the legal constructions defined at other levels which came before: national or international.

The difficulty facing lawyers increases even more when a case might fall to be decided under a series of different legal environments. Thus, a case presented before a national judge can sometimes give rise to proceedings before a European court, for example, a preliminary ruling on the interpretation or validity of EU law brought before the Court of Justice of the European Union or an application made to the European Court of Human Rights after the exhaustion of all national remedies. More rarely, a national conflict may become an interstate conflict brought before the International Court of Justice. In the same way, a situation addressed by a public or private international court may have consequences for European and/or national courts (for example, a sanction announced by the United Nations and executed at a European and national level or an international arbitral award presented to a national judge who decides to apply European Union law and to consult, in that capacity, the Court of Justice of the European Union).

Lawyers may therefore be worried that in spite of all their efforts to put into operation the legal methods and solutions applied in a given context, their analysis could be challenged on the occasion of the re-examination of the case in another national, international or European context. To prevent a new examination from entirely escaping, or weakening, their expertise, what can lawyers (including students training to practise in a global environment) do? Should they open themselves up to other legal environments beyond the one in which they are used to? Or should they revert to the one context that they know best and will therefore provide for a solution with a maximum degree of foreseeability? The book provides a method for tackling these questions.

Abbreviations

AFSJ	Area of Freedom, Security and Justice
Art.	Article or Articles (according to the context)
BIICL	British Institute of International and Comparative Law
Cciv.	Code civil (French Civil Code)
CFI	Court of First Instance of the European Communities, replaced by the General Court of the European Union on 1st December 2009
CFREU	Charter of Fundamental Rights of the European Union
CJCE / CJEU	Court of Justice of the European Communities, replaced by the Court of Justice of the European Union on 1st December 2009.
COE	Council of Europe
CPC	Code de procédure civile (French Code of Civil Procedure)
CPP	Code de procédure pénale (French Code of Criminal Procedure)
Coll.	Collection
Comp.	Compare
Conseil constitutionnel	French Constitutional Council
Conseil d'Etat	French Supreme Court in administrative and public law
Cour de cassation	French Supreme Court in civil, commercial and criminal matters
DDHC	Déclaration des droits de l'homme et du citoyen (French Declaration of the Rights of Man and of the Citizen)
DSB	Dispute Settlement Body (WTO)

EC	European Community, or European Communities (according to context)
ECHR	European Convention for the Protection of Human Rights and Fundamental Freedoms
ECtHR	European Court of Human Rights
EEC	European Economic Community
ERC	European Research Council
EU	European Union
Ed.	Editions or Editor (according to context)
f.	following
GMO	Genetically Modified Organisms
HRW	Human Rights Watch
IACHR	Inter-American Court of Human Rights
ICC	International Criminal Court
ICComm	International Chamber of Commerce
ICCPR	International Covenant on Civil and Political Rights
ICJ	International Court of Justice
ICSID	International Centre for Settlement of Investment Disputes
ICTY	International Criminal Tribunal for the former Yugoslavia
ILO	International Labour Organization
NGO	Non-governmental Organisation
OHIM	Office for Harmonization in the Internal Market
PCA	Permanent Court of Arbitration
PCIJ	Permanent Court of International Justice
Req.	Requête
Rev.	Review or Revue (according to context)
TCFDIP	Travaux du comité français de droit international privé
TEU	Treaty on European Union
TFEU	Treaty on the Functioning of the European Union
TRIPS	Agreement on Trade-Related Aspects of Intellectual Property Rights
Trans.	Translation

UN	United Nations
UNCITL	United Nations Commission on International Trade Law
UNESCO	United Nations Educational, Scientific and Cultural Organization
V°	Verbo
WHO	World Health Organization
WIPO	World Intellectual Property Organization
WTO	World Trade Organization

Table of cases

EUROPEAN COURT OF HUMAN RIGHTS

EUROPEAN UNION

FRANCE

GERMANY

INTERNATIONAL

UNITED KINGDOM

UNITED STATES

Table of legislation

EUROPEAN UNION

FRANCE

GERMANY

INTERNATIONAL

ITALY

UNITED KINGDOM

UNITED STATES

1. Introduction

Imagine a dispute between two German citizens, living in Germany, over an accident that happened in Berlin. The facts call for a given analysis under traditional German law. Should however the analysis be amended in order to take into account legal methods and solutions applied in other contexts, namely the European or even perhaps the international contexts? Imagine a case presented before an international court, be it public (an administration or an international judge) or private (an international arbitrator): should the way a given rule has been applied by national or European courts be taken into account? Imagine a dispute in front of a European Court, the European Court of Justice or the European Court of Human Rights: do the methods and solutions that have been developed over the last 60 years replace or supplement the older legal constructions defined at national or international level?

The domestic, European and international contexts create a complex legal game: far from coexisting in isolation, like Leibnizian monads, rules and legal culture characteristic of each level, intersect, rub against and influence one another. As a consequence, lawyers have to adapt their reasoning to the increasingly global nature of the situations with which they deal. They are confronted more and more frequently by a globalised context such that rules formulated in a national,[1] international,[2] or European[3] environment may all have to be applied to a given case. In any given situation, the laws of several different jurisdictions sometimes come into play, either alternatively or cumulatively, at the same time or at different moments, in or on one or several spaces or levels, by one or by multiple actors. Thus, for example, a case presented before a national judge can sometimes give rise to proceedings before a European court (such as a preliminary ruling on the interpretation or validity of European

[1] Domestic or foreign.

[2] United Nations, World Trade Organization, International Labour Organization, World Health or Intellectual Property Organization, European Union, International Court of Justice, Permanent Court of Arbitration, International Centre for the Settlement of Investment Disputes, the European Court of Human Rights, etc.

[3] EU, ECHR.

Union law brought before the Court of Justice of the European Union or an application made to the European Court of Human Rights after the exhaustion of all national remedies) or, more rarely, an international court (for example, a national conflict that has become an interstate conflict brought before the International Court of Justice). In the same manner, a situation addressed by a public or private international court may have consequences for European and/or national courts (for example, a sanction announced by the United Nations and executed at European and national level or an international arbitration sentence presented to a national judge who decides to apply European Union law and to consult, in that capacity, the Court of Justice of the European Union).

This book seeks to make explicit the analysis lawyers engage in every time they are confronted by the operation of several laws in the following different contexts: national, international or European. It clarifies and classifies the main global occurrences. It provides thereby an intellectual road map to operate law in a global context. It also provides a vade mecum for practising lawyers, who nowadays find themselves advising in what is almost inevitably a multi-jurisdictional context. They may legitimately wonder whether they should adapt their approach to legal environments other than the one in which they principally operate, or whether they should instead adhere strictly to the approach adopted by their home jurisdiction, with which they are most familiar.

The subject matter of the present book is not the definition or description of a so-called 'global' law.[4] The book focuses on the needs of lawyers who need to reach a conclusion in a context that can be described as 'global'[5] in the sense that it is no longer characterised by the Westphalian order in which each nation state has sovereignty over its domestic affairs to the exclusion of all external power or interference.[6] The worldwide movement toward economic, financial, trade and communication integration also influences the way in which the law is

---

[4] For such an endeavour, see John J. Kirton and Jelena Madunic (eds), *Global Law* (Farnham: Ashgate, 2009); Mireille Delmas-Marty, *Global Law: A Triple Challenge*, trans. N. Norbert (Transnational Publishers, 2003).

[5] R.H. Jackson and P. Owens, 'The Evolution of World Society', in John Baylis and Steve Smith (eds), *The Globalization of World Politics: An Introduction to International Relations* (Oxford University Press, 2005), p. 53.

[6] Leo Gross, 'The Peace of Westphalia' (1948) 42(1) *The American Journal of International Law* 20–41.

operated. It has impacted the sources of law:[7] some autonomous transnational law such as the *lex mercatoria*, international and regional treaties have developed; rules and terms promulgated by international organisations are being increasingly incorporated into agreements.[8] In addition to the development of these sources of transnational law, a judicial and legislative cross-influence can also be observed.[9] Parallelism can even develop in an unconscious manner.[10] The globalised context has meanwhile also heightened the perception of remaining differences.[11] Because of these changes derived from the globalisation of the context, legal reasoning has to adapt and to become global as well. Lawyers are expected to take into account more than one legal rule and different levels of geographic integration. This book brings to light the core elements of such a global legal reasoning and stresses its invariant *modus operandi*: comparing, combining and prioritising.

OPERATING THE LAW IN THE NATIONAL, EUROPEAN AND INTERNATIONAL CONTEXT

Conceived by Santi Romano[12] as an instrument for defining legal orders, legal pluralism has been extensively studied by the disciplines of legal theory and sociology or anthropology of law.[13] It allows us to describe

---

7 About the conceptualisation of these developments (globalisation, fragmentation, transnationalisation), see below p. 6 and notes.

8 On these developments, see, Roy Goode, Herbert Kronke and Ewan McKendrick, *Transnational Commercial Law, Text, Cases and Materials* (Oxford University Press, 2007), pp. 25 *et seq.*

9 For instance, the doctrine of state immunity used to give absolute immunity but has progressively not been applied for commercial transactions in which states are involved and has been narrowed to the acts of states in the exercise of their sovereign power.

10 Restatements of contract law have demonstrated that there is high degree of similarity in solutions even if the technicalities are different.

11 For these various traits in the US context, see for instance Jeremy Waldron, *'Partly Laws Common to All Mankind': Foreign Law in American Courts* (New Haven: Yale University Press, 2012).

12 Santi Romano, *L'ordinamento giuridico* (Sansoni, 1946); S. Romano, *L'ordre juridique*, trans. P. Gothot and L. François (Dalloz, 2002). For a commentary of this work, see, J.-S. Bergé and Santi Romano, *Les ordres juridiques* (Dalloz, 2015).

13 For a holistic approach, see in English, John Griffiths, 'What is Legal Pluralism?' (1986) 24 *Journal of Legal Pluralism and Unofficial Law* 1; S. Engle Merry, 'Legal Pluralism' (1988) 22(5) *Law & Society Review* 869; B.Z.

'the existence, in a given society, of different legal mechanisms applying to identical situations'.[14] Lawyers happily refer to it when they study, on the one hand, the different ways in which the law is liable to develop outside the state processes of deliberation or decision and, on the other hand, the diverse modes of interaction that result from the coexistence of a plurality of legal systems or legal orders.

In a globalised environment, legal pluralism has its own particular meaning. The expression 'global legal pluralism'[15] refers to a particular form of legal pluralism brought about by the phenomenon of the globalisation of law and its different forms (globalisation,[16] transnationalisation,[17]

Tamanaha, 'A Non-Essentialist Version of Legal Pluralism' (2000) 27(2) *Journal of Law & Society* 296; R. Macdonald and M.-M. Kleinhans, 'What is a Critical Legal Pluralism?' (1997) 12(2) *Canadian Jounal of Law & Society* 25. See, in French, with the numerous bibliographic references cited, A.-J. Arnaud (ed.), *Dictionnaire encyclopédique de théorie et sociologie du droit* (2nd edn, LGDJ, 1993), *Verbis* 'Pluralisme juridique' by J.-G. Belley and N. Rouland. Compare, D. Alland and S. Rials (eds.), *Dictionnaire de la culture juridique* (PUF, 2003), V° 'Pluralisme juridique' by H. Moutouh.

14 J. Vanderlinden, 'Le pluralisme juridique – Essai de synthèse', in J. Gilissen (ed.), *Le pluralisme juridique* (Université de Bruxelles, 1972), p. 19. Compare from the same author: *Les pluralismes juridiques* (Bruylant, 2013).

15 The expression 'global legal pluralism' has regularly been used since the end of the 1990s by one author: F. Snyder, 'Governing Economic Globalisation Global Legal Pluralism and European Law' (1999) *European Law Review* 334. It has had great success, especially in legal literature in English. See, for example: O. Perez, *Ecological Sensivity and Global Legal Pluralism: Rethinking the Trade and Environment Conflict* (Hart, 2004); P.S. Berman, 'Global Legal Pluralism' (2007) 80 *Southern California Law Review* 1155; R. Michaels, 'Global Legal Pluralism' (2009) *Annual Review of Law & Social Science* 45; P.S. Berman, *Global Legal Pluralism. A Jurispudence of Law beyond* (Cambridge University Press, 2012).

16 Considerable literature has developed on this subject. For different approaches to the phenomenon in different legal disciplines: G. Teubner (ed.), *Global Law without a State* (Dartmouth: Aldershot, 1997); J. Basedow and T. Kono (eds), *Legal Aspects of Globalization* (Kluwer Law International, 2000); J.-B. Auby, *La globalisation, le droit et l'État* (2nd edn, Montchrestien, 2010); M. Faure and A. van de Walt, *Globalization and Private Law* (Edward Elgar, 2010); J.-Y. Chérot and B. Frydman (eds), *La science du droit dans la globalisation* (Bruylant, 2012).

17 Works on the emergence of transnational law are historical. We will mention here two outstanding contemporary publications which reconsider the phenomenon in constitutional law and private law: Ch. Joerges, I.-J. Sand, and G. Teubner (eds), *Transnational Governance and Constitutionalism* (Hart, 2004);

fragmentation,[18] etc.). Although this pluralism has not escaped from forms of standardisation and domination, it describes the multiplication of the sites of the creation and the application of law, which appear outside or transcend the strict state model. Law is not only constructed within national spheres. It results from the particular activity of international and regional organisations, notably European, whether they have a state origin (United Nations, World Trade Organization, International Labour Organization, etc.) or even a private origin (non-governmental organisations such as the International Chamber of Commerce or Human Rights Watch for example, multinationals, professional associations, etc. that can provide for model contracts, recommendations and more generally 'soft law' that has an impact in practice). The national context, which also features forms of legal pluralism, has not disappeared. But it coexists with the legal methods and solutions developed in an international or European context. Most factual situations create a collision between norms stemming from these different levels.

There are ever more cases in which several laws drafted in a national, international or European environment must sometimes be mobilised, alternatively, cumulatively, at the same time or at different moments, in or on one or more spaces or levels, by one actor or by multiple actors. They require the operation of the law in a context of global legal pluralism. The legal rules applied develop, in a variety of global legal situations, their own trajectory. This dynamic cannot result from the mere operation of a method or a legal solution at a given moment, in a predetermined space and on a predetermined level, by a duly identified actor.

A PRACTICAL RATHER THAN A THEORETICAL APPROACH

When questioning how to apply relevant legal rules in the national, international and European context, lawyers may adopt a theoretical and

---

G.-P. Callies and P. Zumbansen, *Rough Consensus and Running Code – A Theory of Transnational Private Law* (Hart, 2012).

[18] This theme has met with great popularity. See, in particular, M. Young (ed.), *Regime Interaction in International Law – Facing Fragmentation* (Cambridge University Press, 2012); M. Forteau, J.-S. Bergé, M.-L. Niboyet and J.-M. Thouvenin (eds), *La fragmentation du droit applicable aux relations internationales – Regards croisés des internationalistes privatistes et publicistes* (Pedone, 2011).

abstract perspective to try to develop legal constructs that may allow them to face the difficulties raised by global legal pluralism.

Such analysis may rely on different methods, such as defining the law, identifying legal systems and their relationships, resolving conflicts of law and, finally, the quest for a global law. We will briefly present these different methods while explaining why none of them underpins the present work.

The first method – *defining the law* – is not the most apt for describing a process of applying the law. If we take the position of normative positivism, which proposes, in simple terms, to define law through law, one could even say that it is the worst method one could adopt. Defining the law by reference to 'norms' makes it impossible to consider the 'applied law' as a separate object of study. It amounts, effectively, to holding that the application of the law is inseparable from the definition of the law itself. As the father of this doctrine wrote:

> application of law is at the same time creation of law. These two concepts are not in absolute opposition to each other as assumed by traditional theory. It is not quite correct to distinguish between law-creating and law-applying acts. Because apart from the borderline cases – the presupposition of the basic norm and the execution of the coercive act – between which the legal process takes place, every legal act is at the same times the application of a higher norm and the creation of a lower norm.[19]

Naturally, other approaches to law exist.[20] But today, none of these have really emerged as making the application of law a truly distinct field of study from the operation of defining law. References to 'the application of law' are most frequently missing from those works (textbooks, handbooks or even treatises) that aim to define law. When it is mentioned, it is in relationship with the procedural, penal and, potentially, contractual tools that accompany the operation of the majority of legal rules. As for the study of case law that, in the civil law tradition, 'applies' the law, this has long been considered, explicitly or implicitly, as a primary source of interpretation, inseparable from the definition of the law itself. In the common law tradition, case law defines the legal rules.

---

[19] Hans Kelsen, *Pure Theory of Law* (1934–1960) (Translation from the Second (Revised and Enlarged) German Edition by Max Knight, University of California Press, Berkeley and Los Angeles, California, 1967).

[20] We refer the reader to general works presenting the main theories of law. See notably: J.W. Harris, *Legal Philosophies* (2nd edn, Oxford University Press, 2011); Dennis Patterson (ed.), *A Companion to Philosophy of Law and Legal Theory* (2nd edn, Wiley-Blackwell, 2010).

Returning to our subject matter, applied global legal pluralism, the approach of defining the law at best leads us to distinguish between those phenomena that participate in a legal process and those which are foreign to it. For example, when lawyers borrow a legal method or solution that is common in another legal system, sometimes at another level of application of law (national, international or European), this can give rise to discussions on the validity of this loan. But these discussions are often misleading: whatever lawyers conclude, more or less confidently, about the legal or non-legal character of the loan, they are no better acquainted, as we shall see, with its status in a dynamic approach to the application of law on a potentially global level.[21]

A second traditional approach relates to *identifying legal systems and the relationships between them.* Santi Romano first introduced this method[22] in a work considered to have given birth to the concept of legal pluralism. Let us recall briefly that the author's ambition was to 'bring into the legal order this fact of the social order which has generally been held to be the antecedent of law'.[23] He proposes a definition of legal order capable of rising above the mere state model. He proposes a criterion of 'relevance' capable of governing relations between two distinct legal orders.

A work on applied global legal pluralism could certainly not have been written if it were not for the legacy of Santi Romano. The existence of a plurality of legal systems and the difficulties arising from defining the relations between them are, in effect, pervasive in any research of this kind.

That said, it is not certain that reflections on the definition of 'legal order' will allow us today to overcome all the difficulties inherent in applying the law in a global context. That it is possible here and there to reconsider the relations between different legal systems through the notion of 'legal order' is one thing. To derive from this a general lesson on the relations between those systems in the triple national, international

---

21 On discussions of this type, notably on the subject of the place of national law in international and European law and on the extensive borrowing of solutions of international and European law in the national context, see *infra*, p. 71.

22 Romano, L'ordre juridique (n. 12). For an analysis of this work in a transnational perspective, see F. Fontanelli, 'Santi Romano and L'ordinemento giuridico: The Relevance of a Forgotten Masterpiece for Contemporary International Transnational and Global Legal Relations' (2011) 2 *Transnational Legal Theory* 67.

23 Note on the second edition, p. 30. Authors' translation.

and European context is another. The 'fact of social order' considered by Santi Romano in the first half of the twentieth century through the prism of the 'institution' that the author borrowed from Maurice Hauriou, no longer corresponds to our contemporary environment. The multiplication of public and private 'institutions' of a national, international and European dimension, the extraordinarily diverse ways in which these institutions interact with each other, and in which situations move from one to the other, etc., justifies the proposition that the starting point of a study whose object is to explain global legal pluralism should be different from that which was considered almost 100 years ago. The only stable anchor for this work is the description and explanation of the phenomenon, and this is preliminary to any *theoretical or abstract* approach.

The same justification can be given for our refusal to carry out this research under the title of any given monism, dualism or pluralism. The explanatory power of these traditional intellectual frameworks has been tempered.[24] An analysis of the relations between legal systems misses the essence of a pluralist approach to legal systems.[25] The variety of situations means that no interpretation – monist, dualist or even pluralist – of the relations between legal systems is to be favoured over the others. The situations we encounter cannot be immutably reduced to one or other of these algebraic figures. According to the context in which they have evolved, according to the result sought by lawyers, the approach can vary dramatically from one state to another. Rather than applying one or other of these theories, it is necessary to consider the factual situations with a fresh eye and to determine in what measure underlying mechanisms that we may not yet be fully aware of animate them.

The third method is that of *resolving conflicts of laws.* The expression 'conflicts of laws' refers, in a global approach, to cases of discrepencies between legal solutions of a national, international and European dimension. It may relate to laws (Italian law conflicting with international or European law, etc.) or rights defined in these different contexts (for

[24] See J. Crawford, 'Chance, Order, Change: The Course of International Law' (2013) 365 *Collected Courses of the Hague Academy of International Law* 260. See also D. Béchillon, *Hiérarchie des normes et hiérarchie des fonctions normatives de l'Etat* (Economica: Paris, 1996), p. 257; M. Virally, 'Sur un pont aux ânes: les rapports entre droit international et droits internes' in Mélanges Rolin (Pedone, 1964), p. 488.

[25] See on this point, the demonstration of D. Boden, 'Le pluralisme juridique en droit international privé' (2006) 49 *Arch. de Philo du droit* (*Le pluralisme*) 275.

example, a conflict between a right to industrial action enshrined in national law and a freedom of economic circulation or competition established by European or international law).

In an environment of applied global legal pluralism, the figure of conflict may seem ubiquitous. The application of law in a triple national, international and European context gives rise to all sorts of formal or material contradictions between the norms that lawyers may want to categorise (for example, by distinguishing true and false conflicts) in order to find solutions to every conflict. We know also that the figure of conflict serves as a real matrix for certain subjects or great legal questions: the law of 'conflict of conventions' in public international law, the rule of 'conflict of laws' in private international law or, the law of 'conflict of norms' in a broader systemic approach. Conflicts refers to the rules applied by a court of a particular national jurisdiction to determine which system of law it should apply in a given situation. It is thus a body of law in its own right.

Without seeking to minimise the importance of 'conflicts', the fact is that no 'general rule of conflict of norms' exists today that can be deployed in all situations. A rule of conflict of laws can be deployed in all situations of private international law or, a rule of conflict of conventions can be deployed in all situations of international public law. In an environment of global legal pluralism, lawyers do not have at their disposal a single tool for resolving conflicts between national, international and European laws. They are obliged to rank the different conflicts by distinguishing situations according to whether they relate to a national, international or even European legal environment. Each of these contexts offers, in effect, legal methods and solutions that can govern potentially conflicting applications of these different laws.

Faced with this situation, the temptation may be to decompartmentalise these legal specialisms 'top-down'. If we follow the methods of private lawyers,[26] we observe an already historical tendency consisting of using and enriching the prism of conflict of international conventions as a tool for resolving the conflicts between international treaties and accords that can arise in situations of private international law. Newer rules have been added to the classical principles for resolving conflicts (*lex posterior, lex*

[26] Public lawyers also use techniques from private law, if not in resolving conflicts of norms, at least in dealing with them. For example, the expressions 'forum shopping' or 'law shopping' have a growing place in works of international public law even though these terms were first popular amongst private international lawyers. See, on this subject, the cross-reflections in Forteau et al. (n. 18).

specialis, res inter alios acta) such as, for example, the theory of *maximum efficiency*.[27]

More recently, the expressions and mechanisms of the conflicts of law rules (*lato sensu*) have been used to describe the process of applying law, not only state or national law, but also non-state, international and, sometimes, European law.[28] The ambition of these different initiatives is to resolve conflicts of law which arise in a national, international and European context by specifying, *a priori*, remodelled rules of conflict and drawing upon the innumerable resources of private international law. Rules of this type have notably developed in all situations, which involve an overlap of the constructions of international public law, private international law and European law. Such overlaps result from the fact that these three legal subjects do not have clear limits. Effectively, international public law and European law are defined by the origins of their rules whereas private international law is constructed through reference to the international private situations to which it applies. It is therefore perfectly feasible for a rule of international public law (an international treaty) or of European law (a secondary legislation) to apply in a situation of private international law, concurrently with one or several national laws. Rules of conflicts of law are also in place regarding transnational law, which develops in certain domains in which private law subjects attempt to govern their relations without having recourse to state mechanisms.

This type of construction, based on conflict of law rules, pursues various objectives. Specialists in a legal discipline may reconsider the foundations of their subject taking into account, to put it briefly, global developments. A more ambitious objective consists of imagining that the concepts developed by one discipline, in this case international private law, are capable of dealing with questions of world or global governance.

Neither of these objectives will be pursued by our work. Other than the fact, already indicated, that we do not believe in the emergence of a global legal science capable of applying, like economics, to all actors in

---

27 On the relationships of conflict between conventional sources, see the work of S.A. Sadat Akhavi, *Methods of Resolving Conflicts between Treaties* (Brill, 2003).

28 On this subject, see H. Muir Watt and D.F. Arroyo (eds), *Private International Law and Global Governance* (Oxford Unversity Press, 2015) and W. van Gerven, 'Plaidoirie pour une nouvelle branche du droit : le "droit des conflits d'ordres juridiques" dans le prolongement du "droit des conflits de règles"' (2011) 350 *Collected Courses of the Hague Academy of International Law* 11.

the world, an analysis in terms of 'legal pluralism' should not, without destroying its own foundations, result in the domination of one legal discipline over all the others.

Dealing with a situation at national level is, historically, the proper domain of private international law: national laws and national judges. This endeavour differs from dealing with a situation in a truly international legal context, of European or *a fortiori* of transnational law. Lawyers who work in these different contexts did not train in the same schools. They do not use the same institutional or substantive tools. They simply do not respond to the same legal questions. This observation is valid for a whole series of subjects that will be tackled in this work (for example: the attribution of nationality to an individual, the recognition of a state's jurisdictional or executional immunity, the exercise of a subjective right, the operation of a rule of public order, etc.). It is also pertinent to the search for law applying in space.[29]

As a consequence, the present work does not adopt the methodological framework of one specialism to the detriment of all the others. In a pluralistic environment, lawyers must learn to consider questions in a pluralistic manner.

A final observation will provide further evidence that the resolution of these conflicts will not resolve, *a priori*, all the inherent difficulties of applied global legal pluralism.

As we have already indicated above, applied global legal pluralism designates the hypotheses in which several laws of a national, international and European dimension apply to a given situation. These hypotheses necessarily exclude cases in which a rule of conflict (conflict of laws, conflict of conventions, etc.) intervenes *a priori* to designate the one and only law applicable. Happily, such cases exist. A permanent environment of pluralism does not surround lawyers. But such cases are beyond our field of study. By definition, we are only interested in those

[29] The same sort of analysis could be pursued in European law. How many decisions of the Court of Justice of the European Union, not ruling on a question of international private law, have been read as containing a lesson in international private law even though, despite the fact international private law handles the 'national'/'foreign' distinction with great dexterity, it has the greatest difficulty in integrating a 'European' dimension into its constructions? We sometimes observe a veritable 'extrapolation' of European law, which, although it may find resonance in international private law, has none at all in European law. This is why it is necessary to dissociate the reasoning according to whether we place ourselves in one territory or another, in avoiding confusing law and the discourse one can have on it through another law.

cases in which several laws, which have developed in different contexts – national, international and European – apply to a given situation.

The diversity of the situations and the examples that will be considered in this work demonstrates that the *a priori* resolution of these so-called 'conflicts of law' cannot be the only, or even the principal, preoccupation of lawyers. The reason for this is not the absence of 'rules of conflict', but the absence of 'true conflict' between laws of a national, international and European dimension, which, very often, cannot be substituted one for the other. They apply together to a given case because very often they do not concern the same object. The idea that such situations may be treated *a priori*, by choosing one applicable law, is an illusion. We abandon here the prism of a conflict to be resolved, understood as the indispensable prelude to any analysis.

The fourth method lawyers may be tempted to use to grapple with the question of how to apply the law in the national, international or European context using an *a priori* construct is *the quest for global law or global governance.* This method does not differ much from the first three methods we have outlined above. But it is part of a dominant trend: a movement notably engaged in by a myriad of national, international and European research programmes which transcends the small world of lawyers, but in which the latter have rightly taken part.[30]

The quest for global law has in recent years become the new holy grail of a global legal expertise. Various perspectives have developed. Our work has no ambition to take part in the definition of global law.

The quest for global law can, first, turn to the figure of a 'law constructed without the state' which aims to respond to global problems (the environment, finance, energy, social responsibility, etc.).[31] It could also take a dialectical approach to law: a 'network of law', putting a multitude of sites of the production of law into contact, an approach which is thus in opposition to the figure of monolithic law, constructed on pyramidal model.[32] Finally, the search for global law can give itself the objective of gathering under one label, that of 'ordered pluralism', all

---

30 As illustrations, consult, for example, the French ANR programmes (http://www.agence-nationale-recherche.fr/) and the European ERC (http://erc.europa.eu/) proposed on these themes.

31 See G. Teubner, 'The Two Faces of Janus: Rethinking Legal Pluralism' (1992) 13 *Cardozo Law Review* 1443; compare by the same author, 'Global Bukowina: Legal Pluralism in the World Society', in *Global Law Without a State* (Dartmouth, Aldershot, 1997), p. 3.

32 F. Ost and M. van de Kerchove, *De la pyramide au réseau? Pour une théorie dialectique du droit* (Brussels, 2002).

the tensions that characterise a contemporary dynamic of the creation of law by all legal actors: international and regional organisations, states and private entities.[33]

Beyond the difficulties raised by theoretical and abstract approaches, the principal reason why we have prioritised a practical analysis relates to the phenomenon studied itself. Instances of applied global legal pluralism, which designates situations in which several laws formulated in a national (domestic or foreign), international[34] or European[35] environment may be applied together to a given case, have developed considerably over the last 30 years. To fully grasp the importance of this evolution, it is enough to remember, for example, what the work of lawyers consisted of at the end of the Second War and what it has become today with the proliferation of international and regional sources of law that may be applied and invoked in different territories. Without being entirely novel, this phenomenon has incontestably attained a previously unequalled scale. Have we, as lawyers, fully grasped the importance of this development? Do we know, if not all, at least the principal situations that give rise to applied global legal pluralism? Though minds broaden, apart from a few specialists, experts and pioneers in these issues,[36] the majority of the community of lawyers appears to largely ignore the phenomenon. It seems that not sufficient attention has been given before now to the great variety of situations of state or non-state, public or private, national, international or European law that participate in the phenomenon of applied global legal pluralism. An effort of description of global legal pluralism through some of its occurrences is, in our view, an indispensable prelude to any *conceptual* analysis of the phenomenon.

None of the three approaches described, defining the law (identifying legal systems and their relationships, resolving conflicts of law or the quest for a global law) will be pursued by this work. Rather than considering the operation of the law in different national, international and European contexts *a priori*, through the construction of the methods and solutions capable of approaching global legal pluralism, it is possible

---

33 M. Delmas-Marty, *Les forces imaginantes du droit, T2. Le pluralisme ordonné* (Seuil, 2006); English translation by N. Norberg, *Ordering Pluralism: A Conceptual Framework for Understanding the Transnational Legal World* (Hart, 2009).

34 UN, WTO, WIPO, ILO, WHO, ICJ, PCA, ICSID, ICC, HRW.

35 EU, ECHR.

36 See in particular, the oldest texts cited in the selective bibliography at the end of this work, p. 221.

to reverse the perspective and pay attention to the operation of law in a global context. This is what we focus on.

APPLIED GLOBAL LEGAL PLURALISM: A NEW FIELD OF STUDY

The suggested shift towards a practical approach to global law requires us to focus on facts.[37] Some legal issues deriving from the facts can be captured without passing through the preliminary definitions of the laws and the legal orders.

More specifically, we propose to adopt the perspective of lawyers who operate the law in different national, international and European contexts. How do they use the law when they are confronted with these different contexts? How does the plurality of contexts affect their manner of applying the law?

Applied global pluralism focuses on how laws with different objects and domains apply to a given situation and how lawyers from different legal cultures deal with it. Applied global pluralism requires a referential shift that can be evidenced with two examples, see Figure 1.1 below. First, the legal context takes precedence over substantive law (treaty, statute or case law) that will govern the solution. Second, the perspective of the lawyers that are involved at the various geographic levels and their legal culture are of greater importance than theoretical hypotheses about the definition of norms and of the legal order.

The operation of the law by lawyers is largely conditioned by the context – national, international or European – in which the law is applied.

National law may permeate this environment. The vast majority of lawyers work in a purely domestic context. But it is also the lot of the international private lawyers when they apply a national law or refer to a state judge designated by a connecting rule. This internal law applied by lawyers is not only composed of laws formulated in writing (e.g., mainly statutes, but also soft written laws such as recommendations of independent agencies). We can also find in it the trace of revelatory law, spontaneous law or soft law, for example.

---

[37] The Perelman Centre of Legal Philosophy (Free University of Brussels) directed by B. Frydman. For a presentation and justification of this method, see by this author: 'Comment penser le droit global?', in J.-Y. Chérot and B. Frydman (eds), *La science du droit dans la globalisation* (Bruylant, 2012), p. 17.

Scheme: a double movement

Sources of law ------------------→ Contexts of operating law

I I

I I

I I

Norms/Legal orders ---------------→ Lawyers/Legal cultures

Comment: in a global context, the most important element is not the law lawyers have to apply but the context in which they have to apply it. Several contexts and several lawyers mean a pluralistic operation of the law in a global context.

Figure 1.1 A double movement

The international context concerns the lawyers' application of legal methods and solutions of an international dimension. This is the lot of international lawyers, public or private, when they operate legal mechanisms adapted to international situations. These mechanisms can have a formal international dimension: an international treaty, an international custom, a procedure before an international court. They can also have a material international dimension, as, for example, a national law destined to apply specifically to international situations: rules of conflicts of law or of jurisdictions, substantially international material rules (such as, for example, a German legal rule of international public order, etc.). This applied international law sometimes has a transnational dimension. It is not the fruit of the labour of states but results from the practice of non-state actors in resolving specific situations.

The European context concerns the application of a law formulated in a legal environment with a European dimension. Two large European organisations aim to create law in this way: the European Union and the Council of Europe (with, under the auspices of the second organisation, the unique position occupied by the European Convention for the Protection of Human Rights and Fundamental Freedoms and its court, the European Court of Human Rights (ECtHR)). The European judge who applies European law every day (which can take the shape of any of the forms of law indicated further above) is thus immersed in the jurisdiction of a law which often asserts itself through its (relative) originality compared to the constructs defined in the national and international context.

These three contexts are evidently not isolated from one another. Lawyers can, through a simple trick of the mind, pass from one context to another. Some actors occupy ambivalent positions. This is very common, for example, for the national judge who presents himself as a European common law judge. This is also the case of the European judge charged with applying national law to a contract concluded by the European Union under the terms of an arbitration clause (art. 272 TFEU). The ICSID Judge is also ambivalent, simultaneously a national and international judge. But each context has its own legal language, its rationality, its institutional or material tools. As a field of study, applied global legal pluralism allows us to pose the question of how lawyers can apply the law, not only in the context that forms their usual sphere of activity, but in other contexts. What tools do lawyers use when they consider how to apply the law in a legal environment other than their own?

In order to distinguish between these three contexts, national, international and European, it is sometimes useful to speak of the 'level of application of law'. This expression does not have a strong theoretical value. It is not meant, notably, to designate a global legal order in which one level of application of law is placed immutably and definitively under the authority of another. But it is sometimes enlightening. It allows us to envisage the hypotheses in which it is possible to approach a case successively at different stages – national, international or European – of law.

This superposition of levels (to which one could add others: local, regional, federated, federal, inter-regional and, perhaps one day, interplanetary, etc.) takes into account the differences that characterise the manner in which the law is applied in distinct contexts. The legal methods and solutions deployed on a national level to tackle legal cases are not the same as those deployed on an international or European level. It matters little that a legal rule drawn from national law (a piece of internal legislation), international law (an international treaty) or European law (a piece of European secondary legislation) can sometimes apply on these different levels. What matters is the legal environment in which lawyers consider that application. If there are several of them, lawyers must show themselves capable of renewing their analysis every time it develops in a new environment.

We propose to focus on the work of lawyers when they apply the law in different national, international and European contexts. How do they use the law when they are confronted with these different contexts? How does this plurality of contexts affect their manner of applying the law?

As understood in this book, lawyers all have in common the pursuit of a practical result: the formulation of a rule, a decision, an argument, an analysis or a theory. In other words, we contemplate lawyers who are either independent (as barrister, consultant, magistrate, solicitor, or professor) or under the authority of a public institution (administration), or subordinate to a private body (such as non-governmental organisation, company, union, association). People refered to as lawyers in this work encompass therefore judges, legal academics, solicitors and barristers from any jurisdiction, legal experts involved in the European institution and, finally, any lawyers who operate within global structures.

A THREE-STEP PRESENTATION: COMPARING, COMBINING, AND PRIORITISING THE APPLICATION OF THE LAW IN THE NATIONAL, INTERNATIONAL AND EUROPEAN CONTEXT

How can lawyers take into account the multiplicity of contexts, national, international and European, when applying the law? They have to take this feature into account. Where should they start? What steps should they take in order to achieve this analysis?

A tempting route might therefore consist in beginning by comparing the application of the law in the different contexts (comparison), to then perhaps (the approach is not inflexible) combine these applications, notably if they allow the attainment of a different result than that obtained in each of the contexts individually (combination), knowing that he potentially has the option of deciding, at any moment, to choose the application of the law in one context, rather than another (prioritisation).

In a general sense, comparison is thus the first step that lawyers must undertake in order to attempt to apply the law in the national, international and European context. Generally confined to the mere study of national laws and a mostly economic exercise, 'comparative law' deserves to be given a broader meaning in a perspective of applied global legal pluralism. The comparison of national, international and European law involves an investigation of the law that may be applied in a national, international or European environment, and how it would be applied (methods, rule of evidence, ...) and with what results. This examination is a necessary first step. It allows lawyers to fully grasp the similarities and differences that characterise the application of the law in contexts that are national and international as well as European.

The step of combining national, international and European law, for its part, requires the lawyers to assemble the methods and solutions identified by the operation of comparison in order to construct their legal reasoning. It may be undertaken in two main situations: that in which the laws considered are complementary and have an operational relationship; and that in which the circulation of situations from one level of law to another can be observed.

The process of the prioritisation of laws enables, finally, every legal system present at national, international or European level to specify which rules have a place in its legal order. This process does not merely have a static value in that it should be considered in an enclosed manner in a national, international or European context. It also has a dynamic dimension in which the application of the methods and solutions derived from national, international or European law leads to interactions. On this point, two scenarios must therefore be carefully distinguished. In the first, lawyers appeal to an application of law on one level, which potentially involves the operation of a hierarchy of legal norms. In the second, lawyers aspire to apply the law at another level, which leads to look for evidence of the materialisation of hierarchical applied law.

THE CHOICE OF A METHOD OF DEMONSTRATION: SITUATIONS, EXAMPLES

Any study on applied global legal pluralism must be articulated around cases. Even though our research does not incorporate any authentic-empirical dimension, it does present situations and examples.

The term 'situation' refers to typical theoretical or practical questions. Pursuant to the method presented in this book, we suggest that situations should be analysed and resolved by reference to legal methods and solutions that can be applied in different contexts. Situations are usually illustrated through one or more examples drawn from the practice of law; results from scenarios are sometimes invented.

In total, almost 89 situations and 142 examples are reviewed in this work. They are presented in boxes.

This method of presentation using situations and examples has three objectives. By describing different scenarios, we hope that the reader, interested by one case in particular, will be able to identify, by means of the summary, tables and index, the instances of comparison, of combination and/or prioritisation that are envisaged. Thus the reader will observe that the case can be dealt with in different ways depending on which method is employed by lawyers. Some cases lend themselves more easily to a multiple treatment than others. But as far as possible, we have tried to proceed so that the same situations and the same examples are presented in the triple light of comparison, combination and prioritisation.

By articulating our demonstration around situations and examples, our second objective is to limit the field of study opened by applied global legal pluralism. Renouncing from the outset any claim to making an exhaustive presentation, we decided to use examples in order to outline the multiple facets of legal pluralism. Our own academic interests have guided the choice of situations and examples, although we have often had to venture out of our specialisms to embrace the different contexts. These situations and examples have not been developed as such. Their treatment and the demonstrations they summon are entirely focused on the purpose of this study.

In short, this work is conducted around situations and examples in response to a scientific need, which is to determine *how the law manifests itself.* In order to answer this essential question, several routes could have been taken.[38] In the context of this study of applied global legal pluralism, it appeared to us clear that the responses had to be found other than at the end of a general and abstract explication. This is why our comments and the few elements of demonstration it attempts to present and organise are systematically grounded in situations and examples.

[38] Two methods, not related to this research, immediately come to mind: the realisation of subjective rights and judicial reasoning.

PART I

Comparing national, international and European law

The comparison of laws in the triple national, international and European context may focus on several different aspects: the methods and solutions they prescribe, which is the most critical aspect (Chapter 2), the scope of application of the laws that are present (Chapter 3), the conditions in which they may be invoked (Chapter 4).

2. Comparing scopes of application

Legal methods and solutions formulated in different legal contexts – national, international or European – do not all necessarily have the same scope of application. It is therefore important to compare the material (Section 1), geographic (Section 2) and temporal (Section 3) scope of the different laws that are present.

1. MATERIAL SCOPE

The material scope of application of the national, international and European laws that may apply to a given situation can be defined with the help of legal classifications (A) which may be organised into a typology (B).

A. Recourse to Legal Classifications

In order to determine the situations to which a legal rule applies, lawyers refer to legal classifications. In general, the operation of classification allows lawyers, in effect, to determine whether a given case falls within the material scope of application of a given legal rule. This scope is defined by reference to legal notions and categories. Generally, we distinguish two steps in this process, according to whether it is necessary to legally define a situation (an action, an event, an object or a person) or to determine the place it occupies in relation to several mutually exclusive legal categories (a contract or a tort; a thing or a person).[1] In both cases, the operation of classification allows us to determine what sort of legal rule applies to a given situation.

In a context of global legal pluralism, the source and content of legal notions and categories can vary according to whether they are drawn from the national, international or European level. It is therefore useful to compare them.

---

[1] On this distinction, particularly in the international context, see notably, with references suggested: B. Ancel, 'Qualification', in *Repertoire de droit international* (Dalloz, 2016).

SITUATION – NATIONAL, INTERNATIONAL OR EUROPEAN CLASSIFICATIONS

An example concerning goods: the case of medicines

Medicines are subject to a specific legal regime that takes their specificities into account. They form a whole separate legal category. The legal classification of 'medicine' can vary according to the law that is applied to it at national, international or European level. For example, a definition of a medicine may be found in a national regulation (in statutes in civil law countries, for example the French Public Health Code; in case law in common law countries, for a historical example, see *Dr. Bonham's Case*, 8 Co. Rep. 114 (Court of Common Pleas [1610]), arising from a dispute relating to the unlicensed pratice of medicine by a Cambridge graduate asserting the absence of jurisdiction of the London College of Physicians over him: the case stands for the principle (since curbed) that legislation passed by the English Parliament is subordinate to the common-law decisions made by trial and appellate court judges, and any statute that is contrary to 'common right and reason' must be declared void[2]). In European Union law, the European Court of Justice has had occasion to interpret a large number of secondary legal texts now codified by Directive 2001/83/EC of the European Parliament and of the Council of 6 November 2001 on the Community Code Relating to Medicinal Products for Human Use (see, for example, one of the Court's first decisions: Case 227/82, *Van Bennekom* [1983] ECR 3883). Even the European Court of Human Rights has ruled on this subject in the triple context of French law, European Union law and Council of Europe Law (App no 17862/91 *Cantoni v France*, (ECtHR, 15 Nov. 1996). The World Health Organisation (WHO) also participates in the development of definitions notably by proposing classifications for different types of medicines.

For comprehensive studies on this topic, see Yann Joly and Bartha Maria Knoppers (eds), *Routledge Handbook of Medical Law and Ethics* (Abingdon, Oxon: Routledge, 2015).

An example concerning contracts: the distinction between the sale of goods and the provision of services

The distinction between the sale of goods and the provision of services poses a well-known problem of legal classification. As the legal regimes governing contracts for sale and contracts for the provision of services do not necessarily obey the same legal rules (for example, in relation to the determination of the price or the competent court), it is important to identify for each situation the corresponding contractual model. The key to the distinction between the two contracts can vary from one context to another according to the legal source under consideration. In English law, the Sale of Goods Act of 1979, as substantially updated in 1994, provides a definition for a contract of sale of

[2] R.A. Edwards, 'Bonham's Case: The Ghost in the Constitutional Machine' (1996) *Denning Law Journal* (annual), 63–90.

goods; it is supplemented by the Supply of Goods and Services Act of 1982. Both Acts were amended in 1994 and have been extensively interpreted by case law. For instance, in *Tata Consultancy Services v State of Andhra Pradesh* (2005) 1 SCC 308, it was held that computer software packages sold off the shelf are 'goods'. In French domestic law, for example, the distinction results notably from the Court of Cassation's interpretation of Articles 1582 and 1792 of the Civil Code. In European law, the distinction is employed in secondary laws (for example, Council Regulation (EU) No. 1215/2012 of 12 December 2012 on jurisdiction and the recognition and enforcement of judgments in civil and commercial matters, art. 7.1.b). In international law, an instrument specifically dedicated to the international sale of goods, for example, distinguishes between contracts for sale and complex contracts, which combine the delivery of goods and services (1980 Vienna Convention on Contracts for the International Sale of Goods – UN – UNICITRAL, art. 3)

An example concerning persons: the definition of a child

Different national, international and European instruments apply specifically to children. In order to determine whether a person falls into this legal category it is necessary to examine the laws present to determine whether they are materially applicable. Sometimes, these laws contain classification criteria. Thus, for example, French law makes parents responsible in tort for the actions of their 'minor children' (art. 1384 paras 4 and 7 of the Civil Code, and as from October 1, 2016 art. 1242 of the new provisions of the Code civil,[3] thus excluding children who have reached the age of 18 and emancipated minors. The New York Convention on the Rights of the Child (UN – 1989), for its part defines children as 'every human being below the age of 18 years unless, under the law applicable to the child, majority is attained earlier' (art. 1). Finally, the Charter of Fundamental Rights of the European Union dedicates an article to the 'Rights of the Child' but does not propose a definition of the notion (art. 24).

An example concerning legal situations: the distinction between domestic situations and international or European situations

In the different contexts of application of the law, an important distinction is sometimes made between domestic situations and international situations. When

[3] Translation into English by John Cartwright, Bénédicte Fauvarque-Cosson and Simon Whittaker, *The Code Napoléon Rewritten: French Contract Law after the 2016 Reforms*: Art. 1242, available at http://www.textes.justice.gouv.fr/art_pix/THE-LAW-OF-CONTRACT-2-5-16.pdf. – One is liable not only for the harm which one causes by one's own action, but also for that which is caused by the action of persons for whom one is responsible, or of things which one has in one's keeping. (…) To the extent to which they exercise parental authority, a father and mother are jointly and severally liable for harm caused by their minor children who live with them (para. 5). The above liability arises unless the father and mother and the artisans cannot prove that they could not have prevented the action which gave rise to this liability (para. 8).

this distinction is made, it has the potential to control the operation of specific legal rules according to whether one is in one category or another. A very characteristic example of this is arbitration in French law which distinguishes clearly between the legal solutions that apply to arbitration in general (arts 1442 *et seq.* Code of Civil Procedure) and international arbitration in particular (arts 1492 *et seq.* Code of Civil Procedure). We also find this distinction in international instruments designed specifically to deal with international situations, such as international transport (for example: The 1999 Montreal Convention for the Unification of Certain Rules for International Carriage by Air) or agency (for example: The 1978 Hague Convention on the Law Applying to Agency, Hague Conference).

The distinction is also present in provisions of European Union law that are intended to apply specifically to traffic flows within the European zone and do not apply to situations that are purely internal to a Member State or to situations involving third-party states (for example: Council Directive 93/7/EEC of 15 March 1993 on the return of cultural objects unlawfully removed from the territory of a Member State).

But this is not a general rule. It is common, in fact, for laws formulated in a national context to apply without distinction to domestic situations or international or European situations (for example, an international contract for sale made subject to French law by the parties). The same phenomenon may be observed at international or European level (for example, a European or international instrument creating a uniform law that applies without distinction to domestic, international and European situations; another example: a European law relating to freedom of movement applied to a situation purely internal to a Member State).

B. The Different Types of Legal Classification

Several lessons may be gleaned from the comparison of different legal classifications developed in a national, international or European context. Lawyers may, first, find themselves in the presence of a classification that is universally recognised at all levels of law or, on the contrary, of classifications that vary according to the context considered.

SITUATION – UNIVERSAL CLASSIFICATIONS AND PARTICULAR CLASSIFICATIONS

An example concerning persons: returning to the definition of a child

The definition of a child has a universal character. Thus, for example, the Charter of the European Union, while it does not define the term, implicitly refers to the definition given in the New York Convention (see, in this sense, the explanations relating to the Charter given by the Praesidium of the European Convention, OJ

C303 of 14 Dec. 2007). But, if we look more closely, we can see that this definition also suffers from particularism. The New York Convention reserves, in effect, the case in which the age of majority is attained before 18 years in virtue of applicable legislation. This solution leaves space for two variables. The first concerns the case in which a regulation fixes the threshold of civil, criminal or sexual majority, for example, at a level below the age of 18 years. The second concerns causes of the emancipation of minors. The result is a heterogeneity of solutions that is not visible at first glance.

Lawyers may, for that matter, observe that the classification they use exists at their own level in an autonomous manner or, conversely, that it is borrowed from another level than their own.

SITUATION – AUTONOMOUS CLASSIFICATIONS AND DEPENDENT CLASSIFICATIONS

An example concerning contracts: returning to the distinction between the contract for sale of goods and the contract for services

The distinction between the contract for sale and the contract for services is a good example of a classification that is sometimes autonomous and sometimes dependent. For an autonomous classification, it is necessary to consider the hypothesis in which a lawyer working in one context (national, international or European) is able to find the classification he seeks at his own level. For example, if we are concerned with applying domestic law in order to determine if we have before us a contract for sale or a contract for the provision of services, it is quite certainly in this domestic context (it does not matter whether it is national or foreign at this stage in the process of comparison) that we must seek the classification in question. For a dependent classification, it is necessary to envisage a different case in which lawyers are compelled to look for the classification in question in a different context from that in which he normally works. For example, if a lawyer of European law wishes to operate the distinction between a contract for sale and a contract for the provision of services used by the Council Regulation (EC) No. 1215/2012 of 12 December 2012 on jurisdiction and the recognition and enforcement of judgments in civil and commercial matters (*supra*), he is compelled, under the case law of the Court of Justice of the European Union, to have recourse to national classifications, insofar as the distinction between a contract for sale and a contract for services is not presently defined at the European level in the specific context of this instrument of private international law.

Solutions can vary from one area of European law to another. For an effort at an autonomous classification in financial matters (VAT), see Case C-497/09, C-499/09, C-501/09, C-502/09 *Bog and Others* [2011] ECR I-1457.

Lawyers may, finally, observe that certain qualifications are supplementary, in the sense that legal subjects may, to a certain extent, opt out of them, whereas others are clearly imperative.

SITUATION – SUPPLEMENTARY CLASSIFICATIONS AND IMPERATIVE CLASSIFICATIONS

Two examples concerning arbitration and the contract for sale of goods

Are the classifications specified in a given law to distinguish, for example, domestic arbitration from international arbitration or the contract for sale from the contract for services inviolable, or can they be modified by a contrary will? In other words, can one derogate from a rule, which is intended to apply only to certain situations when the parties find themselves in another situation? The answer to this question varies according to the nature of the rule that defines the material scope of the law in question. If we consider that the classification is imperative, it will not be possible to derogate from it. Conversely, if it is supplementary, it is possible for the intended subjects of the rule to use it differently. For example, French arbitration laws (*supra*) are imperative in the sense that the parties to a domestic arbitration process cannot voluntarily make themselves subject to the less restrictive rules that apply to international arbitration. On the other hand, it is permissible, under certain conditions, for parties to a contract for services to choose to have the 1980 Vienna Convention on the International Sale of Goods (*supra*) apply to them even though it normally excludes this type of contract.

In different scenarios, the question of the application of national, international or European law does not appear in the same light. The confrontation of legal contexts, their combination and eventual prioritisation[4] are much more relevant than the legal classifications that differ from one space to another. It is therefore necessary to proceed, at the first stage of legal analysis, to their comparison.

2. GEOGRAPHIC SCOPE

The definition of the geographic scope of application of national, international and European law is the subject of a particular inquiry (A) which reveals a great diversity of solutions (B).

[4] On the two processes of combination and prioritisation, see *infra*, Parts II and III.

A. The Question of the Geographic Applicability of National, International and European Law

The legal methods and solutions developed in the national, international or European context do not only have a material scope of application. They also have a scope of applicability in space. This scope allows us to localise from a strictly geographic point of view, the concrete situations that are subject to the materially applicable laws. It is useful for a lawyer to be able to refer to this scope in a context of global legal pluralism in which he may be somewhat disoriented by the profusion of laws on offer.

This geographic scope is sometimes explicitly defined by reference to criteria of location. These criteria have the potential to apply to all elements in a given situation: the location of persons, of goods, of contracts and of torts.

> SITUATION – THE LOCATION OF CASES IN SPACE
>
> **Examples of the criteria used to locate a case in space**
>
> The localisation criteria that may be used to determine the geographic scope of application of the legal methods and solutions developed in the national, international or European context may potentially deal with: natural persons: their nationality, domicile or residence; corporations (in private or public law): the location of their registered office or the law that established them; goods: the place in which they are located or perhaps registered; contracts: the place in which they were adopted, concluded or executed; torts: the place in which they originally occurred and/or the place in which they produced their effects, etc.
>
> According to the legal nature of the situation in question and the context of the application of the law under consideration, lawyers may be invited to use one or other of these criteria.

These localisation criteria are generally incorporated into rules. According to their broadest definition, we call these 'rules of geographic applicability'.[5] They may be present at all levels of law: national, international or European.

---

5 See the major study by M. Fallon, 'Les règles d'applicabilité en droit international privé', in Mélanges offerts à Raymond Vander Elst, ed. (Nemesis, Brussels, 1986), p. 285. See also S. Fatima, *Using International Law in Domestic Courts* (Hart, 2005), pp. 27 *et seq*; J.G. Collier, *Conflict of Laws* (3rd edn, Cambridge University Press, 2001).

SITUATION – THE EXISTENCE OF RULES OF GEOGRAPHIC APPLICABILITY

A few examples from national, international and European law

Geographic applicability rules can concern national, international or European law. Here are a few examples:

- Applicability of domestic law: provisions of domestic law that define the scope of application in space of domestic law (for example, Articles 113-1 *et seq.* of the French Criminal Code which distinguish rules of applicability of the French criminal law according to several criteria, notably whether the crime took place on French or foreign territory, whether the perpetrator and the victim were of French or foreign nationality);
- Applicability of international law: the provisions contained in an instrument of international law which tends to locate the situations to which it applies in space (for example, the 1980 Vienna Convention on the International Sale of Goods (*supra*) which notably applies to contracts concluded between parties established in different State Signatories, art. 1.1.a);
- applicability of European law: the provisions of primary or secondary law which designate situations in space that European law intends to govern (for example, Article 20 TFEU which reserves the benefit of European citizenship and the rights attaching to it to persons with the nationality of at least one Member State; Article 4.1 of Council Regulation (EU) No. 1215/2012 of 12 December 2012 on jurisdiction and the recognition and enforcement of judgments in civil and commercial matters to which the rules of direct competence do not apply, in principle, unless the defendant is domiciled in a Member State).

B. The Diversity of Solutions

A comparison of the criteria and rules of geographic applicability defined in the national, international or European context can reveal a great diversity of solutions that vary according to the legal question posed and the context, or contexts, concerned. To find their way among them, lawyers must try to impose order.

The case we have already encountered is that in which a rule from a national, international or European source is explicitly accompanied by a rule of geographic applicability (see above, previous paragraph, the different examples proposed). These solutions governing applicability may be restricted to public or private law rules, basic rules or procedural rules.

The analysis of some of these rules calls for a deeper examination. Rules of geographic applicability do not all have the same legal meaning and do not all produce the same effects. It is necessary to distinguish certain particularities. Among other possibilities, three particularities are evoked here.

The first particularity concerns rules with a strong institutional dimension. The geographic dimensions of the national, international or European rules that govern the functioning of administrative or judicial institutions normally vary according to the legal system of which they form a part. A national authority is naturally bound by the rules of the state that established it. The same is true for institutions established by an international or European treaty. Their activities are governed by the primary and secondary legal rules that form the legal system that founded them. In these different situations, it is the law that establishes the headquarters of the institution that applies without it being necessary to define it precisely. If this domestic function were to be altered by an external source of law, we would have a situation of a combination of laws.[6] But this applicability of 'foreign' institutional rules belonging to a different legal system from that to which the institution concerned is attached remains an exception to the principle of the applicability of the forum law of the institution.

SITUATION – THE SCOPE OF APPLICABILITY OF INSTITUTIONAL LAWS

Examples concerning national, international or European courts

The functioning of national courts is naturally governed by national law. For an international court, such as the International Court of Justice or the International Criminal Court, for example, the treaty that established the court determines the applicable rules that govern its functioning (the United Nations Charter (1945) and the Statute of Rome (1998)). For a European court, such as the Court of Justice of the European Union (CJEU) or the European Court of Human Rights (ECtHR), it is also necessary to refer to the legal texts that are in force in the legal system in question (EU (e.g., the 1957 European Economic Community, which became the European Community in 1992) or ECHR (1950)).

The second peculiarity distinguishes between rules of geographic applicability according to whether they concern material rules, rules of conflicts of laws or rules of conflicts of jurisdictions. The legal solutions

[6] See *infra*, Part II.

that define the scope of application of a law in the national, international or European legal space can, in effect, concern material rules, which have the purpose of offering a solution to a given basic question, or rules of conflicts of laws, which designate the law that usually applies, or rules of conflicts of jurisdictions, which govern questions of the international competence of national courts and how legal decisions travel. This distinction between three families of rules comes to us from private international law. But it also partly operates in public law which, although it does not employ rules of conflicts of law or of jurisdictions, is often called upon to delimit the scope of application of its material rules.

SITUATION – THE APPLICABILITY IN SPACE OF MATERIAL RULES AND RULES OF CONFLICTS OF LAWS AND JURISDICTIONS

Examples of solutions in national, international and European law

The majority of rules of applicability deal with material rules. In international private law, they are often confused with 'mandatory rules' which, as their name indicates, apply immediately according to their own criteria of applicability, without the need for recourse to a connecting factor. These rules can also be found in European Union law (for an example drawn from European case law, Case C-381/98 *Ingmar* [2000] ECR I-9305).

Sometimes, it is the rule of conflicts of laws itself which is the object of a rule of applicability. The rule that determines the applicable law in a situation of conflict of laws is thus subject to a rule of applicability in space. The most well-known example in international law is an old one: the Hague Convention of 1956 on the law applicable to maintenance obligations towards children, of which Article 6 limits the scope of the Convention to the designation of the applicable law in a state signatory. This type of clause does not appear in the more recent instruments formulated by the Hague Conference of International Private Law. In European Union law, the rule of applicability can affect rules of conflicts of law that have a strong material flavour (see, for example, Directive 96/71/EC of 16 December 1996 concerning the posting of workers in the framework of the provision of services).

Finally, where rules of conflict of jurisdictions are concerned, it is necessary to note several distinctions. National rules in principle have a strictly national foundation. The international competence of French courts or the exequatur of foreign decisions on national soil are naturally subject to national rules of procedure. If the solution to a conflict of jurisdictions is found in a provision of international or European law it is necessary to distinguish whether these concern the direct competence of the courts or the exequatur of the decisions. On the first point, all solutions may be envisaged: some instruments apply to courts in Member States, without any other criterion of applicability (for example,

Council Regulation (EC) No. 2201/2003 of 27 November 2003 concerning jurisdiction and the recognition and enforcement of judgments in matrimonial matters and the matters of parental responsibility); others, on the contrary, add extra criteria, taking into account for example the domicile of the defendant (for example, Council Regulation (EC) No. 1215/2012 of 12 December 2012 on jurisdiction and the recognition and enforcement of judgments in civil and commercial matters). On the second point, it goes without saying that the international or European rules concerning the enforceability of decisions by foreign courts apply only to decisions delivered by the courts of state signatories (see, in relation to European law, the two examples above).

The third peculiarity relates to the vocabulary that may be used to vary the geographic applicability of national, international or European law. A distinction may be made between laws which can apply without geographic limitations and those of a geographically limited applicability. Sometimes the first are referred to using the expression 'universal applicability' whereas the second have the characteristic of being of 'self-limited applicability'. These two expressions are nonetheless misleading. It is rare in fact for one rule to be truly universally applicable and indirect methods exist for defining the geographic scope of application of a rule which do not operate through self-limitation.

SITUATION – ON THE SUBJECT OF SO-CALLED UNIVERSAL AND SELF-LIMITED APPLICABILITY

Examples of solutions in national, international and European law

Situations of the so-called 'universal' applicability of law, which is to say in the absence of *a priori* limitations on the geographical scope of the rules under consideration, exist in all legal contexts. In national law, the term is often used in criminal law matters, whenever a judge is competent to prosecute criminal behaviours that do not have a strict connection with the national territory. That being said, it is necessary to distinguish two scenarios. On one hand are those scenarios in which universal competence is absolute, as has been the case in certain countries (for example, Belgium and in Spain) and on the other are those scenarios in which such competence is more reasoned (for example, France). In the first case, the national judge can have jurisdiction over crimes that have no connection to the national territory. In the second case, the presence on national soil of a person suspected of a crime committed abroad can be one of the minimal conditions of the applicability of the law. Such so-called 'universal' competences in criminal matters are also enshrined in their non-absolute version in several specific international instruments (for example, the 1984 New York

Convention against Torture and other Cruel, Inhuman or Degrading Treatment or Punishment – UN).

The question of universal applicability is also often raised in relation to human rights. The development of these rights, notably in the regional context of the Council of Europe, with the European Convention on the Protection of Human Rights and Fundamental Freedoms (1950) (ECHR), raises vigorous debates on the truly universal character of the Western values contained in this instrument. The debate is not only philosophical or sociological in nature. It also has a legal dimension relating to the geographical scope of the instrument. One question that is notably raised is whether the ECHR should be applied in situations located in countries outside the Council of Europe for the sole reason that they have been presented to a judge in a Member State and that the latter has delivered a decision that could be criticised by the ECtHR.

On the other hand, there is the relatively technical question of whether one or several legal methods exist for limiting the geographical scope of a rule. The answer has been given by a Belgian author who proposed to classify rules of applicability (M. Fallon, 'Les règles d'applicabilité en droit international privé', in Mélanges offerts à Raymond Vander Elst, ed. (Némésis, Bruxelles, 1986), p. 285). He distinguishes between direct and indirect rules of applicability in the following way. The first are provisions of self-limitation of the type we have already presented (see *supra*, p.32). The second are bilateral or unilateral rules of conflicts of laws, which designate the law that normally applies geographically to govern a legal relation (the law governing the residence of a person, the location of a good, the place in which a tort occurred or a legal act was concluded, etc.). The latter exist at every level. At national level, an example is to be found in Article 311-14 of the French Civil Code which establishes a rule of conflict of laws in matters of legitimacy, legitimisation and adoption, or the English Private International Law (Miscellaneous Provisions) Act 1995 which deals with choice of laws in tort). At international level, an illustration is offered by the numerous Hague Conventions that standardise conflicts of laws (http://www.hcch.net). Finally, at European level, the following regulations are also exemplary: Regulation (EC) No. 864/2007 of the European Parliament and of the Council of 11 July 2007 on the law applicable to non-contractual obligations (Rome II); Regulation (EC) No. 593/2008 of the European Parliament and of the Council of 17 June 2008 on the law applicable to contractual obligations (Rome I); and Council Regulation (EU) No. 1259/2010 of 20 December 2010 implementing enhanced cooperation in the area of the law applicable to divorce and legal separation (Rome III). See M. Fallon, 'Les frontières geographiques du droit privé européen selon le droit de l'Union européenne', in E. Poillot and I. Rueda (eds), Les frontières du droit privé européen / *The Boundaries of European Private Law* (Bruylant, 2012), p. 65. See also J.G. Collier, *Conflict of Laws* (3rd edn, Cambridge University Press, 2001).

Finally a fourth and last particularity concerns scenarios in which geographical applicability depends on the will of those who wish to voluntarily submit themselves to the rule. The situation here is similar to the one we encountered earlier in relation to rules of material applicability. In effect, such a choice is sometimes possible whereas in other cases, geographic applicability is imposed imperatively.

SITUATION – OPTIONAL OR MANDATORY APPLICABILITY

Examples of solutions in contract law

In contract law, parties have a certain degree of autonomy which may lead them to choose national, international or European law to apply to their contract which, in the absence of such a choice, would not normally apply. The choice of the parties may thus have the effect of extending or restricting the geographic scope of applicability of the national, international or European law in question. For example, the parties to a purely domestic contract, concluded and executed in one country, may decide to make themselves subject to the law of another country (for example, they might decide to apply Japanese law to a contract located in France) or an international convention creating a uniform law for international contracts (for example, the 1956 'CMR' Geneva Convention on transport by road which normally applies only to international transport) or even European principles which have no binding legal effect (for example, the principles of European contract law devised by the Lando Commission). Are these choices valid? The general answer to this question, which has the potential to vary from one legal system to another, holds true in the context of French law in two main propositions. The choice must not have the effect of allowing the parties to avoid respecting any law. The choice is also restricted by the mandatory rules that normally apply to the contract in the absence of a choice of law by the parties. Subject to these two reservations and in the absence of rules specific to a given area of law, the parties to a contract have a certain control over the geographic scope of applicability of contractual rules. In certain areas (in this case transportation), this practice is referred to as a 'paramount clause' each time the parties to the contract decide to make themselves subject to an international convention even though it does not normally apply given its geographic scope of applicability. For an analysis of this question in the context of Regulation (EC) No. 593/2008 of the European Parliament and of the Council of 17 June 2008 on the law applicable to contractual obligations (Rome I), in particular Article 3, see notably the commentary of F. Ferrari, *Rome I Regulation. Pocket Commentary* (1st edn, Sellier, 2014).

3. TEMPORAL SCOPE

The question of the effects of the law through time naturally arises in the triple national, international and European environment. Every legal system at each of these different levels proposes solutions in this regard.

These solutions may relate to the affirmation of a general principle concerning the important question of the retroactivity of legal texts.

SITUATION – THE QUESTION OF THE NON-RETROACTIVITY OF LAWS

Examples of solutions from national, international and European law

The affirmation of a general principle of the non-retroactivity of a new law or of a new treaty or secondary law may be present at every level of law. We find a general formulation of this principle in French law (art. 2 of the Civil Code), in the Vienna Convention on the Law of Treaties (art. 28) for example and, in a more informal form in English law (*ex post acto* laws are permitted by virtue of the doctrine of the parliamentary sovereignty but they are rare and the *Oxford Dictionary of Law* states that 'there is a presumption that statutes are not intended to have retroactive effect unless they merely change legal procedure'). It is also present, in the narrower case of criminal law, in national law (in France, art. 8 of the 1793 DDHC (French Declaration of Human Rights)), international law (art. 15 of the International Covenant on Civil and Political Rights) and European law (art. 7 of the ECHR and art. 49 of the Charter of Fundamental Rights of the European Union (CFREU)). The legal value of the principle is defined by each legal system. In French law, the principle of non-retroactivity is not considered mandatory, in the sense that another law can derogate from it, on the condition that it respects different rules or principles. The same is true for general international law, which allows states to formulate retroactive solutions within their area of competence. Conversely, where provisions specific to the application of the criminal law in force on the day the crime is committed are concerned, their intangible value is recognised both by domestic laws of a constitutional nature and international and European laws (*supra*). Some legal systems go further by allowing the retrospective application of a more lenient criminal law. The European Union, for example, has thus considered, in the voice of the Court of Justice, that 'the principle of the retroactive application of the most lenient penalty is part of the common constitutional traditions of Member States' (Case C-387/02 *Berlusconi* [2005] ECR I-3565).

The rules governing the temporal scope of application can also concern the date upon which a new law entered into force and the organisation of transitional legal provisions.

SITUATION – THE TEMPORAL SCOPE OF APPLICATION OF NATIONAL, INTERNATIONAL AND EUROPEAN LAW

Examples of provisions on the date of entry into force and transitional law

Each time reference is made to a domestic, international or European text, it is necessary to take into account the general rules of entry into force laid down by every legal system and to verify that the law in question does not derogate from them through the deployment of specific solutions of transitional law. Regarding the first, we find in domestic law (for example, in France, Ordonnance n° 2004-164 of 20 February 2004 modifiying art. 1 of the Code civil; in the United Kingdom the Acts of Parliament (Commencement) Act 1973 provides that laws without explicit commencement provisions will come into effect on the day on which they receive royal assent) and in international law (Vienna Convention on the Law of Treaties, art. 24) general regulations on the modalities of the entry into force of newly adopted laws. Regarding the second, it is necessary to proceed on a case-by-case basis and to verify for each law whether it specifies its date of entry into force and, if relevant, the modalities of its application in time. This practice is particularly frequent in European Union law, which does not contain general rules on this subject equivalent to those found in national or international law (cited above). Notably, where treaties, regulations or directives are concerned, it is very common to find transitional rules which sometimes extend for long periods (for example the construction of the common market followed a calendar lasting a decade and a half; more recently, the accession of new states from Central and Eastern Europe and the development of new European policies have been subject to transitional rules intended to considerably delay the effects of the new legal instruments introduced).

Such rules are, finally, capable of handling the troublesome issue of the limitation of the temporal effects of case law being overturned.

SITUATION – THE TEMPORAL EFFECT OF THE OVERTURNING OF NATIONAL, INTERNATIONAL OR EUROPEAN CASE LAW

An example of a comparative analysis in national and European law

The facts of the problem are well-known. The overturning of a judicial interpretation of a law can have a retroactive effect. We consider, in effect, that the new interpretation of a law is part of the law itself, so that it is to be treated as if it always existed. Except for definitive judicial decisions, which cannot be disturbed, the new interpretation applies to all situations, whether anterior or posterior to the decision that was delivered. In order to prevent the retroactive reversal of case law from suddenly jeopardising a large number of pre-existing situations, the question of whether a judge may limit the effects of his decision in time arises. An initiative led by a high-ranking French judge and a working group composed of academics, judges and lawyers has resulted in the publication of a research paper on this subject. On such a delicate subject as the temporal effect of judicial decisions, it appeared necessary to give a prominent place to European case law. The European courts did, in effect, very quickly (see the first decision delivered in this regard: Case 43/75 *Defrenne* [1976] ECR 455) have cause to limit the temporal effects of their decisions, including in cases in which case law has not technically speaking been overturned (verifying the legality of European Union law or making a preliminary ruling). This European practice could not be overlooked in the context of a study with a more limited object.

3. Comparing conditions of enforceability

Considered narrowly, the possibility for a legal subject to invoke domestic law in the national legal order, international law in the international order and European law in one of the two great European legal systems does not raise any issue in relation to the phenomenon of global legal pluralism considered in this work. The opposite is true every time a legal method or solution derived from one context may be invoked by a legal subject in another context. Different scenarios may be envisaged in this regard (Section 1) which do not all share the same legal implications (Section 2).

1. CASES OF ENFORCEABILITY IN THE TRIPLE NATIONAL, INTERNATIONAL OR EUROPEAN CONTEXT

For the purposes of this analysis, three scenarios may be distinguished according to whether enforceability is at issue in a situation involving the relationship between international law and national law (A), European law and national law (B) or international law and European law (C).

A. Enforceability and the Relationship between International Law and National Law

If we consider, to start with, the relationship between the international and national legal contexts, we observe that the question of enforceability has mainly been addressed from the perspective of the incorporation of instruments of international law into domestic law, particularly international treaties. The most frequently invoked scenario is that of the reliance of a private law subject on an international convention before a national administrative or judicial authority. The claimant pleads international law in an attempt to alter a decision-making process normally governed by the provisions of the domestic law that applies. Several examples exist, one of the most studied being that of the enforceability of the New York Convention on the Rights of the Child (UN, 1989).

SITUATION – THE ENFORCEABILITY OF INTERNATIONAL LAW BY A NATIONAL COURT

The example of the enforceability of the New York Convention on the Rights of the Child in the national context

The possibility for a party to invoke the New York Convention on the Rights of the Child (cited above) for his own benefit depends on the national context taken in consideration.

In France, this question is the subject of abundant case law notably on the part of the two superior courts in administrative and judicial matters. Although the present positions of the Council of State (Council of State 10 March 1995, petition n° 141083) and of the Court of Cassation (1st Civil Chamber, 14 June 2005, appeal n° 04-16942) now converge in the sense that certain provisions of the instrument do apply, this was not always the case. The courts remain hesitant, for the present, concerning certain articles. For each provision of the Convention, a distinction must be made between purely declaratory formulations which may not be used to obtain a particular result and those which, on the contrary, may be enforced in the national context. For example, Article 3.1 of the Convention ('In all actions concerning children, whether undertaken by public or private social welfare institutions, courts of law, administrative authorities or legislative bodies, the best interests of the child shall be a primary consideration') has been recognised to have direct effect, in contrast to Article 24 ('States Parties recognise the right of the child to the enjoyment of the highest attainable standard of health and to facilities for the treatment of illness and rehabilitation of health. States Parties shall strive to ensure that no child is deprived of his or her right of access to such health care services'). See notably on this issue with the numerous cases cited: D. Alland, 'L'applicabilité directe du droit international considérée du point de vue de l'office du juge' [1998] RGDIP 203; P. Courbe, 'L'application directe de la Convention des Nations Unies sur les droits de l'enfant' [2006] D. 1487; B. Bonnet, 'Le Conseil d'Etat et la Convention internationale des droits de l'enfant à l'heure du bilan' [2010] D. 1031.

In other jurisdictions, the situation may be different. A comparative study was published in 2012: based on an analysis carried out in 12 jurisdictions (Australia, Belgium, Canada, Denmark, Germany, Iceland, Ireland, New Zealand, Norway, South Africa, Spain, Sweden), it appears that the application of the NY Convention on children's rights follows specific routes in each jurisdiction (*The UN Convention on the Rights of the Child: a study of legal implementation in 12 countries*, Laura Lundy, by Ursula Kilkelly, Bronagh Byrne and Jason Kang, Centre for Children's Rights School of Education Queen's University Belfast, 2012 – available at https://www.unicef.org.uk/Documents/Publications/UNICEFUK_2012CRCimplementationreport%20FINAL%20PDF%20version.pdf). The conclusion of the study tellingly underlines that:

The review of comparative practice in relation to the implementation of the CRC in the 12 countries included in this study indicates that: each of the countries in the study is taking the implementation of the CRC seriously, albeit in various ways and with varying degrees of commitment; no one country has managed to fully implement the CRC; there is no perfect, one-size-fits-all model for approaching implementation (report, p. 100).

Is the reverse of this first scenario of the enforceability of international law by a domestic court true? Can national law be invoked before an international court? Although considered much less frequently, this question is answered in the affirmative. The taking into account, by an international court, of the existence of national measures for the execution of an international obligation offers an illustration. The most common case is that of a state that invokes the provisions of its national law in order to attempt to demonstrate that it has satisfied its international obligations. In another, very specific, case, national law is invoked before an international court in order to demonstrate the existence of a rule of international customary law.

SITUATION – THE ENFORCEABILITY OF NATIONAL LAW BY AN INTERNATIONAL COURT

The example of national law as a measure of the execution of an international obligation

In international law, it is accepted that a state is held responsible if it fails to incorporate the execution measures required for the respect and performance of its international engagements into domestic law. (PCIJ, opinion of 21 Feb. 1925 on the Exchange of Turkish and Greek populations, series B, no. 10, p. 20). In order to avoid sanctions, the state in question may decide to invoke the provisions of its own national law for its own benefit to demonstrate that the international engagements have been respected. The question of whether national law may be invoked in an international context may be the object of a legal discussion on the ability of national law to satisfy international requirements.

The nature of this type of discussion can vary widely within one international court. This is the case, in particular, of the examinations into the conformity of national law with the law of the World Trade Organization (WTO) carried out by the Dispute Settlement Body (DSB) panels and the Appellate Body that prepare the decisions delivered by the DSB. Depending on the nature of the case, the WTO bodies pursue either a general and abstract examination of the national law, contenting itself with verifying the existence of such law, or an examination of the concrete effects of the application of the national law.

The example of a national law invoked before an international court to demonstrate the existence of a rule of international customary law

When examining the existence of rules of international customary law, the international lawyers scrutinise the practices of all actors involved, including states when they formulate solutions at their own level and when these are capable of having an impact on international situations. This method of analysis has been announced many times by the International Court of Justice (ICJ) (see the frequently cited statement: '[i]t is of course axiomatic that the material of customary international law is to be looked for primarily in the actual practice and opinio juris of States, even though multilateral conventions may have an important role to play in recording and defining rules deriving from custom, or indeed in developing them' (ICJ, 3 June 1985, Continental Shelf Libyan Arab Jamahiriya/Malta, § 27)).

Another decision illustrates this practice (ICJ, 3 Feb. 2012, *Jurisdictional Immunities of the State* – Germany v Italy; Greece (intervening)). On the issue of whether states, by virtue of a rule of international customary law, enjoyed jurisdictional immunity and immunity from execution in respect of actions for compensation taken against them for damage caused in wartime by their armed forces outside national territory, including in cases of grave violations (massacres), the ICJ had recourse to a comparative legal analysis. The International Court reviewed various national legislative and judicial solutions and concluded its comparative analysis by holding, notably, 'that customary international law continues to require that a State be accorded immunity in proceedings for torts allegedly committed on the territory of another State by its armed forces and other organs of State in the course of conducting an armed conflict' (para. 78) and that:

> under customary international law as it presently stands, a State is not deprived of immunity by reason of the fact that it is accused of serious violations of international human rights law or the international law of armed conflict. In reaching that conclusion, the Court must emphasize that it is addressing only the immunity of the State itself from the jurisdiction of the courts of other States; the question of whether, and if so to what extent, immunity might apply in criminal proceedings against an official of the State is not in issue in the present case (para. 91).

B. Enforceability and the Relationship between European Law and National Law

The question of enforceability may also be raised in relation to European law and national law. The most frequently studied case is that of the enforceability of different sources of European law before national courts. Whether European treaties (for example, the TEU or TFEU or the ECHR) or secondary law (notably European Union regulations and directives) are concerned, great attention is paid to the ability of the subjects of national law to invoke European provisions in cases against, for example, national authorities or cases between individuals. The most emblematic case of this enforceability concerns directives that have not been transposed or have been incorrectly transposed.

SITUATION – THE ENFORCEABILITY OF EUROPEAN LAW BEFORE NATIONAL COURTS

The example of European Union directives that have not been transposed or have been incorrectly transposed invoked before a national court

Directives occupy a unique place in the legal order of the European Union. European norms in their own right, they have an obligatory effect. Member States are obliged to transpose them into their national law and a large number of their provisions formulate clear, precise and unconditional legal rules. However, in contrast to regulations, decisions and treaties, directives never have an immediate effect. The Treaty on the Functioning of the European Union expresses this very clearly: 'A directive shall be binding, as to the result to be achieved, upon each Member State to which it is addressed, but shall leave to the national authorities the choice of form and methods' (art. 288 TFEU). The operation of transposition does not pose any problem when the directive has been correctly inserted into national law. In the contrary case, the reconciliation of a directive with an incompatible rule of national law (be it lacunary or otherwise) raises the issue of the enforceability of European law in national law. The binding character of directives requires that they be recognised as effective to a certain degree. However, their lack of immediate effect militates in favour of a certain limit on this effectiveness, particularly in the case of a conflict with a provision of national law. European case law, scrupulously respecting the letter and spirit of the treaty, is careful to highlight this particular feature of directives, especially when compared to regulations. Contrary to the latter, directives do not derive any direct effect from the treaty in principle: they may not be directly invoked except where they are clear and precise and after the period for their transposition has expired (see notably, the ever-cited decision: Case 41/74 *Van Duyn* [1974] ECR 1337). Moreover, their direct effect has been, until now, limited by the important distinction between regulations and directives established by the treaties. Any individual may invoke a directive that satisfies the three conditions of direct applicability in his or her relations with the state (or a dismembered entity), either to avoid a contrary national legal solution, or, where the case may be, to have the solution apply to him or her. Conversely, a directive cannot, in cases between citizens themselves, apply fully in place of an incompatible provision of national law (see, for a particularly explicit reaffirmation of this principle: Case C-91/92 *Faccini Dori* [1994] ECR I-3325). This is not to say that directives cannot be invoked in any cases between citizens. The duty of the domestic judge to apply national law 'in light of' (principle of interpretation in conformity) European Union law can result in provisions contained in directives having an important effect in the context of a private legal action: Case C-106/89

Marleasing [1990] ECR I-4135. Similarly, it is not unusual for a general principle of European Union law to be implied into a directive (see in particular, regarding the principle of non-discrimination: Case C-144/04 *Mangold* [2005] ECR I-9981).

The reverse scenario of the enforceability of national law by a European court also exists. In addition to the related situation described earlier regarding the relationship between international law and national law, which concerned cases in which national law is invoked by a state desirous of demonstrating that it respects its European engagements, one may imagine the less common case in which national law is invoked because it occupies its own special place in European legal reasoning.

SITUATION – THE ENFORCEABILITY OF NATIONAL LAW BY A EUROPEAN COURT

The example of national legal traditions invoked before the CJEU and the ECtHR

The law issuing from national legal traditions has an important position in European law. Solutions from national law are frequently invoked before the Court of Justice of the European Union (CJEU) or the European Court of Human Rights (ECtHR) in order to influence the interpretation of European law. The most significant example in European Union law concerns the definition of the general principles of European Union law. The Court of Justice is often led to compare and contrast the legal traditions of different Member States in order to construct its own general legal principles (for an early application of this method: Joint Cases 7/56, 3/57–7/57 *Algera* [1957] ECR 81). Thus, for example, 'legitimate expectations', 'legal certainty', 'proportionality', 'the principle of respect for acquired rights', 'the general principles of judicial procedure', 'the principle of equality' and the 'principle of good administration' are all of national origin. It is incontestable that European law has been constructed thanks to the aptitude of parties and judges to invoke general principles from national legal systems. See notably on this theme: J. Molinier (dir.), *Les principes fondateurs de l'Union européenne* (PUF, 2005); T. Tridimas, *General Principles of European Union Law* (3rd edn, Oxford University Press, 2016).

Before the ECtHR, the same approach motivates the comparison of national laws in the name of a veritable principle of 'consensual' interpretation, aimed at confirming or disproving the existence of a European consensus on a given legal question (for example the status of illegitimate children, euthanasia, the law applying to homosexual couples, anonymous childbirth etc.). Here also we see that comparative law is invoked to support the formulation of a solution of European law, although judges are not always adept at this exercise.

C. Enforceability and the Relationship between International Law and European Law

The third form of enforceability concerns the relationship between international law and European law. International law is frequently invoked in the context of European law. A law may potentially be invoked by any legal actor: domestic legal subjects, international legal subjects or European legal subjects. All sources of international law may potentially be concerned: international customary law, treaties, secondary law. It frequently features in the area of fundamental rights where international human rights instruments are regularly invoked to aid the formulation of solutions of European law (EU or Council of Europe): the UN Universal Declaration of Human Rights of 1948, the International Covenant on Economic, Social and Cultural Rights and the International Covenant on Civil and Political Rights adopted by the UN General Assembly in 1966, etc. But the enforceability of international law in the European context is sometimes more problematic. The emblematic case is that of the enforceability of agreements or decisions made within the framework of the WTO and DSB being invoked before European Union authorities. But other situations can also present themselves, notably in transportation law and environmental law.

SITUATION – THE ENFORCEABILITY OF INTERNATIONAL LAW BY A EUROPEAN COURT

The example of the enforceability of WTO Agreements and the decisions of the DSB by European Union courts

The rules governing the enforceability of international agreements within the legal system of the European Union derive for the most part from the case law of the Court of Justice. See the oft-cited Cases 21–24/72 *International Fruit Company* [1972] ECR 1219. See also, having recourse to a principle of interpretation in conformity each time an international instrument is not of direct effect: Case C-439/01 *Cipra* [2003] ECR I-745. The Court of Justice sometimes refuses to recognise the direct effect of conventions or international decisions binding on the EU. The best-known example is that of agreements concluded within the framework of the WTO and the decisions of the DSB. The Court of Justice does not wish to allow international trade rules to interfere with the legality of European secondary laws or to support legal actions against the European Union (see notably: Case C-491/01 *BAT and others* [2002] ECR I-11453; on the famous banana case: Case C-377/02 *Van Parys* [2005] ECR I-1465). This attitude is understandable and is, to tell the truth, fair play, insofar as the same practice is engaged in by several of Europe's commercial partners (notably, the USA). The differential treatment given to international norms is nonetheless patent: the European Union intends to favour the resolution of disputes with third-party states by the DSB but also aims to protect its own internal legal system from the potential influences of global trade rules by considerably restricting the possibility for these to be invoked before European courts.

The example of the enforceability of international customary law and international agreements concerning transport by air and environmental protection by the CJEU

The Court of Justice has delivered a spectacular decision relating to general international law and to international transportation law and the environment: Case C-366/10 *ATAA* [2011] EU:C:2011:864. This case concerned a preliminary reference on validity brought by the High Court of Justice of England and Wales in a case between the Air Transport Association of America, American Airlines Inc., Continental Airlines Inc. and United Airlines Inc. (hereafter referred to together as 'ATAA and others') and the Secretary of State for Energy and Climate Change on the question of the validity of the measures adopted by the UK in implementing a European directive. The theme of the interactions between international law and European law (in this instance, European Union law) is central to this case. It fell to the court to identify, with great precision, 'the only principles and provisions of international law, from among those mentioned by the referring court, that can be relied upon, in circumstances such as those of the main proceedings and for the purpose of assessing the validity' of a European directive (Directive 2008/101/EC of the European Parliament and of the Council of 19 November 2008 amending Directive 2003/87/EC so as to include aviation activities in the scheme for greenhouse gas emission allowance trading within the Community, judgment, para.111). In response to this question, the Court of Justice held that only the following principles could be applied, (limited judicial review for principles of customary law and full judicial review for treaty obligations):

> the principle that each State has complete and exclusive sovereignty over its airspace; the principle that no State may validly purport to subject any part of the high seas to its sovereignty; and the principle which guarantees freedom to fly over the high seas and second: Articles 7 and 11(1) and (2)(c) of the Open Skies Agreement (concluded between the European Communities and the United States in 2007 and modified in 2010), and Article 15(3) of that agreement read in conjunction with Articles 2 and 3(4) thereof (paragraph 111 of the judgment).

Conversely, this judicial frame of reference did not include the Chicago Convention on International Civil Aviation (1944), The Kyoto Protocol (1997) to the United Nations Framework Convention on Climate Change or the existence of a rule of international customary law according to which the principle that a ship on the high seas is subject only to the law of its flag applies by analogy to aircraft flying over the high seas.

The question of enforceability was thus notably discussed in this case in relation to the Open Skies Agreement (above). The classical approach of the Court of Justice is composed of two steps. It gauges, first, the general economy of the international instrument:

> Since the Open Skies Agreement establishes certain rules designed to apply directly and immediately to airlines and thereby to confer upon them rights and freedoms which are capable of being relied upon against the parties to that agreement, and the nature and the broad logic of the agreement do not so preclude, the conclusion can be drawn that the Court may assess the validity of an act of European Union law, such as Directive 2008/101, in the light of the provisions of the agreement (judgment, para. 84).

It then proceeds, second, to examine 'whether the provisions of the Open Skies Agreement that are mentioned by the referring court appear, as regards their content, to be unconditional and sufficiently precise, so as to enable the Court to examine the validity of Directive 2008/101 in the light of those particular provisions' (judgment, para. 85). This examination leads the court, notably, to consider that:

> it must be accepted that Article 11(1) and (2)(c) of the Open Skies Agreement, so far as concerns the obligation to exempt the fuel load of aircraft engaged in international air services between the European Union and the United States from taxes, duties, fees and charges, with the exception of charges based on the cost of the service provided, may be relied upon in the context of the present reference for a preliminary ruling for the purpose of assessing the validity of Directive 2008/101 in the light of that provision (judgment, para. 94).

The reverse case of European law being invoked in an international law context is also possible. Certainly, European law has only a regional dimension. It cannot have equal standing with general international law, notably before international courts such as the ICJ. But the enforceability of European law on the international scene is not merely academic. It arises perfectly commonly every time European law is confronted with the demands of international law. This is the case, for example, of confrontations between European regulations and global free market requirements before the dispute resolution body of the WTO. Examples may also be found in recent case law from the ICJ.

SITUATION – THE ENFORCEABILITY OF EUROPEAN LAW BEFORE AN INTERNATIONAL COURT

The example of the enforceability of European law by the WTO dispute resolution body

In the famous *hormone beef* case (DS48 – EC – Hormones (Canada)), European regulations were invoked several times before the WTO dispute resolution body. We know in particular that the European Union had adopted Directive 2003/74/EC of the European Parliament and of the Council of 22 September 2003 amending Council Directive 96/22/EC concerning the prohibition on the use in stockfarming of certain substances having a hormonal or thyrostatic action and of beta-agonists, in order to conform with the recommendations and decisions of the WTO in the case between it and the US and Canada. The enforceability of European law here allowed the WTO to verify that a measure of European secondary law met the requirements of the WTO and thus could put an end to the counter-measures put in place by the European Union's opponents in the case. Furthermore, the former recently reiterated that, in relation to the latest European measures to be introduced, a specific verification procedure had to be followed by the parties to the conflict (procedure established by Article 21.5 of the Understanding on rules and procedures governing the settlement of disputes found in annexe 2 to the WTO Agreement).

The example of European law invoked before the International Court of Justice

We will have the occasion to highlight (see *infra* p. 75 and p. 119) a recent case of the ICJ, finding in favour of an on solutions of regional law, notably European law: ICJ 20 November 2010, *Ahmadou Sadio Diallo* case – Republic of Guinea v Democratic Republic of the Congo; ICJ 3 February 2012, *Jurisdictional Immunities of the State* – Germany v Italy; Greece (intervening); ICJ 19 June 2012, ruling on the issue of compensation in the *Ahmadou Sadio Diallo* case.

2. THE DIFFERENT MEANINGS OF ENFORCEABILITY IN THE TRIPLE NATIONAL, INTERNATIONAL OR EUROPEAN CONTEXT

In every legal system, the ability to call for the application of legal methods or solutions can vary widely according to the maker (A) and the object (B) of the plea.

A. The Variable 'Subject': Who Invokes the Law?

The different scenarios of enforceability envisaged in the triple national, international and European context implies that a wide range of extremely disparate situations can arise according to the characteristics of the legal subject(s) in question.

We can distinguish, in effect, different categories of legal subjects: subjects of public law and subjects of private law; subjects of domestic law and subjects of international law and, as the case may be, subjects of European law. These two groups are liable to overlap. Subjects of domestic law may also be subjects of public law (a state or a public institution) or private law (a natural person or a private corporation). In the case of subjects of international law and, eventually, of European law, it was long considered that these could not be anything but public law subjects (states, international or European organisations, international or European public institutions, holders of legal personality) but the place of private law actors is becoming more commonly recognised (non-governmental organisations, international or European private companies and natural persons).

The type of subject allows us to distinguish two broad types of enforceability: vertical enforceability (between a public body and a natural person) and horizontal enforceability (between private entities). This distinction is not unique to the theme of global legal pluralism. But it presents particular characteristics in the triple national, international and European context.

First, let us consider the issues relating to vertical enforceability.

SITUATION – VERTICAL ENFORCEABILITY

The example of a national public institution confronted with the requirements of international or European law

The term 'vertical' is commonly used in relation to enforceability to designate the relationship between a national public institution and one or more subjects of private law. This relationship is of interest to the theme of global legal pluralism and enforceability where the legal subject wishes to use developments in international or European law to influence and sometimes to alter the position of a public institution on a legal issue. The question of whether the law invoked may be relied upon before that public institution can be crucial. It forms part of the strategic tools that the different actors in the case may use to counter or, on the other hand, maintain a public action. In effect, if a legal rule, the existence of which is not contested, cannot be invoked by a party against a state or a public entity, it is not capable of producing the desired legal effect. The examples are legion. Here we will mention two examples, drawn from the enforceability of international or European law by national courts. The first deals with the aforementioned question (see above, p. 40) of whether the New York Convention on the Rights of the Child may be invoked in national law. The second relates to the possibility for European Union directives to displace domestic provisions when an administrative act is contested (see, the famous French *Cohn-Bendit* case (Conseil d'Etat Ass., 22 Dec. 1978, Rec. Lebon, 524) which is hostile to this possibility and which was abandoned after more than 30 years of resistance by French administrative law judges (Conseil d'Etat Ass., 30 Oct. 2009, Perreux, Req.n° 298348)).

It is also necessary to consider situations of horizontal enforceability.

SITUATION – HORIZONTAL ENFORCEABILITY

The example of the horizontality of human rights and economic freedom of movement

In the international and European context, the term 'horizontal' refers to the applicability of international or European law to the relationship between two private law subjects. For example, the question may be posed whether an instrument of international or European law can be applied to a married couple who wish to divorce, to parties to a commercial contract who contest its validity or, more generally, to a private law dispute. This applicability is notably a function of the recognised ability of private persons to invoke a method or solution of international or European law in their relations.

The question raises relatively few difficulties where the purpose of the international or European legal instrument in question is to govern private legal relations directly (for example, a European regulation or an international convention governing questions of law relating to international divorces or governing a particular type of law).

The issue is more complex, on the other hand, where the provision of international or European law in question concerns something other than a horizontal private law relationship. Two illustrations can be offered. The first concerns what is generally referred to as 'the horizontality of human rights'. This expression refers to the aptitude of these rights to be invoked and, where necessary, recognised in the context of private legal relations. A domestic court could thus be led to consider that fundamental rights of an international or European source have been violated by the actions of private persons and that, for this reason, they ought to be recognised at the domestic level, as otherwise the case might lead to prosecution at another, notably European, level, before the ECtHR (for different examples relating to a clause in a will: App. no. 69498/01 *Pla and Puncernau v Andorra* (ECtHR, 13 July 2004), to a rental agreement: App. no. 35014/97 *Hutten-Crapska v Poland* (ECtHR, 19 June 2006) or to an employment contract: App. no. 39293/98 *Fuentes Bobo v Spain* (ECtHR, 29 February 2000). For an analysis of this horizontal effect, see notably

G. Phillipson, 'The Human Rights Act, "Horizontal Effect" and the Common Law: A Bang or a Whimper?' (1999) 62(6) MLR 824.

The second illustration relates to the enforceability of the economic freedom of movement enshrined in European Union law in relations between private entities. The intrusion of economic freedoms into horizontal relations is incontestably the result of the extensive case law of the Court of Justice which has regularly pronounced on the impact of European law in cases of horizontal litigation brought before national courts (for some still-famous cases: Case 36/74 *Walrave* [1974] ECR 1405 concerning discrimination; Case 58/80 *Dansk Supermarked* [1981] ECR 181 concerning intellectual property; Case C-415/93 *Bosman* [1995] ECR I-4921 concerning sporting activity; Case C-281/98 *Angonese* [2000] ECR I-4139 relating to a private employee recruitment competition; Case C-438/05 *Viking* [2007] ECR I-10779 and Case C-341/05 *Laval* [2007] ECR I-11767 in labour law). In all these cases, it came to the court to decide whether the European law of freedom of movement could be invoked before them to change the direction of a case between private entities. At the heart of the discussion, we find the theme of the enforceability of European Union law in private relations. See on the impact of European law on private law situations: A. Hartkamp, *European Law and National Private Law* (Kluwer, 2012); A. Hartkamp, C. Sieburgh and W. Devroe (eds), *Ius Comune Casebook on the Effects of European Law on Legal Relationships between Individuals* (Hart, 2016).

These two types of enforceability do not cover all of the cases presented previously (see *supra*, this chapter, Section 1). Vertical enforceability does not include situations in which domestic law is invoked in the international or European context. As for horizontal enforceability, this generally excludes relations between public actors. In order to attempt to take these phenomena into account, it is necessary to go beyond this categorisation based on the 'subject' of the enforceability to turn to its object.

B. The Variable 'Object': What is Invoked?

Enforceability has multiple meanings which vary according to what is invoked, which is to say the result desired by the legal subject. This variability is not unique to relations between national, international and European law. In every legal system, the issue of the gradation of the effects a legal rule is capable of producing is raised. Nonetheless, global legal pluralism casts its own light on this question. In the triple national, international or European context, the object of enforceability is, in effect, subject to two main variables.

The first concerns the choice of vocabulary for approaching questions of the enforceability of international or European law, notably in the national context. The expressions 'direct effect', 'self-executing' or 'immediacy' are commonly employed to describe the ability of international or European law to bestow rights and duties upon individuals. Supranational sources of law are of direct effect, self-executing or of immediate effect insofar as they are binding not only on the states that created them, but also on legal subjects who may invoke them. Although direct effect, self-executing character and immediacy remain useful notions, if only due to their theoretical foundations (who is the law aimed at?), one may observe that they are in competition with the term 'enforceability' which, in its different forms, takes into account the variety of legal solutions.

SITUATION – DIRECT EFFECT, SELF-EXECUTING CHARACTER OR IMMEDIACY AND THE DIFFERENT FORMS OF ENFORCEABILITY

Examples drawn from the enforceability of international or European law

The direct effect, self-executing character or immediate effect of European law was envisaged as early as 1928 by the Permanent Court of International Justice (PCIJ, 3 March 1928, Jurisdiction of the Courts of Danzig, series B, n° 15). This was proclaimed very early on to be the cardinal quality of European law, established as such by the treaties (for example, art. 1 of the ECHR and art. 288 TFEU) or affirmed by case law (Case 26/62 *Van Gend en Loos* [1963] ECR 3: see on this case: H. Ruiz Fabri, G.F. Sinclair and A. Rozen (eds), *Revisiting Van Gend en Loos* (SLC, 2014)).

The intensity of the direct effect of European law nonetheless varies strongly from one legal system to another, and sometimes even within each system, and from one norm to another. In international law, it is the intention of the signatories to an international treaty that counts. An international instrument has the potential to be of direct effect if the states that ratified it intended to adopt clear, precise and unconditional provisions creating rights and duties for individuals. Most often, state signatories retain control over the definition of this direct effect. It is often for domestic courts to evaluate the situation case-by-case.

In European Union law and the law of the ECHR the solutions are better supported. The presence of two European courts (ECtHR and ECJ) and the level of integration achieved by the European Union and the ECHR easily explain this. There is abundant case law on the question that has been taken up by national courts. But the solutions are not always uniform. Divergences in interpretation remain between the European context and the national context.

Assuming that these divergences can be overcome, the terms 'direct effect', 'self-executing' or 'immediate' present another disadvantage. They are not always precisely defined. Very often, lawyers who use them are obliged to specify whether they have in mind a vertical or horizontal effect (on this distinction, see *supra*, pp. 49–52) or a partial or total effect. To remedy this situation, European legal scholars have drawn on the case law of the Court of Justice to graduate direct effect by distinguishing different forms of enforceability (see Robert Schütze, *European Constitutional Law* (2nd edn, Cambrige University Press, 2106), especially pp. 77–116). Thus may be distinguished: (1) exclusion, which allows for the avoidance, or disapplication, of a domestic law that would be contrary to a European law of any type: primary law/secondary law, with direct effect or without (for one of the first judgments: Case 48/71 *Commission v Italy* [1972] ECR 529); (2) compensation, which allows the state to be held responsible in tort for failing to meet its European obligations (Cases C-6/90 and C-9/90 *Francovich* [1991] ECR I-5357 and Cases C-46/93 and C-48/93 *Brasserie du Pêcheur and Factortame III* [1996] ECR I-1029); (3) substitution, which involves the direct application of the European law by its pure and simple substitution for the contrary national law (see the landmark decision in Case 106/77 *Simmenthal* [1978] ECR 629); and (4) conforming interpretation, which demands, insofar as possible, an interpretation of the non-European norm (domestic or international) that conforms as closely as possible with European law (see in particular: Case C-106/89 *Marleasing* [1990] ECR I-4135 and Case C-439/01 *Cipra* [2003] ECR I-745). All these distinctions drawn from European law may be extended without problem to international law where it is able to offer an equivalent level of uniformity of legal solutions. But very often, national particularities triumph.

The second variable relates to the nature of the effect sought by enforcement. Schematically, we may consider that in a multilevel approach to law, the act of invoking a legal method or solution developed in another context (national, international or European) may take three different forms.

The enforceability of a norm may, first, proceed from a purely optional attitude in the sense that no legal actor is obliged to take it into account. The law invoked produces, in its strongest form, a simple 'factual effect'. Conversely, the law may be invoked because it has a truly mandatory character in a given situation.

Finally, the third case, closer to the second than to the first, the law may be invoked because it alters the legal situation of the opposing party who, without being the immediate addressee of the law, must take it into account. We may then speak of an opposable effect.

SITUATION – THE FACTUAL EFFECT, THE MANDATORY EFFECT AND THE OPPOSABLE EFFECT

Examples regarding the 'factual effect' in national, international and European law

The invocation of a legal method or solution in a context other than that in which it was formulated is capable of producing a 'factual effect' wherever it does not constitute binding law. Three, very distinct, examples may be envisaged. The act of invoking ECtHR case law before a non-European court, in order to influence the course of national decision-making, may produce a factual effect. The piece of European case law invoked is not legally binding on the foreign court. But the latter may be led to take it into account as a legal fact (see, for a remarkable illustration, the decision of the United States Supreme Court delivered in the case of *Lawrence v Texas* (02-102) 539 US 558 (2003) relating to the criminal prohibition of certain sexual practices). For an analysis of the practices by the judges, see notably: E. Örücü and D. Nelken (eds), *Comparative Law* (Hart, 2007), the contribution of E. Örücü 'Comparative Law in Practice' (p. 411). On the context and the controversies raised by the borrowing of European law by the American Supreme Court: G. Canivet, Les influences croisées entre juridictions nationales et internationales – Eloge de la 'benevolence' des juges (RSCDP, 2005), p. 799.

The second illustration relates to the enforceability of a provision of international law not vested with direct effect in national law. In this situation, the international law provision cannot be invoked by a party to produce a binding legal effect. Despite this, it may be invoked to produce a factual effect, for a remarkable illustration in French case law relating to a United Nations resolution: Civ. 1st, 25 April 2006, appeal n° 02-17344 held that:

> Although the resolutions of the United Nations Security Council are binding on Member States, they do not, in France, have any direct effect insofar as the rules they establish have not been rendered obligatory or transposed into national law; that failing that, they may be taken into consideration by the judge as a legal fact.
>
> (Attendu que si les résolutions du Conseil de Sécurité des Nations Unies s'imposent aux Etats membres, elles n'ont, en France, pas d'effet direct tant que les prescriptions qu'elles édictent n'ont pas, en droit interne, été rendues obligatoires ou transposées; qu'à défaut, elles peuvent être prises en considération par le juge en tant que fait juridique) [2007] RCDIP 113 note S. Lemaire).

A final series of illustrations relates to the circumstances invoked in which a provision of national law is invoked below (see *infra* p. 140) before an international or European court in the context of a discussion on the compatibility of the laws under consideration. Very often, national law does not produce a binding effect strictly speaking, or even an opposable effect. But it exists as a fact that must be taken into account at the stage of the application of international and European law in order to produce legal effects (for an analysis of this phenomenon in the context of the WTO, S. Bhuiyan, *National Law in WTO Law – Effectiveness and Good Governance in the World Trading System* (Cambridge University Press, 2007), especially p. 41).

On the general question of the legal, factual or hybrid statute of foreign law, see the European comparative study: C. Esplugues, J.L. Iglesias and G. Palao (eds), *Application of Foreign Law* (Sellier, 2011).

Examples relating to the distinction between 'mandatory effect' and 'opposable effect' in international and European law

The distinction between the mandatory effect and the opposable effect is well known in contract law. It results from the principle of the relative effect of a contract. A contract is binding on the parties and it may, in certain conditions, be enforced against or by a third party. This distinction is commonly used in the law of international or European treaties in which we distinguish the effects of international conventions for the parties that have adopted them from the effects for third parties, whether these be states, international or European organisations or even private persons. In a context of strong global legal pluralism, this distinction is very interesting. It is common, in effect, for an instrument of international or European law to be invoked by persons who are not direct parties to it. This is the case whenever the instrument is invoked by a natural person (see above, the analysis of direct effect, p. 52). But this scenario of opposability may also concern states or third party international organisations. European Union law is conducive to this type of situation.

The *Bogiatzi* case (C-301/08 [2009] ECR I-10185) is an illustrative example. What did this case concern? The Court of Justice was called upon to make a preliminary ruling on questions raised by a national court dealing with a civil case taken against an air carrier registered in Luxembourg in relation to an accident that occurred while an inter-European flight was boarding. Two of these questions concerned, first, whether the Warsaw Convention (amended at the Hague in 1955) was one of the norms forming the legal order of the European Union that the Court of Justice was charged with interpreting and, second, whether, in any case, this international instrument could be invoked to complete the regime of civil liability established by a European regulation (Regulation (EC) No. 2027/97/EC, in the version that applied to the facts of the case). To the first question, the Court of Justice replied in the negative, considering that the European Community had not succeeded to the Member States that had signed the instrument in question. On the second question, the court considered that the Warsaw Convention could be invoked to complete the regime of civil liability defined by the text of European secondary law, which was silent on this point. These two answers are interesting. The first illustrates a well-known line of case law on the mandatory effect of international conventions signed by Member States in the European legal system (Cases 21–24/72 *International Fruit Company* [1972] ECR 1219). The second answer is part of a strong tendency of European law to interact with the sources of international law that surround it through the concept of opposability. The international convention is opposable to the European legal order as soon as the latter chooses to follow the international instrument in its own legal decisions: '(...) it is clear from (...) Regulation No

2027/97 (…) that, where the regulation does not preclude the application of the Warsaw Convention in order to raise the level of protection of passengers, that protection involves the regulation and the system established by the convention being *complementary and equivalent* to each other' (judgment para. 43, not italics in the text).

4. The comparison of methods and solutions

In the ultimate phase of comparison, lawyers must try to understand the resemblances and differences between the legal methods and solutions retained in the different national, international and European contexts of the application of law. Two recurring questions may present themselves. The first concerns the essential theme of interpretation: in order to compare laws, it is necessary to take into account how they may be interpreted in different contexts (Section 1). The second concerns contextualisation: at some stage in the reasoning, the national, international or European context of the facts and how they compare will have to be taken into account (Section 2).

1. INTERPRETATION

The comparison of the methods and solutions developed in national, international or European law necessarily stumbles over the crucial question of interpretation.[1] A contract, a legal principle or even a piece of case law can be subject to diverging interpretations according to the levels and the legal systems in which they were formulated, without these divergences always necessarily being considered as anomalies (for a few illustrations, see *supra*, p. 24).

When approaching the issue of interpretation in the triple national, international or European context, lawyers may rely upon principles of interpretation established in the national, international and European context. These principles exist in domestic law and in international law in relation to the interpretation of contracts.

[1] For a comparative analysis of the court decision-making process in operation in the United States (Supreme Court), in the European Union (Court of Justice) and in France (Court of Cassation), see M. de S.-O.-L'E. Lasser, *Judicial Deliberations: A Comparative Analysis of Transparency and Legitimacy* (Oxford University Press, 2004).

SITUATION – BASIC PRINCIPLES GOVERNING THE INTERPRETATION OF CONTRACTS

Examples from French, English and international law

French law and international law have both developed, in their own domains, basic principles governing the interpretation of contracts.

The French Civil Code offers a veritable miniature 'guide' to the interpretation of contracts (Arts. 1188–1192 French Civil Code):[2]

Article 1188 – A contract is to be interpreted according to the common intention of the parties rather than stopping at the literal meaning of its terms.

Where this intention cannot be discerned, a contract is to be interpreted in the sense a reasonable person placed in the same situation would give to it.

Article 1189 – All the terms of a contract are to be interpreted in relation to each other, giving to each the meaning which respects the consistency of the contract as a whole.

Where, according to the common intention of the parties, several contracts contribute to one and the same operation, they are to be interpreted by reference to this operation.

Article 1190 – In case of ambiguity, a bespoke contract is interpreted against the creditor and in favour of the debtor, and a standard-form contract is interpreted against the person who put it forward.

Article 1191 – Where a contract term is capable of bearing two meanings, the one which gives it some effect is to be preferred to the one which makes it produce no effect.

Article 1192 – Clear and unambiguous terms are not subject to interpretation as doing so risks their distortion.

These provisions are not legally binding. They content themselves with formulating a few common-sense rules that could help with the interpretation of a private law instrument (search for the common will of the parties, principle of useful effect, contextual interpretation of the contract, reference to customs, etc.).

In English law, important decisions have established rules of a general nature to be applied by courts in order to interpret written agreements. The three main rules are the following. First, words should be understood in their plain and literal meaning, that is to say not the dictionary sense of the word but the sense in which it is generally understood (*Robertson v French* (1803) 4 East 130, at p. 135), unless this creates an inconsistency with the rest of the agreement (*Watson v Haggit* [1928] AC 127) or an absurdity (*Abbott v Middleton* (1858) 7 HLC 68; *Investors Compensation Scheme Ltd v West Bromwich BS* [1998] 1 WLR 898 (HL)). Secondly, words susceptible of two meanings should be

[2] Translation into English by John Cartwright, Bénédicte Fauvarque-Cosson and Simon Whittaker, *The Code Napoléon Rewritten: French Contract Law after the 2016 Reforms*.

interpreted to make the instrument valid rather than void. For instance, in a case (*Haigh v Brooks* (1839) 10 A & E 309) in which a guarantee was to be given to the plaintiffs 'in consideration of your being in advance' the court held, to avoid the risk of past consideration, that the words were to be understood as equivalent to 'in consideration of your becoming in advance'. Thirdly, construction shall be based on the instrument as a whole (*Baron v Fitzgerald* (1812) 15 East 529 at 541. See more generally J. Beatson, A. Burrows, and J. Cartwright, *Anson's Law of Contract* (30th edn, Oxford University Press, 2016), pp. 184 *et seq.*

In international law, similar provisions exist. These have been codified in the Vienna Convention on the Law of Treaties (1969) which devotes an entire section to the issue. Notably, the following provisions may be found:

Article 31 General rule of interpretation

1. A treaty shall be interpreted in good faith in accordance with the ordinary meaning to be given to the terms of the treaty in their context and in the light of its object and purpose.
2. The context for the purpose of the interpretation of a treaty shall comprise, in addition to the text, including its preamble and annexes:
   (a) any agreement relating to the treaty which was made between all the parties in connection with the conclusion of the treaty;
   (b) any instrument which was made by one or more parties in connection with the conclusion of the treaty and accepted by the other parties as an instrument related to the treaty.
3. There shall be taken into account, together with the context:
   (a) any subsequent agreement between the parties regarding the interpretation of the treaty or the application of its provisions;
   (b) any subsequent practice in the application of the treaty which establishes the agreement of the parties regarding its interpretation;
   (c) any relevant rules of international law applicable in the relations between the parties.
4. A special meaning shall be given to a term if it is established that the parties so intended.

Article 32 Supplementary means of interpretation

Recourse may be had to supplementary means of interpretation, including the preparatory work of the treaty and the circumstances of its conclusion, in order to confirm the meaning resulting from the application of article 31, or to determine the meaning when the interpretation according to article 31:

(a) leaves the meaning ambiguous or obscure; or
(b) leads to a result which is manifestly absurd or unreasonable.

These provisions are used quite often by judges who do not hesitate to use several principles of interpretation whilst trying to reconcile them with each other (for a synthetic and illustrated presentation, see O. Corten, *Méthodologie du droit international public* (ULB, 2009), especially pp. 210 *et seq.*; R. Gardiner, *Treaty Interpretation* (Oxford University Press, 2015).

In European law, these rules do not apply. But early on, European courts sought to promote their own principles of interpretation.

SITUATION – PRINCIPLES OF INTERPRETATION DEVELOPED IN EUROPEAN UNION LAW

Example of the theory of 'useful effect'

The so-called theory of 'useful effect' is a principle of interpretation that relies on the idea that a legal act is necessarily the fruit of the will of its author, such that it cannot remain useless or without effect. The principle is reputed to be of Roman origin (Ulpien) and features clearly in certain national legislative provisions (see for example, art. 1157 [or new art. 1191] of the French Civil Code noted above). It does not only belong to European law, all the more so given that it occupies an important position in legal scholarship on international law (Rousseau). It does, however, play a unique role in the European legal order. The European Court of Justice has made a veritable legal doctrine of it and has systematically relied upon it in the formulation of a certain number of decisions establishing the European legal order. Thus, for example, the possibility for European law to substitute itself for a national legal rule was justified with reference to the theory of useful effect: Case 106/77 *Simmenthal* [1978] ECR 629. The same is true, for example, of the wide autonomous definition given by the Court of Justice to the notion of 'workers' benefitting from freedom of movement: Case 53/81 *Levin* [1982] ECR 1035. The court has also relied upon the theory of useful effect in recognising, in the name of European citizenship (art. 20 TFEU), the right of a parent who is a citizen of a third-party state to remain in the European Union with his or her minor child, who is a European citizen: Case C-200/02 *Kunqian Catherine Zhu* [2004] ECR I-9925.

The ECtHR has also demonstrated from its earliest decisions a strong will to make the protection of fundamental rights effective, which is reminiscent of the 'theory of useful effect'. The method of interpretation is therefore deliberately purposive or teleological (see notably, relying on Articles 31–33 of the Vienna Convention of 23 May 1969 on the Law of Treaties, the oft-cited case: App. no. 4451/70 *Golder v United Kingdom* (ECtHR (Grand Chamber), 21 Feb. 1975)) even though this approach is counterbalanced by what are referred to as 'moderating concepts'.

For a philosophical study of the methods of interpretation used by the ECtHR, see G. Letsas, *A Theory of Interpretation of the European Convention on Human Rights* (Oxford University Press, 2008). For a comprehensive approach to the process of interpretation in a European law context, see: S. Besson, N. Levrat and E. Clerc (dir), Interprétation en droit européen – *Interpretation in European Law* (Bruylant – LGDJ – Schulthess, 2011).

Nonetheless, the existence of principles or rules of interpretation does not allow us to predict which interpretation will be made by one legal actor or another, situated at one level of law or another. The comparison of legal methods and solutions used in national, international and European law demands an exacting and often delicate decryption of all the interpretations of the law suggested at different levels by the competent actors.

In order to prevent lawyers from becoming lost in this maze of interpretations, they will have to distinguish those which are capable of having particular importance and influence. Tools exist to help them do this: instruments with an interpretive value and the presence of privileged interpreters. These tools exist at the different levels of application of law. But their respective importance and the realities they cover can vary widely from one level to another. It is therefore interesting to compare them.

Now, what about these instruments with interpretive value?

SITUATION – INSTRUMENTS WITH INTERPRETIVE VALUE

Examples from national, international and European law

At all levels of law, legal actors have the option of adopting instruments with interpretive value. In national law, we are familiar with the practice of interpretive statutes which remain, however, exceptional (for example, French Law n°47-898 of 23 May 1947 interpreting article 16 of the law of 16 April 1946 giving amnesties) and strictly circumscribed (the prohibition on validating laws having the effect of contradicting an interpretation of the law given by the courts for on-going situations without any imperative motive in the public interest: for example, Court of Cassation, ass. plén., 23 Jan. 2004, appeal n° 03-13.617). In international law, this practice is more widespread. Parties to an international treaty may adopt an interpretive statute for the treaty they have concluded. This may be a collective act (for example, the Interpretive Protocol, of 30 July 1936, to Article 10 of the Hague Convention of 20 January 1930 regarding the immunities of the Bank for International Settlements) or, more frequently, a unilateral act (for example, a unilateral declaration by a state which, at the signing of a treaty, wishes to indicate to the other parties present the manner in which it intends to interpret the treaty). In European law, notably in European Union law, the phenomenon took on an unequalled amplitude with the adoption of the latest constituting treaties (for example, the Treaty of Lisbon (2009) includes no less than 37 protocols and 65 declarations, some of which clearly have an interpretive value). It is also found in secondary law (for example, the numerous guidelines adopted by the Commission in competition law).

The question of interpretation is also deeply marked by the presence of privileged interpreters.

SITUATION – THE PRESENCE OF PRIVILEGED INTERPRETERS

Examples from national, international and European law

At all levels, certain actors occupy the position of privileged interpreter. In international law, and more precisely in the law of treaties, states retain the position of 'authentic interpreters' in the sense that only they have the power to clarify the meaning of their will as expressed in a treaty. But there is nothing to prevent them from temporarily or permanently delegating this power to a third party and notably to a judge (for example, the International Court of Justice, the Dispute Resolution Body of the WTO, the International Tribunal for the Law of the Sea, the International Criminal Court, etc.; on the multiplication of international courts and its consequences in terms of litigation strategies at national, European and international level, see Y. Kerbrat (ed.), *Forum Shopping et concurrence des procédures contentieuses internationals* (Bruylant, 2011); O. Kristian Fauchald and A. Nollkaemper (eds), *The Practice of International and National Courts and the (De-)Fragmentation of International Law* (Hart, 2014).

In national and European law, judges clearly occupy the position of privileged interpreters. But distinctions must be made. In the European context, the two great European courts are undeniably favoured: the ECJ for the interpretation of European Union law and the ECtHR for the interpretation of the ECHR.

In a national context, for example in the French context, priority is undeniably accorded to three institutions: the Constitutional Council, whose importance has continued to grow with the exercise of the preliminary reference procedure first established in 2009 (art. 61-1 of the French Constitution on preliminary rulings on constitutionality) and the two upper courts of the administrative and judicial court systems: the Council of State and the Court of Cassation (in the French academic tradition of case commentaries on 'grands arrêts' we find notably: H. Capitant, F. Terré and Y. Lequette, *Les grands arrêts de la jurisprudence civile* (2nd supp, tome 2, 13th edn, Dalloz, 2015); P. Gaïa, R. Ghevontian, F. Mélin-Soucramanien, E. Oliva and A. Roux, *Les grandes décisions du Conseil constitutionnel* (17th edn, Dalloz, 2013); M. Long, P. Weil, G. Braibant, P. Delvolvé and B. Genevois, *Les grands arrêts de la jurisprudence administrative* (20th edn, Dalloz, 2015).

In an English national context, judges are recognised as making the law as they interpret it. The Supreme Court, the Court of Appeal and the High Court are, in that order, the three most prominent judicial bodies.

The questions raised, in the national context, by global legal pluralism greatly challenge the relationship between the forces present. Thus, we may give the example of the controversy provoked by the position taken by the French Court of Cassation when, faced with a potential conflict between French criminal law, on the one hand, and the French Constitution and European Union law on the other, it sought to respond to the question that had been posed to it, after a preliminary ruling by the Court of Justice: Cases C-188/10 and C-189/10 *Aziz Melki and Sélim Abdeli* [2010] ECR I-5667, without referring the question of the constitutionality of the national law to the Constitutional Council (notably: C. Cour de cassation, QPC, 16 April 2010 and ass. plén., 29 June 2010, appeal n°

10-40002). The Constitutional Council (Cons. const., 12 May 2010, n° 2010-605 DC) and the Council of State (Conseil d'Etat, 14 May 2010, Req. n° 312305) clearly disapproved of the defiant attitude of the Court of Cassation, preferring to apply the letter of French law, which accords priority to the preliminary ruling on constitutionality.

2. CONTEXTUALISATION

According to the context, a law may not necessarily always be interpreted or applied in the same manner. At the stage of multilevel comparison, it is essential to determine the influence exerted by the national, international or European legal environment on the legal methods or solutions under consideration. This process can reveal many things: exposing strong differences or, on the other hand, the presence of great similarities, bearing in mind that situations sometimes change.

In order to illustrate this point, it may be interesting to examine the significance of a given word in the triple national, international or European context. Sometimes we find, in effect, that an expression used very commonly to convey one meaning at one level of application of the law does not have the same meaning at all at another level.

SITUATION – THE USE OF THE SAME LEGAL TERM IN A NATIONAL, INTERNATIONAL AND EUROPEAN CONTEXT

The example of the term 'constitution'

Used in domestic law to refer to the fundamental law, that which establishes the authority of the state and that can be written (such as the French Constitution of 4th October 1958 which established the Fifth Republic) or unwritten (such as the English Constitution), the term 'constitution' and its derivatives have gradually gained ground in international and European law in the name of 'constitutional pluralism' (on the origins of this doctrine and the reflections it inspires in modern law, see M. Avbelj and J. Komárek (eds), *Constitutional Pluralism in the European Union and Beyond* (Hart, 2012)). The borrowing of a piece of vocabulary specific to the national context by these two levels of law is not uncontroversial. In international law as in European law, it gives rise to two types of discussions on the aptitude of the expression to move from one level to another and on the transformations that such movements induce in the true meaning of the word. In international law, see for an historical and critical approach to this phenomenon, H. Ruiz-Fabri, 'Les "contaminations" disciplinaires' in J. Bois de Gaudusson and F. Ferrand (eds), *La concurrence des systèmes juridiques* (PUAM, 2008), p. 123; see also the different in-depth analyses offered in L. Klabbers, A. Peters and G. Ulfstein, *The Constitutionalization of International Law* (Oxford University Press, 2009); H. Ruiz Fabri and M. Rosenfeld (eds), *Repenser le constitutionnalisme à l'âge de la mondialisation et de la privatisation* (SLC, 2011); and S. Hennette-Vauchez and J.-M. Sorel (eds), *Les droits de l'homme ont-ils constitutionnalisé le monde?* (Bruylant, 2011). In European law, see the ever-cited case: *Opinion 1/91* Draft agreement between the Community, on the one hand, and the countries of the European Free Trade Association, on the other, relating to the creation of the European Economic Area [1991] ECR I-6079: 'the EEC Treaty, albeit concluded in the form of an international agreement, none the less constitutes the constitutional charter of a Community based on the rule of law.' Compare Joint Cases C-402/05 and C-415/05 *Kadi and Al Barakaat* [2008] ECR I-6351: 'In this connection it is to be borne in mind that the Community is based on the rule of law, inasmuch as neither its Member States nor its institutions can avoid review of the conformity of their acts with the basic constitutional charter, the EC Treaty' (para. 281). For a critical approach to the phenomenon of the constitutionalisation of European law, particularly in relation to the Treaty of Rome (2004) Establishing a Constitution for Europe (not in force), see notably, P. Craig, *The Lisbon Treaty: Law, Politics and Treaty Reform* (Oxford University Press, 2010); J.-CL Piris, *The Lisbon Treaty: A Legal and Political Analysis* (Cambridge University Press, 2010); P. Norma, *The Accidental Constituton: the Making of Europe's Constitutional Treaty* (EuroComment, 2003); and O. Beaud, A. Lechevalier, I. Pernice and S. Trudel (eds), *L'Europe en voie de constitution. Pour un bilan critique des travaux de la Convention* (Bruylant, 2004).

The example of the term 'codification'

Another legal term lends itself well to multilevel comparison: the word 'codification' and its derivatives. Forged in the context of the unification of national law, notably in civil and criminal matters, the idea of codification has spread to the international and European levels (we speak, for example, of the international or European codification of international private law or contract law). This passage from one level to another has the potential to modify the meaning of the term used (see among abundant reflections on this subject, H. Collins, *The European Civil Code. The Way Forward* (Cambridge University Press (Cambridge Studies in European Law and Policy), 2008); P. Lagarde, M. Fallon and S. Poillot Peruzzetto (eds), *Quelle architecture pour un code européen de droit international privé?* (Peter Lang, 2012). For a classical study on codification, see B. Beignier (ed.), *La codification* (Dalloz, 1996). Discussions can be lively, particularly when what is usually a domestic legal term is used at European level: changes in national legal culture might be expected, see H. Collins, cited *supra*, pp. 130 *et seq.*, and critical positions are no surprise (see e.g., P. Legrand, 'A Diabolical Idea' in A. Hartkamp (ed.) *Towards a European Civil Code* (4th edn, Kluwer, 2010); Y. Lequette 'Vers un code civil européen?' in *Le Code civil* (2003) 107 Pouvoirs 97.

The sometimes problematic migration of legal vocabulary and concepts between different levels demonstrates that one must always be very careful when applying a legal method or solution outside the context in which it was developed. A law formulated in a national, international or European context may, when applied in another context, be confronted with a different legal environment. This difference in context must be taken into account at the stage of comparison.[3] To apply a law on another level is to be obliged to compare potentially different contexts.

European law is particularly favourable to this type of analysis. Thus one may envisage two cases representing a European law approach out of its usual context.

SITUATION – EUROPEAN LAW OUT OF ITS USUAL CONTEXT

The example of European food law projected on national private law constructs

An 'ERC' research programme, directed by F. Collart-Dutilleul (http://www.droit-aliments-terre.eu/), was the occasion of a workshop in January 2009 on the manner in which a European regulation (Regulation (EC) No. 178/2002 of the European Parliament and of the Council of 28 January 2002 laying down the general principles and requirements of food law, establishing the European Food Safety Authority and laying down procedures in matters of food safety) could be projected onto private law constructs of an essentially national origin ('Le droit spécial de l'alimentation à l'épreuve du droit privé', Nantes – 29 Jan. 2009). This seminar, among other things, highlighted the necessity of mastering the legal context of a European legal text before attempting to extrapolate it to another level, in this case domestic private law. In effect, every provision of European secondary law must conform to the Treaties (TEU and TFEU) which constitute their legal basis. If, for example, a law infringes the free movement of goods within the European economic area, it must be justified by the pursuit of an objective in the general interest allowed by the treaty (for example, art. 36 TFEU) as interpreted by the Court of Justice in its case law (for example Case 120/78 *Rewe-Zentral* [1979] ECR 649). The regulation mentioned above is not exempt from this rule, and this is why it must first be understood as having the aim of reconciling the principle of freedom of movement with the imperative of the protection of public health. Situating the text in the context of the European internal market also helps us to understand why the consumer is considered in a process of market regulation. If the regulation does not distinguish, for example, between a contracting consumer and a non-contracting consumer, if it seems to state that once the consumer has been informed, he or she becomes responsible, this is because European law is trying to define the status of the European consumer as an independent economic agent, the same as a professional

[3] We will also find it in the later stages of combination and hierarchisation. See *infra*, Parts II and III.

operator. But the analysis must be pushed even further. Two important observations must be made in this regard. First, the material and geographic scope of application of the law is extremely wide. The regulation appears to establish a legal framework, it establishes general principles and seems to be a 'basic law' upon which more developed texts depend. Moreover, although it is not of universal application, we observe that the regulation does not concentrate only on the internal market and that it creates effects both within and beyond the European Union. Now, the extent of its scope of application is not without effect on its normative force. Generally, we observe that the wider the scope of application of a law, the less restrictive it is and, inversely, the more restrictive the law is, the narrower its scope of application is likely to be (see for an often misunderstood example, Case C-285/08 *Leroy Somer* [2009] ECR I-4733). Second, it seems clear that the regulation does not aim to construct a private law system for governing food as such. It is too general for this to be its objective. Thus, one must not commit the error of taking European law for something it is not and to apply it, in the national legal order, as if it dealt with the same subject as national legal institutions do. As a law of the European internal market, regulations are different from national law. They coexist with each other. The relationship between regulations and the private law of each Member State is measured less in terms of the influence of European law on national law than in terms of the articulation between European law and national law. This is not the same thing.

The example of the European internal market compared with international rules on free trade

The regional law of the European Union is in part modelled on pre-existing international rules. For example, it is common for European primary or secondary legal texts to take inspiration from older international legal texts. The most remarkable case, without doubt, is that of the provisions of the EEC Treaty of 1957 relating to freedom of movement compared with the, sometimes very similar, provisions of the GATT of 1947 relating to global free trade (see, in particular, the present Article 36 TFEU and Article XX of the GATT which, using very similar formulations, define justifications for the restrictions). These textual similarities must not erase the specificities of each of these legal systems, however. For example, there is an undeniable difference between the legal nature of the case law of the Court of Justice of the European Union applying Article 36 TFEU and that of the decisions of the DSB applying Article XX of the GATT. The first is part of a process of legal integration which aims to create a legal community. Thus, it has a strong normative value. The second relates more modestly to the resolution of commercial disputes. The objective is not so much to bring the laws of Member States closer together but to facilitate exchanges between State Parties (for a systematic comparison, see L. Bartels and F. Ortino (eds), *Regional Trade Agreements and the WTO Legal System* (Oxford University Press, 2006).

But national law can also be interpreted differently when it is implemented in a different context.

SITUATION – NATIONAL LAW OUT OF ITS USUAL CONTEXT

The example of the interpretation of national law in the context of European human rights protections

Civil law is subject to regulation at different levels: notably national, international and European. In essence, it continues, even today, to be inspired by national law. The interpretation that is given to it may vary nonetheless depending on the context. One author offers an illustration in the shape of a study of a decision of the ECtHR (J.-P. Marguénaud: 'La stigmatisation européenne de l'application mécanique des principes d'interprétation d'un Code civil' [2010] RDC 981 (on the subject of App. no. 64301/01 *Velcea and Mazare* (ECtHR, 1st Dec. 2009)). According to the suggested reading of this decision:

> By calling for the mechanical application of the principles of interpretation in a Civil Code to be avoided, the ECHR has declared open season not only on interpretations that do not conform with the aim of the legal provision applying to a contract but also to those which do not take into account economic and social upheaval. The refusal to endorse the theory of frustration or hardship seems to be directly endangered by this daring new European interpretation.

European law thus offers a technique of interpretation that the domestic lawyers may use to apply national law in a manner that conforms with the demands of European human rights law. Thus, it is for the domestic lawyers to take into account the European context surrounding national law.

The same is true for international law

SITUATION – INTERNATIONAL LAW OUT OF ITS USUAL CONTEXT

The example of international public order

International lawyers handle the distinction between domestic public order and international public order with great dexterity. Although we may observe the development of a public order of a truly international or regional source (on this phenomenon, see, with the references cited, M. Forteau, 'L'ordre public "transnational" ou "réellement international"' [2011] JDI 3; F. Hoffmeister and Th. Kleinlein, 'International Public Order' (2013) *Max Planck Encyclopedia of Public International Law*) the latter often emanates from the former: a rule of domestic public order, due to its essential character, applies to international situations and thus transforms into a rule of international law. This international public order may be applied in a given national context. This double national or European projection of an international rule puts the plurality of contexts of application that impact on the very definition of public order into perspective. The latter may, in effect, vary depending on what is envisaged in a national, international or European legal framework. Thus, the reference to the operation of a domestic rule of public order (that international private lawyers call a 'public order exception') may, according to the context in which the rule in question is applied, refer to a rule defined by the law of the country in which the judge sits (lex fori), to a European legal rule or to a legal rule with a truly international dimension.

PART II

Combining national, international and European law

The first step in the process of comparison has allowed us to enumerate the principal methodological tools that are useful for analysing the similarities and differences between the methods and solutions offered in different contexts of the application of law – national, international or European. One of the next steps may be that of combination,[1] in which lawyers try to gather these methods and solutions together in order to construct his legal reasoning.

The combination of national, international and European law may be seriously envisaged by lawyers in two main situations: that in which the laws present complement each other and that in which the phenomenon and the constraint of the circulation of legal situations is at work.

---

[1] The other step envisaged in this work is that of prioritisation, see *infra*, Part III.

5. The complementarity of laws

Combination is meaningless unless the laws in question complement each other, which is to say that the methods and solutions defined by one law may be combined with those defined by another law in order to produce an independent legal effect. This complementarity is not always present. But it is still relatively common, insofar as at the stage of the application of the law, national, international and European legal systems are rarely expected to deal with situations alone.

This complementarity may be institutional or material (Section 1). We may explain it through the existence of relationships of application (Section 2). It is frequently guided by the search for an effect (Section 3).

1. INSTITUTIONAL AND MATERIAL COMPLEMENTARITIES

A. Institutional Complementarities

It is common (and therefore commonplace) for a law developed in one context to be applied by an institution at another level. This phenomenon may be observed when national, international or European institutions apply laws originating from a context other than their own.

SITUATION – THE APPLICATION OF A LAW ORIGINATING FROM ANOTHER CONTEXT BY NATIONAL, INTERNATIONAL OR EUROPEAN INSTITUTIONS

The example of the application of international and/or European law by national institutions

The way international, or European Union law, is applied in national contexts is influenced by the constitutional structure of the domestic jurisdiction. In the European context, the constitutional structure itself is partly moulded by European Union law or the ECHR. For a case of the application of an international convention binding the European Union through a European directive and the national implementing provisions to which it refers: see Case C-240/09

Lesoochranárske zoskupenie VLK [2011] ECR I-1255 (Arhus Convention on Access to Information, Public Participation in Decision-making and Access to Justice in Environmental Matters – 1998) in which it was held that:

> in so far as concerns a species protected by European Union law, and in particular the Habitats Directive, it is for the national court, in order to ensure effective judicial protection in the fields covered by European Union environmental law, to interpret its national law in a way which, to the fullest extent possible, is consistent with the objectives laid down in Article 9(3) of the Aarhus Convention (para. 50).

In France, for example, all national institutions may potentially be affected by the application of international or European law. It may concern the legislature (the Parliament) or the executive (the President of the Republic or the Government) responsible for authorising an international or European agreement (for example, a ratifying law or a decree of approval) or for transposing an international or European secondary law into national law (for example, a law bringing national law in line with an international treaty or a national law or regulation transposing a European directive). National administrations (the services under the responsibility of the Prime Minister (General Secretariat for European Affairs (SGAE)), the Ministries of State (notably the Ministry of Foreign Affairs and the Ministry of Justice) and independent administrative authorities and territorial administrations (the regions, departments or communes) also contribute to the application of international and European law on French soil (for a detailed presentation of the role of national and territorial administrations in the European context, see E. Dubout and B. Nabli, *Droit français de l'intégration européenne* (LGDJ, 2015)). Moreover, national public courts and tribunals and private arbitrators are also called upon to apply the methods and solutions of international and European law. In France, all judges may be called upon to apply international and European law, whether they belong to the constitutional court or the court of jurisdiction, administrative courts or judicial courts, whether they are ordinary judges, superior judges or judges of first instance, sitting in a collegiate court or a single judge court, and whether they are state judges or arbitrators subject to French arbitration rules (for an annual analysis of French state court decisions delivered in international or European law, see the regular publication of the *Annuaire français de droit international* (ed. CNRS) and the *Annuaire de droit européen* (ed. Panthéon-Assas).

An increasing number of studies focus on how European Union law is applied in the various Member States. Publishers have developed specific series relating to this topic. For instance, Hart Law Publishing created the series European Union Law in the Member States, which includes M. Freedland and J. Prassl, *Viking, Laval and Beyond* (Hart, 2014), M. Bobek, *Central European Judges Under the European Influence. The Transformative Power of the European Union Revisited* (Hart, 2015), M. Bobek and J. Prassl, *Air Passenger Rights* (Hart, 2016).

The situation is different in countries that are not part of the European Union nor signatories of the ECHR. In the US, international law obeys special rules of application as a consequence of two combined factors: first, the absence of regional rules, secondly, the federal structure of the country. See C.A. Bradley, *International Law in the U.S. Legal System* (2nd edn, Oxford University Press, 2015).

For a comparative perspective on domestic judiciary practices, see D. Sloss (ed.), *The Role of Domestic Courts in Treaty Enforcement: A Comparative Study* (Cambridge University Press, 2014).

The example of the application of a national law by an international or European institution

Instances of the application of national law by an international or European institution are less common than those discussed previously. Despite this, cases do exist in which national law is applied by an international or European court responsible for examining its implementation.

Three types of cases may be envisaged. The first concerns circumstances in which an international (International Court of Justice, WTO Dispute Settlement Body) or European court (European Court of Justice or the European Court of Human Rights) examines the compatibility of the application of national law. This compatibility is sometimes evaluated concretely. Then the issue is the application of a national law with regard to the demands of international and European law (national regulation producing an effect contrary to the demands of international or European law). In this situation, the application of the national law is discussed before an international or European institution. For an illustration of a case before the ICJ concerning the legality of a national measure of expulsion: ICJ, 30 November 2010, *Ahmadou Sadio Diallo* case – Republic of Guinea v the Democratic Republic of Congo. For an illustration from WTO law concerning a case of discrimination, see, DSB, Appellate Body, 13th Dec. 1999, *Chile – Taxes on Alcoholic Beverages*, WT/DS87 and DS110/AB/R. For an illustration of a case before the CJEU and the ECtHR, concerning the compatibility of the effects of French regulations with the demands of European law, see, on the national legislation granting priority to an interlocutory procedure for the review of constitutionality: Joint Cases C-188/10 and C-189/10 *Melki and Abdeli* [2010] ECR I-5667, and on the functioning of the French Public Prosecutor: App. no. 37104/06 *Moulin v France* (ECtHR, 23 Nov. 2010).

The second type of case also concerns public or private courts acting in an arbitral or similar capacity. Two scenarios may be highlighted: first, cases in which the CJEU is called upon to apply a national law that has been declared applicable to a contract concluded by the European Union (art. 272 TFEU); second, cases in which the ICSID arbitrator, called upon to apply a national law to a contract concluded by a state and a foreign investor (see on this phenomenon, the analysis of M. Forteau, 'Le juge CIRDI envisagé du point de vue de son office: juge interne, juge international, ou l'un et l'autre à la fois?' in Mélanges J.-P. Cot (Bruylant, 2009), p. 95).

The third type of case concerns the particular scenario in which an international court agrees to evaluate the validity of the ratification of a treaty having regard to the respect of national constitutional provisions by the ratifying state (for the articulation of this rule, see Article 46 of the Vienna Convention on the Law of Treaties – 1969; for an example: Resolution 1757 (2007) by the United Nations Security Council establishing the Special Tribunal for Lebanon).

The example of the application of international law by a European institution

The space occupied by international law in European Union law is growing. Considering only the international agreements binding the EU, the statistical data reveal that: between 1950 and 1974 only 18 agreements were signed, 450 were signed between 1975 and 1999 and more than 700 found a place in the European legal order between 2000 and 2010 (source: http://eur-lex.europa.eu). We are witnessing a veritable explosion of international instruments binding the EU, resulting in the ever-more frequent application of these instruments by the various European institutions (notably: the Commission, the Council of Ministers, the European Council, the European Parliament and the Court of Justice), each according to their respective remits. See as an illustration, the reference made by the Court of Justice to the general rules of international law in relation to nationality: CJEU, 2 March 2010, Case C-135/08 *Rottmann* [2010] ECR I-1449. This phenomenon is not without its consequences for the development of international law in the European context. In effect, the question whether a European approach to international law exists is posed more and more often. See notably on this theme: Ch. Kaddous, *The European Union in International Organisations and Global Governance* (Hart, 2015); J. Wouters, A. Nollkaemper and E. de Wet (eds), *The Europeanisation of International Law* (TMC Asser Press, 2008).

The Council of Europe takes a more modest part in this phenomenon. In the area of fundamental rights in which the Council of Europe can pride itself on the existence of a European court – the European Court of Human Rights – the ECtHR has on occasion applied international treaties. See for an illustration: App. no. 34503/97 *Demir and Baykara v Turkey* (ECtHR, Grand Chamber, 12 Nov. 2008), concerning the ILO conventions on the freedom to form trade unions and the right to strike. On the phenomenon from a fundamental rights perspective: E. Dubout and S. Touzé (eds), *Les droits fondamentaux: charnières entre ordres et systèmes juridiques* (Pedone, 2010).

The example of the application of European law by an international institution

Cases of the application of European law by an international institution remain rare. There are two main reasons for this. The first relates to the regional character of European law, which is often judged to be incompatible with the administration of international justice. The second is linked to the manner in which the CJEU interprets its exclusive competence in an absolute manner concerning, notably, the resolution of disputes between Member States, thus refusing to recognise any competing competence on the part of any other international court (see, the particularly remarkable example of the *Mox* case: Case C-459/03 *Commission v Ireland* [2006] ECR I-4635, concerning referrals to the International Tribunal of the Law of the Sea and other international arbitration bodies; see more recently, in a different configuration, CJEU, 8 March 2011, *Opinion 1/09* concerning the creation of a unified European and European Union patent litigation system [2011] ECR I-1137; compare, also, the terms of withdrawal claimed by Belgium in its conflict with Switzerland regarding the

Lugano Convention on jurisdiction and the enforcement of judgments in civil and commercial matters, a withdrawal that took place 'in concert with the Commission of the European Union' (ICJ, 5 April 2011, order, p. 2); see also *Opinion 2/13* [2014] ECLI:EU:C:2014:2454 in which the CJEU decided that:

> The agreement on the accession of the European Union to the European Convention for the Protection of Human Rights and Fundamental Freedoms is not compatible with Article 6(2) TEU or with Protocol (No 8) relating to Article 6(2) of the Treaty on European Union on the accession of the Union to the European Convention on the Protection of Human Rights and Fundamental Freedoms.

But things are changing. The ICJ recently agreed for the first time to refer to the law of the European Convention for the Protection of Human Rights and Fundamental Liberties (ICJ, 30 November 2010, *Ahmadou Sadio Diallo* case – Republic of Guinea v the Democratic Republic of Congo). Strictly speaking, this law was not 'applied' by the ICJ. It simply referred to it. But it is an interesting beginning which explains, doubtlessly, the reinforcement of the position of regional law before the international court in a more recent decision (ICJ 3 February 2012 *Jurisdictional Immunities of the State* – Germany v Italy; Greece (intervening)). Effectively, the ICJ, in this case, undertook an analysis of the case law of the ECHR, on the same footing as national case law, with the aim of finding within it international customary rules relating to the scope of the jurisdictional immunities enjoyed by States. This practice of comparison, developed by the highest international court in the place of regional law, has become more important in the aftermath of another decision (ICJ, 19 June 2012, ruling on the question of compensation in the *Ahmadou Sadio Diallo* case (cited *supra*)) which makes abundant reference to the practices of the ECHR in relation to the awarding of damages (and, for that matter, the Inter-American Commission on Human Rights (IACHR)).

Moreover, the application of the law of the European Union is occasionally disputed before international tribunals in the context of arbitration proceedings concerning one or several states. We think here of one case between Belgium and the Netherlands, in which the Permanent Court of Arbitration examined the applicability of European Union law in deciding its own competence (CPA, 24 May PCA 2005, *Iron Rhine Railway* case). We think also of the ICSID arbitration decision in which the judges applied a European Union directive (ICSID, *Giovanna a Beccara and others v Argentina*, ARB/07/5, 27 January 2010).

This type of institutional complementarity is sometimes established as a 'principle'. This was true for the difficult and sensitive question of the relationship between the International Criminal Court and State Parties.

SITUATION – INSTITUTIONAL COMPLEMENTARITY ESTABLISHED AS A PRINCIPLE

The example of the relations between the International Court of Justice and the judges of Member States

The Rome Statute of the International Criminal Court (1998) specifies that cases are inadmissible where: (a) the case is the subject of an investigation or proceedings on the behalf of a state with jurisdiction over the case, insofar as that state is not willing or is incapable of seeing the investigation or proceedings through; (b) the case has been the subject of an investigation on the behalf of a state with jurisdiction over it and that state has decided not to prosecute the person concerned, insofar as that decision was not the result of an unwillingness or inability to see the investigation or proceedings through; (c) the person concerned has already been prosecuted for the actions forming the basis for the accusations, and that he cannot be prosecuted by the Court by virtue of Article 20, paragraph 3; and (d) the case is not sufficiently serious for the Court to pursue (Article 17(1)).

This tendency is judged by specialists of the subject to be an expression of a 'complementarity principle' which allows the international legal order to interact with domestic public orders. This interaction is intended to ensure the continuity of prosecutions in order to avoid impunity. For a deeper analysis and critique of the use made of this mechanism, see V. Chetail, 'Tous les chemins ne mènent pas à Rome (la concurrence de procédures dans le contentieux international pénal à l'épreuve du principe de complémentarité)' in Y. Kerbrat (ed.), *Forum Shopping et concurrence des procédures contentieuses internationals* (Bruylant, 2011), p. 126. Compare M.M. El Zeidy, *The Principle of Complementarity in International Criminal Law* (Brill, 2008).

This institutional complementarity is the subject of veritable coordinating rules, as is the case in international arbitration in which national legislative provisions are introduced to govern the relationship between international arbitration and state justice.

SITUATION – INSTITUTIONAL COMPLEMENTARITY GOVERNED BY COORDINATING RULES

The example of the relationship between international arbitration and state justice

International law specialists have notably developed important reflections on the issue of the relationship between arbitration and state justice (see, for example, with the works cited: Ph. Fouchard, E. Gaillard and B. Goldman, *International*

Commercial Arbitration (Kluwer Law International, 1999), especially Parts 4 and 6). A balance is sought to allow the two systems to work in harmony and to complement each other, although competition between them cannot be excluded (see on this question: B. Darmois and E. Glucksmann (eds), Procédures parallèles et decisions contradictoires (Bruylant, 2015; for a presentation in English, see: http://www.iccwbo.org/Products-and-Services/Arbitration-and-ADR/Articles/2014/Report-on-the-conference-on-Parallel-Proceedings-and-Contradictory-Decisions-in-International-Arbitration/). These reflections have notably led to the adoption of rules of civil procedure intended to coordinate the actions of the state judge with those of the arbitrator.

Specifically concerning international arbitration and its relationship with French judges, Articles 1505 *et seq.* of the Code of Civil Procedure (and the legal provisions to which they refer) regulate the supporting role of the national judge responsible for intervening in support of arbitration proceedings (for example, concerning the resolution of a difficulty in deciding the composition of the arbitration tribunal) and establish the conditions under which an arbitration decision may be recognised and executed on French soil (exequatur procedure).

In the UK, the English Arbitration Act 1996 provides a straightforward approach to the legal regime governing international arbitration agreements. The Act treats both domestic and international arbitration agreements as the same: both categories are subject to the Act. Basic provisions regarding the presumptive validity of arbitration agreements and the specific enforceability of such agreements (by means of a stay of litigation) (sections 9–11 of the English Arbitration Act) are applicable to arbitration agreements regardless of the arbitral seat. The Act makes the fundamental requirement that arbitration agreements be recognised and specifically enforced applicable regardless of the arbitral seat, while limiting other provisions (regarding competence–competence and separability) to agreements to arbitrate in England. See Gary B. Born, *International Commercial Arbitration* (2nd edn, Kluwer Law International, 2014), pp. 334 *et seq.*

B. Material Complementarities

The institutional approach to the complementarity of laws from different contexts may be complemented by a material approach. Here, lawyers attempt to capitalise on the similarities and differences that exist between the methods and solutions of national, international or European material law in order to build composite structures intended to produce a particular legal effect. Complementarities of this type are all the more interesting in that they allow lawyers to attain a different result than that which would have been obtained by applying each law separately.

This type of complementarity is rare in relations between national laws, which are generally conceived in terms of substitution rather than combination.

SITUATION – THE RARE CASE OF THE COMBINATION OF NATIONAL LAWS

An example from national case law

The application of national laws to a given factual situation is rarely conceived of in terms of combination. Save in particular cases, such as, for example, the theory of dépeçage (which notably allows the parties to a contract to choose several applicable laws by distinguishing the laws that apply to particular issues from those that would otherwise apply; on this possibility, see Article 3 of the Regulation (EC) No. 593/2008 of the European Parliament and of the Council of 17 June 2008 on the law applicable to contractual obligations (Rome I)) or the 'partial' (and generally accidental) displacement of the law that usually applies through the operation of a public order exception or, potentially, a police law (for example: Articles 9 and 21 of Regulation (EC) No. 593/2008, *supra*), international private law attempts to designate a single applicable national law according to category (which is to say according to general legal question: capacity, marriage, divorce etc.).

One author[1] has nonetheless identified a case in which the solution resulted from the combination of two national laws (the taking into consideration of one and the application of the other):

> Where a foreign State [Brazil] concedes that its legislation allows for the application of the social security legislation in force in the employing country to local consular assistants and, by virtue of circulars n° 285 SS of 31 December 1946 and n° 101 SS of 16 August 1956, it had the opportunity to affiliate its employee with the French social security regime, the decision that declared the State responsible for the damage caused to that employee due to her non-affiliation and directed it to pay compensation was legally justified.

Cases of complementarity are much more frequent in relations between laws conceived in different contexts. The explanation is simple: international and European laws are subject to a principle of speciality such that they, by their nature, have an incomplete character. It is common, therefore, for combinations to arise that bring together the material content of the laws that are present. Here we develop two examples: the first historical and the second more contemporary.

---

[1] L. D'Avout, case note: Cour de cassation (Ch. soc). – 24 février 2004, République fédérative du Brésil c. Mme L. de Azevedo Werneck, pourvoi: 01-47113, [2005] RCDIP 62.

SITUATION – THE MOST COMMON CASES OF THE COMBINATION OF NATIONAL AND INTERNATIONAL LAW

The historical example of the *Boll* decision of the International Court of Justice

In 1958, the ICJ had the occasion to decide on the correct application of an international convention of international private law (the 1902 Guardianship Convention) in a dispute between the Netherlands and Sweden (ICJ, 28 Nov. 1958, Rec. 1958, 66). The main question to be decided was whether a state (Sweden) could take a protective education measure intended to protect a minor whose status was determined, by virtue of the aforementioned Convention, by the law of another state (the Netherlands). In deciding that Sweden had not violated its international obligations, the ICJ held that:

> in spite of their points of contact and in spite, indeed, of the encroachments revealed in practice, the 1902 Convention on the guardianship of infants does not include within its scope the matter of the protection of children and of young persons as understood by the Swedish Law of June 6th, 1924. The 1902 Convention cannot therefore have given rise to obligations binding upon the signatory States in a field outside the matter with which it was concerned, and accordingly the Court does not in the present case find any failure to observe that Convention on the part of Sweden.

The solution of the international court relies upon a combination of two laws, the national law on measures for the protection of minors being considered complementary to the rules of private international law which permits the identification of the law applying to guardianship.

This historical example of complementarity between the provisions of an international legal instrument and a national law may be usefully completed by other, more contemporary, examples, notably arising from the case law of the CJEU or European Union law.

SITUATION – OTHER CASES OF THE COMBINATION OF NATIONAL, INTERNATIONAL AND EUROPEAN LAW

An example of the combination of national, international and European law in relation to transportation

The case law of the CJEU offers several examples of the material combination of national, international and European law. The *Bogiatzi* decision (CJEC, 22 Oct. 2009, Case C-301/08 [2009] ECR I-10185) to which we have already referred and to which we now return is one such example. Let us recall that preliminary references were made to the Court of Justice by a national court seized of a civil suit against an air carrier arising from an accident that took place during the boarding of an inter-European flight. These questions brought together three potentially applicable legal texts: (1) the Warsaw Convention for the Unification of Certain Rules Relating to International Carriage by Air (as amended at the Hague in 1955); (2) Regulation (EC) No. 2027/97 of the Council of 9 October 1997 on air carrier liability in the event of an accident (in the version applying to the facts of the case); and (3) the domestic procedural rules allowing the victim to bring a legal action before a national court. The application of the national and European law was not disputed before the Court of Justice. It was apparent nonetheless. Only national law allowed the victim to seize a state court and to appeal to higher courts. The legal basis for the civil suit directed towards the air carrier lay only in European Union law. Conversely, the application of the Warsaw Convention was in dispute as it established a limitation period of two years and legal action was taken five years after the accident. In deciding that this convention was 'applicable' in the context of this case, the Court of Justice held that the resolution of the case before the national court depended on the combined application of three laws: national law (which allowed the court to be seized), European law (which gave the action its legal basis) and international law (which established a limitation period). The legal solution thus obtained was the consequence of the cumulative application of three laws, a result that none of the laws concerned could have obtained on its own. In this sense, we may speak of material complementarity.

An example of the combination of national, international and European law in the area of the protection of cultural objects

The protection of cultural objects, which is to say the fight against illegal exports of objects that lessen the cultural heritage of a state, is the subject of much regulation in the triple national, international and European context. Without claiming to make an exhaustive list, we may notably highlight the existence, at international level, of the Unidroit Convention on Stolen or Illegally Exported Cultural Objects (Rome, 1995), at European level, of the European Parliament and the Council Directive 2014/60/EU of 15 May 2014 on the return of cultural objects unlawfully removed from the territory of a Member State and, at the national level, of specific administrative or criminal provisions for the protection of national treasures and general civil law rules governing claims taken by victims for the recovery of stolen property. This three-level stratification of the applicable legal regime is conducive to material combinations. We note, in effect, that the Unidroit Convention establishes a procedure for the restitution of cultural objects stolen from their owners which depends simultaneously on civil rules laid down by national legislation and absent from the European directive. Conversely, where the procedure for returning cultural goods to their country of origin is concerned, the Unidroit Convention is not, in principle, applicable to relations within the European Union, and the directive takes its place. The juxtaposition of these two rules show that where relations within Europe are concerned, the fight against illicit trafficking in cultural goods is governed simultaneously by an international convention, a European directive and national legal rules. For an analysis of the interactions between these three normative levels, see

J.-S. Bergé, 'La Convention d'Unidroit sur les biens culturels: retour sur un texte majeur dans la lutte contre un fait international illicite de circulation' (2015) 1 *Uniform Law Review* 26 (doi: 10.1093/ulr/unv022). On the Unidroit Convention, see notably: UNIDROIT Convention on Stolen or Illegally Exported Cultural Objects: Explanatory report [in English and in French], (2001) 6 *Uniform Law Revie* 476.

An example of the combination of national, international and European law in the area of the protection of fundamental rights

Article 53 of the Charter of Fundamental Rights of the European Union states that:

> Nothing in this Charter shall be interpreted as restricting or adversely affecting human rights and fundamental freedoms as recognised, in their respective fields of application, by Union law and international law and by international agreements to which the Union or all the Member States are party, including the European Convention for the Protection of Human Rights and Fundamental Freedoms, and by the Member States' constitutions.

Generally understood to be a non-regression clause (the European Union text cannot be used as an instrument for reducing the protection of fundamental rights), this provision may be read as an affirmation of the complementary character of different national, international and European instruments for the protection of fundamental rights. As the text states, this complementarity operates through the juxtaposition of such instruments in their respective domains of application. But one cannot exclude phenomena of combination in which lawyers seek to apply the texts cumulatively, in order to produce a particular effect (on the different possible effects see Section 3 of this chapter)

2. THE EXISTENCE OF RELATIONSHIPS OF APPLICATION

The expression 'relationships of application' refers to a particular process of combination. Whenever institutions or laws issuing from distinct legal systems present differences that necessitate their combined application, none of the institutions or laws concerned may efface or supplant the methods and solutions of the others. The institutions (A) and laws (B) coexist in a durable manner in a relationship of application.

A. Institutional Relationships of Application

Institutional complementarities sometimes participate in a process of execution. From this perspective, one institution in a given legal context is charged with determining the mode of application of a law issuing from another legal context.

This phenomenon is particularly common for national institutions which try to adapt legal rules in order to allow the application of international and European law. The complementarity between the laws is clear here. It is the national law that allows national courts to realise the rights and obligations established by the international and European sources of law.

SITUATION – THE EXECUTION OF INTERNATIONAL OR EUROPEAN LAW BY NATIONAL INSTITUTIONS

The execution of international law: the example of the incorporation of international treaties into the national legal order

A relatively obvious way of describing a national procedure for the execution of international law is to present the manner in which a source of international law is incorporated into a national legal system. This incorporation sometimes follows a formalised procedure. This is the case in France for international treaties and agreements that are subject to a ratification or approval procedure governed by Articles 52 and 53 of the 1958 Constitution. These provisions create a double distinction: (1) the first distinction is made between 'treaties' and 'agreements', the first requiring ratification by the President of the Republic and the second subject only to the approval of the authority that led the negotiations; and (2) a second distinction, which does not overlap with the first, between those commitments that are subject to enabling legislation, either voted by parliament or approved by referendum (Article 11 of the 1958 Constitution) and those that are not. Respect for these procedural rules had long been outside the jurisdiction of the courts. But things are changing. The Council of State has been called upon to examine the constitutionality of the incorporation procedure that is followed (see for example: Conseil d'Etat, ass. 18 déc. 1998, Req. n° 181249, aff. Parc d'activité de Blotzheim, Conseil d'Etat, 23 fév. 2000, Req. n° 157922, aff. Bamba Dieng). The Court of Cassation has followed suit (Civ. 1re, 29 mai 2001, pourvoi n° 99-16673, aff. ASECNA). See, for a more recent illustration, Conseil d'Etat 9 juill. 2010, Fédération nationale de la libre-pensée et autres, Req. n° 327663: '(…) Considering that it results from the combination of these provisions that treaties or agreements falling within the scope of Article 53 of the Constitution that have been ratified or approved without legal authorisation cannot be regarded as properly ratified or approved within the meaning of Article 55 cited *supra*; that it is for the Council of State, in deciding the case, where it is claimed that a decree publishing a treaty or agreement was ultra vires, to receive submissions, on one hand, based on the defects of the decree and, on the other hand, based on the contention that, by virtue of Article 53 of the Constitution, the ratification or approval of the international agreement in question ought to have been authorised by law; that a treaty or agreement modifying provisions of a legislative nature consists, in the terms of that Article, of an international agreement touching on matters reserved for the law by the Constitution or introducing rules that differ from those established by legislative provisions (...)'.

In the US, the Constitution provides, in Article II, Section 2, that the President has the power to make treaties with the advice and consent of the Senate. An alternative way consists of the possibility used to a large extent to adopt executive agreements which are international agreements concluded by the US without resort to the senatorial process.

In Germany, various constitutional provisions relate to the formal reception of international law. Typically, Article 59§2 provides that: 'Treaties that regulate the political relations of the Federation or relate to subjects federal legislation require the consent or participation, in the form of a federal statute, of the bodies competent in any specific case for such federal legislation'.

In Italy, statutes incorporate international treaties into the national law. Such statutes must be in conformity with the national Constitution: a few provisions deal with the topic, including Article 117 relating to the specific power of the national Parliament and of the regions.

In the UK, Treaties to which the state is a party do not automatically become part of UK law: an Act of Parliament is required to incorporate them into the domestic law. As a consequence, there is no distinction in UK law between self-executing and non-self-executing treaties, with, priorto the Brexit, the exception of treaties concluded by the institutions of the European Union with outside states, pursuant to the powers possessed by those institutions under relevant European Union law. These treaties have been held, as a matter of European Community law, to be directly enforceable within the Member States. There has, however, not been case law in British courts applying this exception. Incorporation is usually a legislative enactment, but in some instances merely the executive acts (orders) of a Minister, who has been previously delegated authorisation to act by legislation. Depending on the occasion, legislative enactments may stand alone and be more detailed than the treaty language or may refer to the treaty being included as a schedule. Finally, the most usual practice is for the statute to state that it gives effect to the treaty, the full text of which is scheduled to the Act. In such instances, the substantive part of the domestic legislation is the text of the treaty itself, which has been transformed into domestic law: see Case 87/75 *Bresciani* [1976] ECR 129; and Case 104/81 *Kupferberg* [1982] ECR 3641. *In Re Westinghouse* [1978] AC 547, the House of Lords opinions revealed that all of them were aware that the Evidence (Proceedings in other Jurisdictions) Act 1975 was adopted to give effect to the Hague Convention on the Taking of Evidence abroad in Civil or Commercial Matters 1970, but the 1975 Act failed to refer to the treaty. See F.A. Mann, *Foreign Affairs in English Courts* (Oxford: Clarendon, 1986), p. 97. In at least one case, *Wilson Smithett and Co. Ltd v Terruzzi* [1976] 1 QB 683, 711, Lord Denning is said to have assumed that the entire Articles of Agreement of the International Monetary Fund had been incorporated, although the legislation only referred to certain provisions.

See also R. Higgins, 'United Kingdom,' in Francis G. Jacobs and Shelley Roberts (eds), *The Effect of Treaties in Domestic Law* (London: Sweet and Maxwell, 1987). For a systematic comparative analysis of the incorporation of international law in the different national legal orders, see: D. Shelton (ed.),

International Law and Domestic Legal Systems: Incorporation, Transformation, and Persuasion (Oxford University Press, 2011).

To these formal methods of transposition may be added methods of material transposition, which may go so far as to adopt veritable domestic measures of execution. These measures are the expression of the duty that international law imposes on states to fulfil their obligations (PCIJ, opinion of 21 Feb. 1925 on the Exchange of Turkish and Greek Populations, series B, n° 10, p. 20: it is self-evident, that a state 'which has contracted valid international obligations is bound to make in its legislation such modifications as may be necessary to ensure the fulfilment of the obligations undertaken'). Such obligations may take multiple forms. The most frequeent case is that in which the national legislation is modified so as to allow the full application of an international instrument concluded by the state.

The execution of European law: examples of the recognition of institutional or procedural autonomy of European Union Member States and the transposition of directives

European law provides a body of rules that commonly require recourse to a national procedure. In this case, national law intervenes alongside European law. It plays an absolutely essential operational role: without national laws, their jurisdictional organisation and the body of procedural rules, European law would be frozen, incapable of movement except within European procedures. In European Union law, this vital role is known as 'the principle of institutional (or procedural) autonomy'. For more than 30 years, it has been the subject of regulation by the Court of Justice (see notably for the first judgments handed down concerning the duplication of taxes and charges illegitimately obtained by Member States: Case 33/76 *Rewe* [1976] ECR 1989; Case 45/76 *Cornet* [1976] ECR 2043; and see more recently, relying on the principle of an effective judicial protection flowing from the constitutional traditions common to Member States: Case C-432/05 *Unibet* [2007] ECR I-2271). The reasoning underlying this principle is twofold: first, in the absence of European regulation, the domestic legal order of each Member State is responsible for designating the competent court and for regulating procedures to safeguard the rights parties derive from the direct effect of European law; and second, those procedures, however, must not be less favourable than those that apply to similar domestic legal proceedings (principle of equivalence) and, above all, they must not make the exercise of the rights conferred by the European legal order impossible or unduly difficult (principle of effectiveness). In other words, when European law does not offer the means for its application, it relies on different national laws. It does not fade away completely; on the contrary, it continues to ensure the respect of its rules in the name of a double imperative of legal effectiveness and uniform application.

The transposition of directives offers a second illustration of the role of execution played by national and European law. A distinctive instrument of the EU's legal structure dominated by the interactions between the European and national levels, the directive is 'binding, as to the result to be achieved, upon each Member State to which it is addressed, but (...) leave(s) to the national authorities the choice of form and methods' (Art. 288 TFEU). National law must implement the directive. This implementation is necessary for the directive to have full effect.

This logic of execution may also be envisaged for European institutions when they are responsible for establishing the manner in which international law is implemented.

SITUATION – THE EXECUTION OF INTERNATIONAL LAW BY EUROPEAN INSTITUTIONS

The execution of international law: the example of the implementation of international law by the European Union institutions

The implementation of international law by the institutions of the European Union sometimes requires a formal act of incorporation. For this purpose, the Treaty on the Functioning of the European Union provides precise rules on the procedure for concluding agreements with third party states and international organisations (see notably, Article 216 *et seq.* TFEU).

In addition, it is quite common for secondary legislation (e.g., a regulation or directive) to facilitate the implementation of an international agreement within the European Union. For example, a European regulation establishes the internal procedural rules allowing European Union institutions to intervene before an international court in cases of disputes between states (the Dispute Resolution Body of the WTO, for example: the Regulation (EU) No. 2015/1843 of the European Parliament and of the Council laying down Union procedures in the field of the common commercial policy in order to ensure the exercise of the Union's rights under international trade rules). In a similar manner, a European directive was adopted with a view to harmonising the positions of Member States to ensure respect for international norms (for example: Regulation (EC) No. 216/2008 of the European Parliament and of the Council of 20 February 2008 on common rules in the field of civil aviation and establishing a European Aviation Safety Agency, which relies on international security norms contained in a convention on international civil aviation).

But more complex scenarios emerge when the execution of international law concerns both the European and national levels. Thus we sometimes see a veritable structure governing the relationships between the three contexts of the application of law.

SITUATION – THE EXECUTION OF INTERNATIONAL LAW BY EUROPEAN AND NATIONAL INSTITUTIONS

The execution of international law: the example of the organisation of the relationships between national and European institutions in cases of mixed agreements

It sometimes happens that an international legal text envisages that its execution will require the shaping of the respective roles assigned to the European and national contexts. This is the case for the Convention on Access to Information, Public Participation in Decision-making and Access to Justice in Environmental Matters (known as the Aarhus Convention, 1998). This Convention confers a right of legal action on any person who has had a request for information refused by a public authority. This right cannot be effective unless measures of execution are adopted by the signatories of the international instrument. Now, a provision of the Convention provides for the possibility of the instrument being simultaneously approved by an organisation for regional integration and its members (we refer then to a 'mixed agreement'). In such a case, in effect, the Convention states that the signatories must arrange their relationships in such a manner as to guarantee the effective exercise of the right to legal action. After the European Union and its Member States signed the Aarhus Convention, a question arose as to how the roles were divided by the different European secondary laws in the area. The Court of Justice responded to this question in an important preliminary reference decision: Case C-240/09 *Zoskupenie* [2011] ECR I-1255 at the end of which it held that if European secondary law had not directly resolved the issue, it was for national courts:

> to interpret, to the fullest extent possible, the procedural rules relating to the conditions to be met in order to bring administrative or judicial proceedings in accordance with the objectives of Article 9(3) of that convention and the objective of effective judicial protection of the rights conferred by European Union law, so as to enable an environmental protection organisation to challenge before a court a decision taken following administrative proceedings liable to be contrary to European Union environmental law.

The execution of the international norm thus resulted from the combination of national law ('procedural rules') and European law ('effective judicial protection of the rights conferred by European Union law'). This case is one of several examples of the, sometimes formidable, difficulties that arise at institutional and/or material level for mixed agreements. For further discussion on this subject, see notably: E. Neframi (ed.), *Les accords mixtes de la Communauté européenne: aspects communautaires et internationaux* (Bruylant, 2007); M. Möldner, 'European Community and Union, Mixed Agreements' (2011) *Max Planck Encyclopedia of Public International Law*.

A third logic, undoubtedly the most advanced, may be capable of explaining institutional complementarities. It concerns the circumstances in which institutions belonging to different legal contexts cooperate with each other in a more or less deliberate manner. Examples are numerous. Here we mention two: the first from trademark law, the second concerning the fight against terrorism.

SITUATION – COOPERATION BETWEEN NATIONAL, INTERNATIONAL AND EUROPEAN INSTITUTIONS

An example of cooperation between national, international and European institutions in the area of trademark law

In trademark law, the Madrid Agreement of 1891 (amended several times) concerning the international registration of trademarks facilitates close cooperation between the national administrations responsible for registering and delivering trademarks and an international administration located in Geneva: the International Bureau of Intellectual Property contained within WIPO. This cooperation is two-way. National administrations send international requests for protection aimed at one or several foreign countries to the international bureau. After registration, the bureau sends those requests it deems admissible to the national administrations of the country or countries concerned. National administrations are responsible for establishing the conditions of the national protection of the trademark. This cooperation between the two levels of the administration gives rise to various communications or notifications (communication of initial and modifying requests, notifications of refusals of national protection, etc.).

The international system of trademark registration put in place by the Madrid Agreement of 1891 (cited *supra*) was modified by a protocol adopted in 1989. The aim of this protocol was to make the Madrid Agreement system interoperable with the European Union Trademark. Following the signing of the protocol by the European Union (2004), a request for international registration can now be sent through or to the EUIPO (cited *supra*).

In relation to trademarks, institutional cooperation may thus concern relations between all the contexts of the application of law: national, international and European.

An example of cooperation between national, international and European institutions in relation to the fight against terrorism

Following the September 11 attacks in New York in 2001, the UN Security Council developed a system of 'targeted sanctions' aimed at fighting terrorism. The implementation of these sanctions can notably involve three distinct institutional contexts: international (UN), European (EU) and national (Member States). The multiplicity of contexts of intervention is justified by a concern for effectiveness. Sanctions agreed at international level do not have direct effect. They therefore require the assistance of regional and national measures of execution (see in particular, Article 48 of the Charter of the United Nations –

1945). When these measures are taken at European level, the European Union institutions endeavour to ensure the effective implementation of the sanctions, sometimes adding their own sanctions to those imposed by the UN. The double role played by the European institutions therefore has an impact on that of the national institutions of Member States, responsible in turn for implementing European law. The result is a multitude of interactions between the different institutional levels.

B. Material Relationships of Application

The interactions between laws in the process of their application often go unnoticed. They are nevertheless important. In effect, such relationships demonstrate that laws developed in different systems, that coexist with and are applied alongside each other, do not disappear. Whatever the result of these joint applications may be, the laws in question continue to exist in the legal context from which they originate. It is therefore necessary to see their application as part of the enduring coexistence of legal rules if we wish to master all the effects the process of combination can produce. These effects are not exhausted by the application of one law alongside another. They are long lasting. That is why it is necessary to understand these exchanges as forming part of an enduring relationship of application.

Several illustrations of this type of relationship of application exist. Here we will develop two series of examples. The first relates to international judicial cooperation in civil and criminal matters.

SITUATION – INTERNATIONAL JUDICIAL COOPERATION IN CIVIL AND CRIMINAL MATTERS

Example drawn from the application of the European right to due process in the context of the European Union law of judicial cooperation in civil matters

The right to due process consists, in the broad sense (due process, right of access to a court, the principle of legality, *ne bis in idem*), of the rights and guarantees contained in Articles 6, 7, 13 and Article 4 of Protocol 7 of the ECHR. Articles 47 to 50 of the Charter of Fundamental Rights of the European Union are also dedicated to due process. In substance, as we know, the right consists of institutional and procedural guarantees (the right of access to a court and to the enforcement of judgments are of particular interest here). It also has a substantive dimension. In the European Union, the law of judicial cooperation in civil matters, together with judicial cooperation in criminal matters, immigration policy and cooperation in police matters, forms the area of freedom, security and justice (AFSJ, arts 81 *et seq.* of the TFEU) which is one of the main goals of the European Union (art. 3.2 TEU). What type of relationship exists between the right to due process and the law of judicial cooperation in civil matters in the European area? Will these bodies of law continue to coexist as two distinct legal structures or, on the contrary, will one be absorbed by the other (the right to due process moulding the law of judicial cooperation in civil matters or, conversely, the law of judicial cooperation in civil matters imposing its own structures on the right to due process)? The question is not merely academic and its discussion is not purely of interest to specialists. It also has scientific value. The right to due process and the law of judicial cooperation in civil matters each have their own rationales. They appeal to two different 'core businesses'. The examination of the accuracy of reasoning that suggests, more or less consciously, that one will be absorbed by the other is therefore not without interest. Rejecting this intellectual approach, which proceeds exclusively through the prioritisation of laws (on this prioritisation, see *infra*, Part III), the hypothesis we would like to prove here is the presence of a 'relationship of application' between these two great legal subjects, which is to say the necessary and long-term coexistence of these two bodies of law with different sources, institutional resources, modes of reasoning and solutions. From this perspective, there would be something irreducible about these two subjects and it would be the greatest mistake to attempt to fuse them. In order to verify this hypothesis, we will analyse an example from the law of judicial cooperation in civil matters (see further on this theme, our study in Le droit à un procès équitable au sens de la coopération judiciaire en matière civile et pénale: l'hypothèse d'un rapport de mise en œuvre, in C. Picheral (ed.), *Le droit a un procès équitable au sens du droit de l'union européenne* (Anthémis-Némésis (collection Droit et Justice), 2012), p. 249).

The example concerns the operation of what is known as the procedural public order reservation within the scope of the Convention and Regulation (EU) No. 1215/2012 on jurisdiction and the recognition and enforcement of judgments in civil and commercial matters (known as 'Brussels I bis'). These texts have, in effect, given rise to a difficulty of interpretation (art. 45 of the regulation). The question was, in substance, whether the violation of defence rights could be invoked as a reason for the non-recognition or non-execution of a foreign decision in cases other than that of the defaulting defendant, the only one envisaged by the law? (For an overview of these discussions, see with the works cited, H. Gaudemet-Tallon, *Compétence et exécution des jugements en Europe* (5th edn, LGDJ, 2015), Title 3; A. Dickinson and E. Lein (eds), *The Brussels I Regulation Recast* (Oxford University Press, 2015), section 13.) The Court of Justice replied in the affirmative; Case C7/98 *Krombach* [2000] ECR I-1935. The solution of the Court of Justice demonstrates that the application of a flagship instrument of judicial cooperation in civil matters is inseparable from the application of the ECHR: the application of the first does not exhaust that of the second.

There are different arguments in favour of this reading of the international right to due process and the right to a fair trial in terms of relationships of application. The first argument that comes to mind is drawn from the procedural nature of the right to a fair trial. Insofar as the latter serves the realisation of fundamental rights, it is logical to consider its relationship with the law of judicial cooperation in this manner. This argument is not entirely convincing, however, for two reasons. The right to a fair trial has a substantive dimension which is difficult to obscure. It therefore cannot be reduced to its mere procedural function. Furthermore, the law of judicial cooperation has a procedural element, which, in the majority of cases, is enough in itself, in the sense that it does not demand an appeal to the right to a fair trial.

The second argument is more interesting even though it has been overtaken to some extent. The right to a fair trial is inseparable from the work of the ECtHR. Now, this court has its own way of working: it reviews the concrete application of the ECHR *a posteriori.* For this institutional reason, which concerns the manner in which the Strasbourg Court is seized and intervenes, it is tempting to present the right to a fair trial as a right against which the application of the law of judicial cooperation may be evaluated. There is a risk, however, that this argument will not stand the test of time. With the systematic and binding application of the Charter of Fundamental Rights of the European Union and the prospective adhesion of the European Union to the ECHR, the validity and interpretation of the legal instruments of the European Union may, in effect, be appreciated after some future intervention by the Strasbourg Court. It is therefore possible for the monitoring of respect for the demands of the right to a fair trial to take institutional routes other than those available at the European level. It may in any case take place following a future *a posteriori* examination by the Strasbourg Court.

The third argument has our vote. If these two bodies of law – the law of judicial cooperation and the right to a fair trial – have a close relationship of application, it is simply because they do not concern the same subject matter. There are strong differences between these bodies of law and there is therefore the potential for them to be complementary, such that one cannot be substituted for the other. In the international legal process, the law of judicial cooperation needs the right to a fair trial and vice versa.

An example drawn from the application of the European right to due process in the context of the European Union law of judicial cooperation in criminal matters

As an extension of the previous example, taken from the law of judicial cooperation in civil matters, it may be interesting to confront the law of judicial cooperation in criminal matters established in the European Union by the area of freedom, security and justice (AFSJ) and the right to due process drawn notably from the ECHR and the special rules, notably from European Union secondary law, intended to encourage judicial cooperation in criminal matters in the European area. Effectively, European Union law brings into play mechanisms for the mutual recognition of contracts and torts that move from one Member State to another. This mutual recognition has one foundation: mutual trust. Our question here is what sort of right to a fair trial can found this mutual trust?

Part of a possible answer concerns the capacity of the right to a fair trial to guide the conditions of the application of the instruments of European Union secondary law that animate the process of mutual recognition which is at work in judicial cooperation in criminal matters. The principle of mutual recognition has an important place in the law of the AFSJ. It has a prominent place among the new treaties in force (see in particular Articles 67, 81 and 82 of the TFEU) and is the subject of numerous associated measures in secondary law. In criminal matters, the flagship instrument of mutual recognition is none other than the famous framework decision 2002/584/JHA on the European arrest warrant and the surrender procedures between Member States.

In applying these instruments of secondary law, the question arises whether the right to a fair trial is capable of interfering with the European Union law of judicial cooperation in criminal matters. At issue here is the automatic character of the recognition and execution of a judicial or extrajudicial instrument in another Member State as well as the sole jurisdiction of courts in the Member State of origin. These possibilities of circulation increase the opportunities for the execution of judicial decisions (absence of formalities, shortening of time periods, cooperation between states). They therefore reinforce the right to execution. But at the same time, they are a potential threat to the right of access to justice and defence rights. How then may we envisage the combination of these instruments of secondary law with the solutions derived from the right to a fair trial?

In answering this question, two different approaches may be taken: a 'systems' approach and an 'application' approach. We will examine them in turn in demonstrating our preference for the latter.

Structures of the 'systems' variety aim to understand the relationship between the right to a fair trial and the law of judicial cooperation in criminal matters in terms of institutional relations. Responses to the difficulties that result from confrontations between these two bodies of law are sought here in the tools or resources offered by the institutional architecture of the European Union and/or the ECHR. This approach offers two possible routes. The first consists of relying upon the simple presumption, established in the celebrated *Bosphorus* case (App. 45036/98 ECHR, 20 June 2005), that European Union law meets the demands of the ECHR. This would involve the presumption that the European Union generally respects the standards established by the right to a fair trial such that if the application of a European regulation were contested before the ECtHR, it would be for the applicant to prove a violation. The second route involves the, still unprecedented, triggering of a clause that allows the rights of a Member State to be suspended for persistent and serious violations of human rights (Article 7(2), in conjunction with Articles 2 and 6 TEU). An instrument of secondary law concerning judicial cooperation in criminal matters expressly refers to this possibility (see, Framework Decision 2002/584/JHA on the European arrest warrant, cited *supra*, reason no. 10).

These different 'systems' approaches, which willingly participate exclusively in the prioritisation of laws (see *infra*, Part III), lead to a certain compartmentalisation of the legal mechanisms capable of sanctioning an attack on a due process right in the context of European Union policy on judicial cooperation in criminal matters. They reveal a sort of reflex, which consists of systematically seeking a tool capable of offering a response to a case of the violation of this right in institutional structures.

Another intellectual approach is possible which follows what we call an 'application' procedure. Effectively, a second series of responses considers that the instruments of secondary law concerned with judicial cooperation in criminal matters are inseparable, in their application, from the systematic and concrete application of the right to a fair trial as developed historically by the interpretation of the ECHR and which we nowadays find notably formulated in the Charter of Fundamental Rights of the European Union. According to this thesis, wherever secondary law does not in itself satisfy the demands of the right to a fair trial on a practical level, it must be possible to invoke the different European sources of this right (ECHR and Charter of Fundamental Rights of the European Union), to which the European Union secondary law expressly or implicitly refers.

This proposal was discussed in relation to judicial cooperation in criminal matters in the context of the framework decision on the European arrest warrant (cited *supra*). The question is, in effect, whether it is permissible to refuse to execute a European arrest warrant where there has been a violation of due process rights (see for an illustration: Case C-399/11 *Melloni* [2013] ECLI:EU:C:2013:107).

Another case of a material relationship of application may be found in the area of free movement on the European level.

SITUATION – EUROPEAN FREEDOM OF MOVEMENT

Example drawn from the application of national law by European Union law on freedom of movement

The concept of a relationship of application allows us to understand the profound nature of the process of negative integration which has characterised, and continues to characterise in those areas in which accompanying measures have not yet been introduced in secondary law, the operation of the freedom of movement as defined by European Union law (arts 26 *et seq.* TFEU) in its relations with the national laws of Member States. These freedoms, far from being sufficient in themselves, participate in a continual relational dialectic in national law. The free movement of people, goods, services or capital acts on the manner in which personal rights derived from national sources are applied, without being able, or even seeking, to establish alternative European personal rights. They aim to respect legal pluralism: European law is not sufficient in itself, it relies on national law and is intertwined with it.

The intervention of European law operates through the well-known mechanism of placing limits on national law. But this mechanism has a specific focus. It involves, in the case of European law, limiting the application of national law, hence the expression 'relationship of application'. This relationship is unusual. Often, it is national law that is presented as capable of facilitating the application of European law through its institutional and procedural tools. As European law is, by its nature, incomplete, it is for national law (its institutions, its procedures) to assist its application (on this point, see the illustrations *supra*). Without seeking to draw an overly symmetrical representation, one could say that the relationship is inverse. It is European law, in effect, that facilitates the application of national law in a European context. Thus, for example, in the first decisions on intellectual property: Case 24/67 *Parke Davis* [1968] ECR 55; Case 40/70 *Sirena* [1971] ECR 69; Case 78/70 *Deutsche Grammophon* [1971] ECR 487; and Case 58/80 *Dansk Supermarked* [1981] ECR 181, freedom of movement never abrogated the exclusive prerogatives established at national level. It was content to modify the manner in which these rights established at a national level could be exercised by distinguishing those situations in which the holders of intellectual property rights can invoke the benefit of their rights and those in which, on the contrary, their exercise is excluded by the principles of freedom of movement.

A question nonetheless arises today regarding the utility of the notion of 'relationship of application', as European secondary law has not ceased expanding and it is increasingly capable of facilitating the exercise of personal rights at a European level, without resorting to national legal instruments. Contrary to what one may think, this sort of relationship has lasted into the second and third generations of European law. Even where secondary law is involved, it sustains a relationship between the spirit of the freedom of movement, introduced by the European treaties, and the practical exercise of personal rights through secondary law. Here we offer an illustration.

This illustration is drawn from the *Dior* case (Case C-59/08 [2009] ECR I-3421) relating to a question of the interpretation of former Directive 89/104/EEC to approximate the laws of the Member States relating to trade marks (a consolidated version of this text has been produced, integrating amendments to the original text: Directive (EU) 2015/2439 of the European Parliament and of the Council of 16th December 2015 to approximate the laws of the Member States relating to trade marks). This legal text defines, in a classic manner, the conditions of the granting of industrial property rights over distinctive symbols, exclusive rights of commercialisation and limits on, or exceptions to, such rights. Its aim is not to regulate contracts in this area in a general manner. It contents itself with dedicating a single Article (art. 8) to the trademark licence which notably provides that the licensor can take legal action (counter-claim) against a licensee who does not respect its contractual obligations in a certain number of cases listed exhaustively by the directive. It is this provision that was notably the subject of a preliminary reference brought before the Court of Justice in a case taken by the Dior Company against a licensee that had sold goods outside its network in contravention of the selective distribution system put in place by the manufacturer. In substance, the question was as follows: does the breach of a contractual restriction constitute a violation of trademark rights such that the owner of the trademark can oppose the circulation of its merchandise outside the network? The Court of Justice's answer to this question reflects the capacity of the European law on freedom of movement to limit the manner in which trademark rights may be exercised, even though this right was established not at national but at European level. Effectively, in coming to the conclusion that:

> the proprietor of a trade mark can invoke the rights conferred by that trade mark against a licensee who contravenes a provision in a licence agreement prohibiting, on grounds of the trade mark's prestige, sales to discount stores such as the ones at issue in the main proceedings, provided it has been established that that contravention, by reason of the situation in the main proceedings, damages the allure and prestigious image which bestows on them an aura of luxury (para. 37),

the Court of Justice confronts the letter of the directive, particularly its Article 8(2), with the very purpose of protecting trademarks in the law of the European Internal Market, what specialists in the subject call the 'essential function of the trademark'. The reasoning is as follows: in the European area, the trademark notably has the function of guaranteeing the quality of the origins of the product bearing the mark; that quality may flow from the prestigious or luxurious image of the product; consequently the violation of a contractual prohibition on selling outside the network is a threat to the trademark, insofar as the manner in which the product is distributed outside its network threatens this image of luxury or prestige; in these circumstances, the rights holder may counterclaim against its licensee (see for the details of the reasoning behind the decision, paras 15–36 of the judgment). The qualification 'breach of licence', in the sense of the 'trademark' directive is thus derived from the justifications given by the law of the European Internal Market for the protection of exclusive intellectual property rights. Two laws coexist – the secondary law and the primary law that survives it – and these two laws have a 'relationship of application'. See further on this theme, J.-S. Bergé, 'Existence et exercice des droits subjectifs et libertés de circulation: l'hypothèse (à nouveau) d'un rapport de mise en œuvre' in E. Dubout and A. Maitrot de la Motte (eds), *L'unité des libertés de circulation – In varietas concordia* (Bruylant-Larcier, 2013), p. 139.

3. THE QUEST OF AN EFFECT

The combination of national, international and European law frequently forms part of a purposive approach in which lawyers seek to benefit from global legal pluralism or to protect themselves from it, depending on which strategy they pursue. It therefore has a functional (the search for a result) and a dynamic (the interaction between different possible results) character. The effects can be several: sometimes equivalent and sometimes different (A), sometimes global and sometimes limited (B).

A. The Quest for Either an Equivalent or Different Effect

The method according to which lawyers seek an equivalent or, on the other hand, a different effect is similar to the approach proposed by modern doctrines of natural law, which do not exclude that the search for universal solutions may be tinted with particularities in the context of a law confronted by globalisation.[2]

One common scenario may be envisaged in which lawyers placed in one context of application of the law seeks a means of supporting his legal analysis in other contexts. One application illustrates this approach particularly well: the development of customary rules or general principles.

[2] For an analysis of this phenomenon, see D. Lochak, *Le droit et les paradoxes de l'universalité* (PUF, 2010), esp. pp. 45 *et seq.*

SITUATION – THE SEARCH FOR AN EQUIVALENT EFFECT

The example of the identification of an international custom having regard to the solutions applied on the national and European levels

We have already had the occasion to observe the manner in which the ICJ tries to identify the existence of international customary rules in the legislative and judicial practices of states in situations involving the international legal order (see *supra*, p. 42). In such cases, international courts seek an equivalent effect produced by the practices of states. This search has expanded with the decision in ICJ, 3 Feb 2012, *Jurisdictional Immunities of the State* – Germany v Italy; Greece (intervening). In this case, in effect, the ICJ expanded its search to the practices of the ECtHR. Although the goal has remained unchanged (to confirm or disprove the theory that an equivalent legal practice exists which in turn reveals the existence of an international customary rule), the method used aspires to be ever more global. It integrates the different levels (national, international and regional) of application of the law (see further our discussions *infra*, p. 97, on the search for a global effect).

The example of the formulation of general principles of European law from national legal traditions and the principles of international law

General legal principles exist at all levels of the application of law: national, international and European. Their essentially judicial formulation, often proceeds from the combination of different laws in which lawyers seek a source of inspiration. The phenomenon may notably be observed in European Union law.

It is common, in effect, for the Court of Justice to have recourse to a comparison between the legal traditions of different Member States in order to construct its own general legal principles (for an early application: Joint Cases 7/56, 3/57–7/57 *Algera* [1957] ECR 39). For example, it has been decided that 'the principle of the retroactive application of the more lenient penalty forms part of the constitutional traditions common to the Member States' such that it 'must be regarded as forming part of the general principles of Community law which national courts must respect when applying the national legislation adopted for the purpose of implementing Community law' (Case C-387/02 *Berlusconi* [2005] ECR I-3565).

The proximity of international law to European law is such that, within the European Union, we also sometimes see combinations of these two bodies of law. Very early on, the Court of Justice relied upon principles of international law (for the first decision delivered by reference to a general principle of international law: CJEC, 13 July 1972, Case 48/71 *Commission v Italy* [1972] ECR 529). This reference to international law notably allowed the court to develop its own general legal principles. A particularly notable case takes account of this:

> (...) the Court holds in this connection, first, that the principle of good faith is a rule of customary international law whose existence is recognized by the International Court of Justice (...) That principle has been codified by Article 18 of the first Vienna Convention, which provides as follows (...). The principle of good faith is the corollary in public international law of the principle of protection of legitimate expectations which, according to the case-law, forms part of the Community legal order (...)

(Case T-115/94 *Opel Austria* [1997] ECR II-39). Compare Case C-162/96 *Racke* [1998] ECR I-3655.

The example of the equivalent interpretation of the ECHR and the CFREU

The search for an equivalent effect amongst laws formulated in different contexts is sometimes stated as a principle of interpretation. Thus one may read in Article 52 of the Charter of Fundamental Rights of the European Union that:

> In so far as this Charter contains rights which correspond to rights guaranteed by the Convention for the Protection of Human Rights and Fundamental Freedoms, the meaning and scope of those rights shall be the same as those laid down by the said Convention. This provision shall not prevent Union law providing more extensive protection.

The justification for this provision stems from the desire expressed by the European Union Member States not to create an instrument for the protection of fundamental rights that would compete with the pre-existing one in the Council of Europe. Save for the particularities of the European Union system, the effect produced by the instruments must be equivalent, insofar as the same rights are protected, which is largely the case (although the CFREU innovates on certain aspects, it repeats the core of the rights protected by the ECHR). See for a recent example, Case C-256/11 *Dereci* [2011] ECR I-11315:

> As a preliminary point, it must be observed that in so far as Article 7 of the Charter of Fundamental Rights of the European Union (...), concerning respect for private and family life, contains rights which correspond to rights guaranteed by Article 8(1) of the ECHR, the meaning and scope of Article 7 of the Charter are to be the same as those laid down by Article 8(1) of the ECHR, as interpreted by the case-law of the European Court of Human Rights. (Case C-400/10 *PPU McB.* [2010] ECR I-8965, para. 53).

But the methods used are sometimes misleading. Under the cover of searching for common or similar solutions in the different contexts of application of the law, sometimes the lawyers are looking for a different effect. One must therefore be vigilant about the meaning of these borrowings. This phenomenon has also been observed in relation to general legal principles.

SITUATION – THE SEARCH FOR A DIFFERENT EFFECT

The example (again) of the development of general legal principles

The existence of cooperation between national judges and the European courts and even of a constructive dialogue cannot disguise, however, the complexity of the relationships formed between different levels. The relationship between national courts and the Court of Justice are subtle by nature, sometimes marked by allegiance, and on other occasions, by resistance or misunderstanding, deliberate or otherwise. Cases of this type are legion. In the course of dialogue between courts, we sometimes see veritable struggles, as national courts, for example, seek to remain master of the concepts they use in a similar context to that of European law.

We have thus demonstrated that in adopting a more extensive concept of legal security than that of the Court of Justice, the French Council of State created an autonomous concept for itself and gave itself the means to no longer apply a principle of legitimate expectations, a principle which it may always say in future applies uniquely to the field of European law (see, regarding the French Council of State, Ass., 24 mars 2006, KPMG ea, Req. n° 288460, P. Brunet and O. Dubos, 'Approche critique du vocabulaire juridique européen: la pratique des juges' [2008] n° 164-165 LPA 7; see also more generally on this phenomenon of national appropriation: J. Sirinelli, *Les transformations du droit administratif par le droit de l'Union européenne – Une contribution à l'étude du droit administratif européen* (LGDJ, 2011).

In a similar manner, the General Court of the European Union has been tempted to give general international law principles an independent European interpretation: Case T-115/94 *Opel Austria* [1997] ECR II-39, this attitude having been firmly resisted by the Court of Justice: Case C-162/96 *Racke* [1998] ECR I-3655.

B. The Quest for Either a Global or Limited Effect

The time and space that separates the pronouncement of a legal question from its solution in a context of the application of the law at several levels – national, international or European – is an invitation to the lawyer to utilise a global approach to anticipate the effects produced by his invention in all the other contexts of application of the law. These situations are particularly visible in the international or European arenas, which form many delocalised spaces for the treatment of a legal question that finds its source in another context. In these configurations, lawyers anticipate the effects produced by his legal invention, by incorporating into his frame of reference not only the law applying on his level but also the law applying on other levels.

These practices notably concern national law when it is invoked in an international or European arena.

SITUATION – THE SEARCH FOR A GLOBAL EFFECT

Examples of the taking into account the application of domestic law in the international or European context

The status of national law before international or European courts takes into account this search for a global effect. By agreeing to consider national law, its application and even sometimes its interpretation, the international or European institution hopes to anticipate the reception of its decision in the national context in question.

This is how we may explain the case law of the ICJ which willingly recalls that although it is not the master of the application of national law, it may first, censure obvious errors of interpretation and second, scrutinise the application of domestic law whenever it interferes with the structures of international law. Thus, for example, in the *Diallo* case (ICJ, 30 November 2010, *Ahmadou Sadio Diallo* case – Republic of Guinea v the Democratic Republic of Congo, cited *supra*) the court notably considered that:

> although it would be possible in theory to discuss [its] validity, it is certainly not for the Court to adopt a different interpretation of Congolese domestic law for the purposes of the decision of this case. It therefore cannot be concluded that the decree expelling Mr. Diallo was not issued 'in accordance with law' by virtue of the fact that it was signed by the Prime Minister although it would be possible in theory to discuss the validity of that interpretation, it is certainly not for the Court to adopt a different interpretation of Congolese domestic law for the purposes of the decision of this case. However, the Court is of the opinion that this decree did not comply with the provisions of Congolese law for two other reasons (…). The Court thus concludes that in two important respects, concerning procedural guarantees conferred on aliens by Congolese law and aimed at protecting the persons in question against the risk of arbitrary treatment, the expulsion of Mr. Diallo was not decided 'in accordance with law'. Consequently, regardless of whether that expulsion was justified on the merits, a question to which the Court will return later in this Judgment, the disputed measure violated Article 13 of the Covenant and Article 12, paragraph 4, of the African Charter.

A similar attitude may be found in the European context. Every time the Court of Justice or the ECtHR is called upon to evaluate whether national law has been applied in accordance with the demands of European law, the discussions to which national law may give rise incidentally enter into the courts' legal analysis even though the European courts willingly admit that they are not entitled to directly intervene in the debate on or legal discussion of domestic law. By way of example, we may cite the Court of Justice's evaluation of the compatibility of the French preliminary ruling on constitutionality mechanism with the demands of European Union law: Joint Cases C-188/10 and C-189/10 *Aziz Melki and Sélim*

Abdeli [2010] ECR I-5667. In that case, French law is literally discussed before the Court of Justice, which reasons in terms of the impact of the application of the domestic regulation on European Union law. In the same manner, when the ECtHR assessed the compatibility of the status of the French Prosecutor's Office with the rights of detained persons to be brought before a judge, all the effects produced by the French judicial structure were closely scrutinised in light of the demands of the ECtHR (see, notably, App. no. 37104/06, *Moulin v France* (ECtHR, 23 Nov. 2010)).

They also concern international law when it is invoked in a European arena and vice versa.

SITUATION – THE SEARCH FOR A GLOBAL EFFECT

Examples of international law taken into account in the European context

The different examples given in presenting cases in which a piece of international law that does not apply in the legal system of the European Union may be relied upon perfectly illustrates this search for a global effect (on these examples see, *infra*, p. 129, our discussions on the subject of the historical case law of the Court of Justice relating to the ECHR – which could not be classified in European law at the time – and the *Bogiatzi* (Case C-301/08 [2009] ECR I-10185), *Gottardo* (Case C-55/00 [2002] ECR I-413) and *SCF* cases (Case C-135/10 [2012] ECLI:EU:C:2012:140).

In these four scenarios, the Court of Justice interprets European law from the point of view of its application to situations specific to national courts. Now these national situations have an international dimension insofar as the norms of international law, which are not binding on the European Union or its predecessor, the European Communities, apply to them. The manner in which the Court of Justice takes this applicable international law into account in the national context reflects the search for a global effect. The Court of Justice anticipates the applicability of international law so as to better control its effects. This allows the Court of Justice to ensure the compatibility between its law and the law that applies in the different Member States. This issue was crucial where the protection of fundamental rights were concerned. The Court of Justice had to show that it was capable of taking into account the demands of the ECHR applicable in the different Member States, to avoid the latter challenging the legal value of its decisions. The Convention is also important in the other areas we have studied (transport, social welfare and intellectual property). European law would not be very effective if it was incapable of interacting with its national and international legal environment.

Examples of taking into account in the international context of European law

It is a recent phenomenon for a court such as the ICJ to take European regional law into account in its decisions. This is demonstrated by the *Ahmadou Sadio Diallo* (ICJ, 30 November 2010, Republic of Guinea v the Democratic Republic of Congo, cited *supra*) and *Jurisdictional Immunities of the State* (ICJ, 3 February 2012, Germany v Italy; Greece (intervening), cited *supra*) cases, in which the international court, for the first time in its history, referred to the case law of the ECtHR, thus placing its decisions in a global context. The phenomenon is particularly remarkable in the *Jurisdictional Immunities of the State* decision, in which it was for the ICJ to characterise the existence of a rule of customary international law by relying, not only on the practice of states, but also on the case law of the ECtHR.

Neither do they spare national institutions when they seek to broaden their frame of reference as much as possible.

SITUATION – THE SEARCH FOR A GLOBAL EFFECT

Examples of taking into account in the national context of international and European law

One case, which had a great impact in France on the issue of jurisdictional immunities, is a good illustration of the capacity of national courts to, very broadly, take into account the whole of the resources offered by international and European law in deciding a case. In the *African Development Bank* case (Cour de cassation, ch. soc., 25 janv 2005, pourvoi n° 04-41012), the issue was a conflict between the treaty establishing this international organisation ('accord de siège') and the ECHR. By virtue of the first text, the international organisation benefitted from a total jurisdictional immunity, including in the ordinary course of employment disagreements between the bank and its international officials. By virtue of the ECHR, a right of access to justice was established in the name of the right to due process, a right which allows, according to the ECtHR's interpretation, a jurisdictional immunity to be set aside when it exposes the plaintiff to a complete denial of justice (notably: ECHR, 18 Feb. 1999, App. n° 28934/95, *Beer and Regan*: 'For the Court, a material factor in determining whether granting [the international organisation] immunity from [national] jurisdiction[s] is permissible under the Convention is whether the applicants had available to them reasonable alternative means to protect effectively their rights under the Convention', § 58). In argument, the appellant asserted that the ECHR did not apply to an international organisation that was not bound by that instrument, such that the right of access to justice could not be invoked to defeat the immunity established by the international treaty. The Court of Cassation avoided this difficulty by integrating a solution dictated by the ECHR into French international public order:

> But held that the African Development Bank cannot avail of a jurisdictional immunity in a case between it and an employee it had dismissed where, at the time of the events in question, it had not established an internal tribunal with the power to rule on cases of that nature, the impossibility for one party to gain access to a court responsible for deciding its case and to exercise a right that forms part of the international public order constitutes a denial of justice that gives jurisdiction to the French courts where there is a link with France.

We see here a case of the appropriation of a solution of European law by a national court that intends to give it a global effect. For an analysis of this solution in terms of the circulation of situations, see our discussions *infra*, pp. 108–20.

See also, *infra*, p. 110, the analyses proposed by: the Council of State, 11 March 2011, Req. 324071, which successively refers to the European Convention for the Protection of Human Rights and Fundamental Freedoms, the Franco-Algerian Agreement of December 27, 1968 relating to the movement, employment and residence in France of Algerian nationals and their families, the Convention on the Rights of the Child, signed in New York on 26 January 1990 and various French legal texts. Compare (notably), Court of Cassation, ch. soc., 16 février 2011, pourvois n° 10-60.189 et 10-60.191, which begins as follows:

> In view of Articles 3 and 8 of Convention n° 87 of the International Labour Organisation (ILO), Article 4 of Convention n° 98 of the ILO, Article 5 of Convention n° 135 of the ILO, Articles 11 and 14 of the European Convention for the Protection of Human Rights and Fundamental Freedoms, Article 6 of the European Social Charter, Article 11 of the Charter of Fundamental Rights of the European Union and Articles L. 2122-1, L. 2122-2 and L. 2143-3 of the Employment Code.

This global approach is not always appropriate. It is counterbalanced by more contained approaches. In international or European arenas, it may be, in effect, that a legal system decides to restrain itself ('self-restraint'), which is to say to restrict the impact of its decisions as far as possible to a limited frame of reference. The reasons for this may be several. They often have a political dimension. The judges seek to contain their power. In the absence of democratic legitimacy, they take care not to break the social contract that binds them to a society.[3]

[3] See, notably on this theme: S. Brondel, N. Foulquier and L. Heuschling (eds), *Gouvernement des juges et démocratie* (Publication de la Sorbonne, 2001), esp.: L. Pech, 'Le remède au gouvernement des juges: le judicial self-restraint', p. 63; see also p. 304, the explanation offered by a former judge of the former Court of Justice, J.-P. Puissochet, concerning the celebrated '*Grant*' decision on the rights of same-sex couples (Case C-249/96 [1998] ECR I-621). See also, A. Torres Pérez, *Conflicts of Rights in the European Union – A Theory of Supranational Adjudication* (Oxford University Press, 2009), esp. pp. 168 *et seq.*

This is how one may interpret, for example, the principle, or more modestly, the concept of subsidiarity when it is applied by the two superior European courts.

SITUATION – THE SEARCH FOR A LIMITED EFFECT

Examples of judicial subsidiarity, notably in relation to the principle of proportionality in European case law

A veritable doctrine has been forged with the aim of containing the ECHR within certain limits. Contrary to received wisdom, the European protection of human rights is not intended, by its essence, to be absolutely uniform. National (see for example, in relation to the regulation of advertising by lawyers, App. no. 15450/89 *Casado v Spain*, ECtHR, 24 Feb. 1994) or local (see for example, in relation to the definition of a restricted electorate for the self-determination ballot of an overseas country, New Caledonia in this case, App. no. 66289/01 *Py v France*, ECtHR, 11 Jan. 2005) particularities are allowed so that states can develop their own system of protection based on a common European model: 'Again, the court cannot hold that the injunction was not "necessary" simply because it could or would not have been granted under a different legal system. As noted in the judgment of 9 February 1967 in the 'Belgian Linguistic' case, the main purpose of the Convention is "to lay down certain international standards to be observed by the Contracting States in their relations with persons under their jurisdiction" (...). This does not mean that absolute uniformity is required and, indeed, since the Contracting States remain free to choose the measures which they consider appropriate, the court cannot be oblivious to the substantive or procedural features of their respective domestic laws (see, *mutatis mutandis*, judgment of 23 July 1968 in the '*Belgian Linguistic*' case, Series A no. 6, pp. 34–35).' (App. no. 6538/74, *Sunday Times v Royaume-Uni*, ECtHR (Grand Chamber), 26 April 1976). Such a margin of appreciation is not left to the complete discretion of Member States. It can vary considerably from one fundamental right to another: certain rights demand veritable guarantees from Member States, whereas others, on the contrary, offer greater flexibility. The exercise of this margin of appreciation, along with recourse to derogations offered by the Convention (for example in the name of public order) are subject to judicial scrutiny. Different tests are applied by judges (tests of necessity and above all of proportionality) to detect abuses. See further on this subject, B. Delzangles, *Activisme et autolimitation de la Cour européenne des droits de l'homme, Fondation Varenne* (LGDJ, 2009); A. Legg, *The Margin of Appreciation in International Human Rights Law* (Oxford University Press, 2012). For a critical approach (seeing proportionality as an instrument for resolving conflicts of laws), see E. Georgitsi, La proportionnalité comme instrument de 'conciliation' des normes antagonistes, [2011] RIDC, 559.

In European Union law, there is no general rule governing the division of labour between the Court of Justice and national courts on the exercise of freedom of movement. Sometimes, the test of proportionality prompts the court to undertake a detailed analysis of the legal basis for the legislation, concluding with a judgment on whether the measure was proportionate or not (see for example, Case 382/87 *Buet* [1989] ECR 1235, on the proportionality of a ban on the door-to-door selling of educational material to the aim of protecting consumers relied on by the French government; Case C-366/04 *Schwarz* [2005] ECR I-10139, on a ban on selling unwrapped confectionery in vending machines). However, the review conducted by the Court of Justice is not always so in-depth. The court sometimes contents itself with indicating to national courts the points to take into account when evaluating respect for the proportionality principle. Concerning restrictions on the use of additives in food, for example, the court has indicated that such restrictions must be limited to what is necessary for the protection of public health, and their evaluation must take into account the results of international scientific research and eating habits in the importing Member State; Case 174/82 *Sandoz* [1983] ECR 2445. Similarly, in establishing the proportionality of a ban on the sale of newspapers containing prize competitions to the goal of maintaining a pluralistic press, the court indicates to national courts that it is best to examine the national newspaper market with a view to establishing the market of the product in question, to take into account the parts of the market held by each publisher and market trends, and to measure the extent to which it is possible in the eyes of the consumer of the product concerned to substitute a newspaper that does not offer the possibility of winning a prize; Case C-368/95 *Familiapress* [1997] ECR I-3689. It also sometimes happens that the Court of Justice gives no instructions to national courts and is content to entrust them with the task of reviewing proportionality (Cf. for example, Case C-275/92 *Schindler* [1994] ECR I-1039, on the proportionality of banning lotteries for the protection of social order). The Court of Justice is thus often led to entrust national courts with the task of reviewing proportionality which assumes a perfect knowledge of the national context in which a measure restricting commerce in the public interest is embedded (for a particularly striking illustration, concerning the Italian legislation governing upper limits on the remuneration of lawyers: Cases C-94/04 and C-202/04 *Cipolla* [2006] ECR I-11421). The Court of Justice, which does not always have as thorough a knowledge of the material and legal context of a case as the national courts, does not have all the means that are at the disposal of the legislature to appreciate the appropriateness of the choice made. Furthermore, and this is a more serious objection, the legitimacy of the review of proportionality, which authorises the European judge to undo the work of the national legislature, is contested. Under these conditions, judicial subsidiarity allows the European judge to restrict the exercise of his power of interpretation. Rather than centralising reviews of proportionality, the Court of Justice allows national courts to form their own judgments of the compatibility of a given restriction with the demands of the European treaties. For a critical approach of the use of the principle of proportionality by the CJEU, see A. Marzal Yetano, *La dynamique du principe de proportionnalité* (Fondation Varenne, 2013).

We also encounter cases of self-restraint in the international case law on the principle of speciality, a self-restraint which may have the aim of encouraging the international legal system to take a global approach.

SITUATION – THE SEARCH FOR A LIMITED EFFECT

Examples drawn from the reading of the principle of speciality by the International Court of Justice

Three authors (P. Daillier, M. Forteau and A. Pellet, *Droit international public* (8th edn, LGDJ, 2009) n° 389, p. 668) offer a very interesting comparison of two requests for an advisory opinion submitted to the ICJ by the UN General Assembly and the World Health Organisation (WHO).

The first was deemed admissible on the grounds that:

> The question put to the Court has a relevance to many aspects of the activities and concerns of the General Assembly including those relating to the threat or use of force in international relations, the disarmament process, and the progressive development of international law. The General Assembly has a long-standing interest in these matters and in their relation to nuclear weapons. This interest has been manifested in the annual First Committee debates, and the Assembly resolutions on nuclear weapons; in the holding of three special sessions on disarmament (1978, 1982 and 1988) by the General Assembly, and the annual meetings of the disarmament Commission since 1978; and also in the commissioning of studies on the effects of the use of nuclear weapons. In this context, it does not matter that important recent and current activities relating to nuclear disarmament are being pursued in other fora.

(ICJ, 8 July 1996, Legality of the Threat or Use of Nuclear Weapons, Advisory Opinion, ICJ Reports 1996, p. 226, esp. para. 12).

In the second advisory opinion, delivered on the same day, the ICJ held that:

> to ascribe to the WHO the competence to address the legality of the use of nuclear weapons even in view of their health and environmental effects – would be tantamount to disregarding the principle of speciality; (...). The World Health Organization is, moreover, an international organization of a particular kind. As indicated in the Preamble and confirmed by Article 69 of its Constitution, 'the Organization shall be brought into relation with the United Nations as one of the specialized agencies referred to in Article 57 of the Charter of the United Nations'. (...). It follows from the various instruments mentioned above that the WHO Constitution can only be interpreted, as far as the powers conferred upon that Organization are concerned, by taking due account not only of the general principle of speciality, but also of the logic of the overall system contemplated by the Charter. If, according to the rules on which that system is based, the WHO has, by virtue of Article 57 of the Charter, 'wide international responsibilities', those responsibilities are necessarily restricted to the sphere of public 'health' and cannot encroach on the responsibilities of other parts of the United Nations system. And there is no doubt that questions concerning the use of force, the regulation of armaments and disarmament are within the competence of the United Nations and lie outside that of specialized agencies. (...). For all these

reasons, the Court considers that the question raised in the request of an advisory opinion submitted to it by the WHO does not arise 'within the scope of [the] activities' of that Organization as defined by its Constitution.

(ICJ, 8 July 1996, Legality of the Use by a State of Nuclear Weapons in Armed Conflict, Advisory Opinion, ICJ Reports 1996, p. 66, esp. paras 25 and 26).

According to the ICJ, the limitations on the powers of the WHO are expressly justified by the 'logic of the overall system', which militates in favour of the recognition of wider powers on behalf of the United Nations.

On the principle of speciality, considered in a more general manner concerning relations between the different international and regional jurisdictions, see M. Forteau, 'Forum shopping et fragmentation du droit applicable aux relations internationales – Le regard de l'internationaliste publiciste' in M. Forteau, J.-S. Bergé, M.-L. Niboyet and J.-M. Thouvenin (eds), *La fragmentation du droit applicable aux relations internationales – Regards croisés des internationalistes privatistes et publicistes* (Pedone, 2011), p. 143. See also on this theme: Y. Kerbrat (ed.), *Forum Shopping et concurrence des procédures contentieuses internationales* (Bruylant, 2011); M. Andenaes and E. Bjorge, *A Farewell to Fragmentation: Reassertion and Convergence in International Law* (Cambridge University Press, 2015); M. Young, *Regime Interaction in International Law: Facing Fragmentation* (Cambridge University Press, 2012).

Such cases of self-restraint may also be found in the national context.

SITUATION – THE SEARCH FOR A LIMITED EFFECT

Examples drawn from national case law elaborated in a strongly internationalised context

In international environmental law, for example, one author has studied the practices of national (mainly American) courts which echo the *forum non conveniens* doctrine which allows one court to declare that it does not have jurisdiction when it decides on a discretionary basis that it would be in the interests of justice and of the parties for it not to decide the case (O. Perez, *Ecological Sensitivity and Global Legal Pluralism* (Hart, 2004), especially pp. 194 *et seq.*). This doctrine is notably used in the fight against forum shopping practices which sometimes prompt plaintiffs to choose a court in the (right or wrong) belief that they are more likely to win their case. The author notably demonstrates that the use of this doctrine is inappropriate in an international market governed by free trade principles. Economic actors find themselves effectively barring the access of certain state jurisdictions even though where investments are concerned access to the territory is totally free and threats to the environment can have a cross-border dimension.

These contentious strategies, which consist of restricting the jurisdiction of a given national court in consideration, notably, of the jurisdiction exercised in another state, are studied increasingly frequently by specialists of international private judicial law and are becoming more popular in the world of international arbitration where it is becoming more and more common for cases to be opened on multiple fronts by the parties to a disagreement (for an overview of this phenomenon in state and arbitration case law, see, notably, with the references cited: F.-X. Train, 'Forum shopping et fragmentation du droit applicable aux relations internationales – Le regard de l'internationaliste privatiste' (cited *supra*), p. 131). These practices are most often located on one level (before national judges or in the context of international commercial arbitration). But interference may occur between the national and international level as is frequently the case, in international arbitration in which state courts find themselves in a supporting role (see, for example, in French international arbitration law, Article 1505 in the Code of Civil Procedure which mentions the role of the 'juge d'appui').

6. The phenomenon and the constraint of circulation

The combination of national, international and European law may be seriously envisaged by the lawyer in which the phenomenon (Section 1) and the constraint (Section 2) of the circulation of legal situations is at work.

1. THE PHENOMENON OF CIRCULATION

Lawyers are largely unaware of the phenomenon of circulation. First, it is necessary to define it and the concept of 'legal framework of reference' (A) and then to distinguish between circulation within one legal context (B) and in different contexts (C).

A. The Definition of Circulation and Legal Framework of Reference

'Circulation' (or 'movement') is not a term commonly used by lawyers; nor does it necessarily feature in specialist dictionaries.[1] Here, it has a relatively precise meaning. Circulation refers, in effect, to the range of phenomena, which allow lawyers to approach a legal situation in a different legal space to that in which it originated. The effect produced by these movements from one normative space to another may be perfectly identical, as circulation gives birth to a given legal effect in the exact same manner – in the broad sense: mandatory effect, opposable effect or even factual effect – in two distinct environments. But this effect often involves differences, and circulation is therefore partial, bearing upon a given aspect of the situation in circulation. The phenomenon of circulation is at play every time a legal effect of a situation that arose in one legal environment appears again in a legal environment other than that in which it originated. If the effects produced are entirely foreign to one

[1] The expression is, for example, absent from the *Dictionary of Globalization* (A. Jones (ed.), Polity Press, 2006) or the Dictionnaire de la globalisation (A.-J. Arnaud (ed.), LGDJ, 2010).

another, or are similar purely by chance,[2] it is not helpful to speak of circulation.

SITUATION – EARLY APPROACHES TO THE CIRCULATION OF SITUATIONS

Examples of the circulation of legal situations

The phenomenon of circulation does not necessarily follow an organised process. It has an eminently factual dimension in which a person, an object, a legal instrument, a judgment or a tort moves from one normative space into another and in which the question arises whether the approach taken to the situation in the receiving space stems from the legal solutions applied in another normative space, notably the place of origin. For example, a ship – whether public or private – flying the flag of a given country and carrying on board its crew and goods – sails from port to port, in territorial waters, in regional zones and on the high seas. This practical situation of circulation interests the law for two reasons. Does the legal status of the ship, that of its crew and of the goods it carries move from one place to another, or does it change completely depending on the successive legal environments it travels through? In the first case, it may be useful to speak of circulation to show that the situation retains the same legal effects, but not in the second, in which the situation changes according to movement from one space to another. The two solutions coexist. All depend on the nature of the question posed. For example, the ship must retain its flag and the rules that attach to it wherever it is found. Conversely, the legal status of the merchandise it is carrying may change (legal here, illegal there) according to the legal environment in which it is found.

Sometimes, circulation is regulated or encouraged by the rule of law. Thus, for example, international or regional rules (notably European) may aim to regulate this circulation by establishing a right of free movement (or a right to mobility). For example, a rule may dictate that merchandise from country A may move within country B so long as it is legal in its country of origin or that a judicial decision delivered in country A produces a legal effect in country B without the need for a formal procedure. From another perspective, furthermore, the circulation of situations is written into the very procedure for accessing the majority of supranational courts, which is dominated by the rule of the prior

[2] For a critique of the random character of the overlapping of legal orders in certain situations: P. Brunet, 'L'articulation des normes – Analyse critique du pluralisme ordonné', in J.-B. Auby, *L'influence du droit européen sur les catégories du droit public* (Dalloz, 2010), p. 195, spec. pp. 200 *et seq*. Here we will be careful to distinguish the scenarios of the circulation of legal situations that we refer to in this chapter under the heading of the combination of laws from the more general scenarios of the circulation of legal methods and solutions that participate in a process of the comparison of laws (on which, see *supra*, Part I).

exercise or exhaustion of domestic legal remedies. Thus we see that the same legal situation may be handled in turn by judges situated in different contexts.

The circulation phenomenon is not unknown to judges. Expressions describing it such as 'legal framework of reference', or its derivatives 'framework of reference' and, more modestly, 'legal framework', are used quite often in European law. The European Court of Justice (CJEU) and, to a lesser extent, the European Court of Human Rights (ECtHR) use the term to refer to the legal context – European or national or international – in which the legal question before them is situated.

SITUATION – THE DEFINITION OF A LEGAL FRAMEWORK OF REFERENCE BY JUDGES

Examples from European case law

The CJEU refers almost systematically to the 'legal framework' and, more rarely, the 'framework of reference' or 'reference framework' (for an example: Case C-371/08 *Ziebell* [2011] ECR I-12735, especially para. 78), which forms a sort of prelude to its legal analysis. This practice is common in decisions delivered in the context of preliminary references. In this manner, the laws that potentially apply are listed at the beginning of the decision, whether they are from a national, international or European source. See, as an example, Case C-478/07 *Budějovický Budvar* [2009] ECR I-7721, which cites, under the title of international law, the Lisbon Agreement of 31 October 1958 for the Protection of Appellations of Origin and their International Registration, under the title of community law, Regulation (CEE) No. 2081/92 of the Council of 14 July 1992 on the protection of geographical indications and designations of origin for agricultural products and foodstuffs and, under the title of 'national law' (sic), a bilateral treaty concluded on 11 June 1976 between the Republic of Austria and the Czechoslovak Socialist Republic on the protection of indications of source, designations of origin and other designations referring to the source of agricultural and industrial products.

The ECtHR adopts a similar practice, if only to specify the national, international and European regulatory context in which the alleged violation of the European Convention for the Protection of Human Rights and Fundamental Freedoms (ECHR) took place. The expression 'framework of reference' was employed in a noteworthy judgement (App. no. 34503/97 *Demir and Baykara v Turquie*; ECtHR, Grand Chamber, 12 Nov. 2008: 'the Court has never considered the provisions of the Convention as the sole framework of reference for the interpretation of the rights and freedoms enshrined therein. On the contrary, it must also take into account any relevant rules and principles of international law applicable in relations between the Contracting Parties (see Bosphorus Hava Yolları Turizm ve Ticaret Anonim Şirketi v Ireland [GC], no. 45036/98, § 150, ECHR 2005-VI; see also Article 31 § 3 (c) of the Vienna Convention)'.

This practice of the two great European courts finds a certain echo in the international and national contexts. We know that the Vienna Convention of 1969 on the Law of Treaties established, under the title of a general rule of interpretation, a principle of 'systemic interpretation', according to which the context of treaties must be taken into account, and in particular 'any relevant rules of international law applicable in the relations between the parties' (art. 31.3(c) of the Convention;[3] compare Article 293 of the United Nations Convention on the Law of the Sea of 1982). National law, for its part, may, by different means, invite lawyers to mobilise all legal principles capable of contributing to their reasoning. For example, a national law may impose a professional obligation to undertake such a task upon a barrister or require a judge to automatically examine all the legal rules applying to a case.

Examples from international and national case law

International courts do not, to our knowledge, use the expression 'legal framework of reference' or its derivatives. But the search for the applicable law is a natural preoccupation which may lead an international institution to refer, in addition to the applicable international law, to a regional law, or even to a national law. For example, a judgment of the International Court of Justice (ICJ) (ICJ, 30 November 2010, *Ahmadou Sadio Diallo* case – Republic of Guinea v the Democratic Republic of Congo), after having applied the International Covenant on Civil and Political Rights of 16 December 1996, referred to the African Charter on Human and Peoples' Rights of 27 June 1981 and to national constitutional provisions (see also, more recently: ICJ 3 February 2012 *Jurisdictional Immunities of the State* – Germany v Italy; Greece (intervening); ICJ, 19 June 2012, which ruled on the question of compensation in the *Ahmadou Sadio Diallo* case (cited above).

These practices of the European courts and, to a lesser extent, of international courts, have clearly inspired our national judges, notably those sitting in our highest courts. Despite the brief format of their decisions, the French Council of State and Court of Cassation do not hesitate to multiply references to national, international and European legal sources. See, for example, Conseil d'État, 11 mars 2011, Req. 324071, which successively cites the ECHR, the Franco-Algerian Agreement of 27 December 1968 relating to the free movement, employment and residence of Algerians and their families, the International Convention on the Rights of the Child, signed in New York on 26 January 1990 and various French laws. The reference to the two multilateral conventions is interesting in this case: the New York Convention allowed the Council of State to exercise its power of censure in the name of the interests of the child; the ECHR

[3] For an in-depth and updated analysis of this provision, see J. Cazala, 'Le rôle de l'interprétation des traités à la lumière de toute autre "règle pertinente de droit international applicable entre les parties" en tant que "passerelle" jetéeentre systèmes juridiques différents', in H. Ruiz Fabri and L. Gradoni (eds), *La circulation des concepts juridiques: le droit international de l'environnement entre mondialisation et fragmentation* (SLC, ed. Sté de législation comparée, 2009), p. 95.

allowed the court to recall that infringements of the right to private and family life must satisfy the demands of proportionality. Compare, Cour de cassation, ch. soc., 16 février 2011, pourvoi n° 10-60.189 10-60.191, which begins as follows:

> In view of Articles 3 and 8 of Convention no. 87 of the World Trade Organization (WTO), Article 4 of Convention no. 98 of the WTO, Article 5 of Convention no. 135 of the WTO, Articles 11 and 14 of the European Convention for the Protection of Human Rights and Fundamental Freedoms, Article 6 of the European Social Charter, Article 11 of the Charter of Fundamental Rights of the European Union, and L. 2122-1, L. 2122-2 and L. 2143-3 of the Labour Code ('Vu les articles 3 et 8 de la convention n° 87 de l'Organisation internationale du travail (OIT), 4 de la convention n° 98 de l'OIT, 5 de la convention n° 135 de l'OIT, 11 et 14 de la Convention européenne de sauvegarde des droits de l'homme et des libertés fondamentales, 6 de la Charte sociale européenne, 11 de la Charte des droits fondamentaux de l'Union européenne et L. 2122-1, L. 2122-2 et L. 2143-3 du code du travail').

In this case, the decision of a lower court was censured for having seen in these international and European legal texts, a reason not to apply the new French law, which made trade unions capable of holding elections of employee representatives subject to a condition of representativeness. It emerges, in effect, from the decision and the annexed appeal that one of these instruments did not apply to this situation and that the others were not contradicted by the French legal provision. By citing all of these legal texts, the Court of Cassation fully assumed its power to verify the absence of a violation of the law, mixing all national, international and European laws together. For a critical analysis of the judicial practice (in social protection matters) to refer confusedly to international and European sources, see S. Robin-Olivier, 'European Legal Method from a French Perspective. The Magic of Combination: Uses and Abuses of the Globalisation of Sources by European Courts' in U. Neergaard, R. Nielsen and L. Roseberry (eds), *European Legal Method – Paradoxes and Revitalisation* (Djøf, 2011), especially p. 307; see also, B. Teyssié (ed.), *L'articulation des normes en droit du travail* (Economica, 2011), especially pp. 223 *et seq.*

See also 'Decisions of British Courts during 2013 Involving Questions of Public or Private International Law', as described by A. Sanger, in (2013) 84(1) *British Year Book Of International Law* 395.

B. Circulation at One Level

The phenomenon of circulation may first be observed within each context of the application of law: national, international or European. It has an essentially concrete character (for a more abstract approach to circulation in the context of the application of the law at different levels, see *infra*, p. 116). Within each national, international or European legal context, situations may be led to move from one normative space to another such that phenomena of combination may be observed.

Within a specific vocabulary, the phenomenon of circulation is considered to describe the mobility of situations (persons, goods, contracts or torts) between national legal systems. Whether we are concerned with 'mobile conflicts', questions relating to 'the international enforceability of judicial or extrajudicial legal instruments or judgments' delivered at national level by a public or parapublic court or, above all, the issue of the 'recognition of situations', very much debated at the moment, international private law doctrine has been and very much remains heavily involved in all these subjects.

SITUATION – CIRCULATION BETWEEN NATIONAL SPACES

The case of the mobile conflict

The expression 'mobile conflict' ('conflit mobile'), attributed to Etienne Bartin by private international law specialists, refers to cases in which the lawyers ponder whether it is appropriate to take into account a change in a connecting factor following the displacement or modification of a person, a good or, potentially, a legal instrument or a judgment. Thus the question of whether a property right ought to be governed by the law relating to the previous location of the good or that relating to its present location or whether the status of a person is governed by the law relating to his or her previous domicile at a given moment (when the person was born or married for example) or the law relating to his or her current domicile (upon death, for example) is posed. The answers to these questions vary according to the aim pursued and the method of reasoning employed. Sometimes, lawyers reason by analogy with the principles of the application of the law in time, which govern, in principle, the immediate operation of the new law (for an in-depth analysis of the institution, see, with the numerous works cited: M. Souleau-Bertrand, *Le conflit mobile* (Dalloz, 2005)). In these different cases, it may be useful to think of the situation in terms of circulation, above all as we know that legal instruments have intervened to encourage the movement of goods and persons (for a comparison of the approaches of international law and European Union law, see *supra*, p. 66).

The example of the recognition of foreign judicial or extrajudicial public legal instruments and judgments

The case of the circulation of foreign judicial decisions and, to a lesser extent, of foreign public or parapublic legal instruments (for example, birth certificates or authenticated documents), are well-recognised cases of legal circulation in private international law. Whether or not this circulation requires a preliminary procedure of exequatur or of recognition, it tends, in every case, to allow a legal document or a judgment issued by a judicial or extrajudicial public authority from state A to produce a legal effect in state B. The legal circulation of judgments has increased considerably in the European context. Instruments of European Union law have notably been introduced to facilitate this circulation in the civil law context by strictly limiting the cases in which a receiving state may refuse to recognise foreign decisions (Regulation (EU) No. 1215/2012 of the European Parliament and of the Council of 12 December 2012 on jurisdiction and the recognition and enforcement of judgments in civil and commercial matters (recast), OJ 2012 L351/1; Regulation (EC) No. 2201/2003 of 27 November 2003 concerning jurisdiction and the recognition and enforcement of judgments in matrimonial matters and the matters of parental responsibility). Circulation is also common in the international context and is spreading to extrajudicial decisions (see notably: Répertoire de Droit international – Dalloz, V° Acte public étranger, by Ch. Pamboukis, 2009; J. Rodriguez-Arena Munoz (ed.), *Recognition of Foreign Administrative Act* (Springer, 2015)).

The example of the recognition of a factual situation constituted abroad

Another case of circulation is envisaged in the context of international private relations: that of the recognition of a factual situation constituted abroad. When the situation in question has not given rise to a foreign public legal instrument, whether judicial or extrajudicial, but arises from an essentially private legal instrument (for example, the creation of a body corporate through a private law instrument, or the conclusion of a private law instrument affecting the personal status of a natural person) the question, very much debated among specialists of private international law, is under which conditions is it possible for that situation to produce a legal effect in another state? Some authors have shown themselves, effectively, to be favourable to the extension of the method of recognition, which disregards the verification of, and therefore the search for, the national law which presided over the situation constituted abroad (on this proposition, see in particular: P. Lagarde, 'La reconnaissance, mode d'emploi' in Mélanges en l'honneur de H. Gaudemet-Tallon, *Vers de nouveaux équilibres entre ordres juridiques* (Dalloz, 2008), p. 481; on the principle of recognition in general, see J. Basedow, *The Law of Open Societies – Private Ordering and Public Regulation in the Conflict of Laws* (Brill, 2015), especially pp. 321 *et seq.* Such an extension of the technique of recognition would open up new possibilities for the circulation of situations from one state to another.

Circulation also takes place at international level, although it corresponds to different realities than those we have observed in the national context. The international level is not as fragmented as national legal systems are. It is characterised by a certain unity of the applicable law: international law. If divisions exist, these result mainly from the multiplication of actors, notably international institutions, responsible for applying international law in a given domain. The phenomenon of circulation is thus limited to exchanges between these international institutions.

SITUATION – CIRCULATION IN THE INTERNATIONAL CONTEXT

An example of circulation between international institutions: the relationship between the United Nations and the International Criminal Court

As one author has observed, the fragmentation of public international law is a different phenomenon from that which may be observed at a national level, notably by private international lawyers (M. Forteau, 'L'influence du choix de la juridiction sur le droit applicable aux relations internationales', in J.-S. Bergé, M. Forteau, M.-L. Niboyet and J.-M. Thouvenin (eds), *La fragmentation du droit applicable aux relations internationales – Regards croisés des internationalistes privatistes et publicistes* (Pedone, 2011), p. 143). It essentially results from the multiplication of institutions, which cooperate with each other and allow legal decisions, legal instruments and torts to circulate at international level.

Thus for example, in the context of the Libyan civil war, we know that in February 2011 the UN Security Council unanimously decided to refer a suspected case of on-going crimes against humanity, that had begun in the Libyan Arab Jamahiriya on 15 February 2011, to the Prosecutor of the International Criminal Court. Thus, a legal instrument – in this case a resolution of the UN Security Council – summoned the authority of international criminal law – the Prosecutor of the International Criminal Court, which did not recognise the state concerned at the time. In this sense, we may refer to circulation between two international institutions.

The European context also presents peculiarities in terms of circulation. Institutional fragmentation is particularly marked in this context given the presence of two large organisations (the Council of Europe and the European Union) and two European courts (the CJEU and the ECtHR). Between these two organisations, the forms of circulation are numerous. Legal decisions and instruments adopted on each side circulate from one organisation to the other. Very close cooperation is at work, including at an informal level as is the case today for European courts which may be led to consider comparable situations which circulate from one normative space to another.

SITUATION – CIRCULATION IN THE EUROPEAN CONTEXT

Examples of circulation between the institutions of the Council of Europe and the European Union

The Council of Europe maintains particularly close ties with the European Union. These ties are partly of an institutional nature: cooperation between them was formalised through the exchange of letters (1987 and 1996), so-called 'European' clauses were inserted into the Council of Europe conventions so as to allow the European Union to sign them, the Brussels Commission assists the Committee of Ministers of the Council of Europe, meetings are regularly held between the management of the principle institutions of the two organisations and a permanent system for exchanging information has been established. These exchanges also have a jurisdictional dimension. In effect, the ECtHR has had the occasion to consider cases involving a European Union law or a national measure applying a European Union law (see, for example, App. no. 36677/97 *Dangeville v France* (ECtHR, 16 April 2002); compare on the subject of the implementation of the 'Dublin II' European Union Regulation on matters of immigration by Member States: App. no. 30696/09 *M.S.S. v Belgium and Greece* (ECtHR, 21 January 2011), which directly influenced the case law of the Court of Justice: Joint Cases C-411/10 and C-493/10 *NS* [2011] ECR I-13905), even though, for the moment, the court has refused to recognise the existence of a violation of the European Union itself or of the ECHR by all of its Member States, taken collectively.

Compare, in a case in which the ECtHR and the CJEU successively considered the compatibility of the same national situation (in Italy) from the angle of the ECHR and then European Union law, where the press office of the CJEU, in order to explain the absence of a response from that court to one of the questions before it, clarified in a press release (press release no. 80/11 relating to Case C-108/10 *Ivana Scattolon* [2011] ECR I-7491) that:

> (t)hat question, which has in the meantime been considered by the European Court of Human Rights (App. no 43549/08, 6107/09 and 5087/09 *Agrati and Others v. Italy* (ECtHR 7 June 2011), has not been answered by the Court of Justice. The latter has held that, having regard to the answers given to the other questions referred, there is no longer any need to examine the case from the angle of general principles of law.

Even though this press release has no legal value, it is interesting to note that in it the solution is presented in a global manner as though it was the object of two successive analyses by the ECtHR and the CJEU, although the judgment of the Court of Justice does not explicitly mention this point. The circulation of the legal situation in question from one institution to the other may explain the position of the judge in Luxembourg, taking into account the previous decision of the judge in Strasbourg. This shows, at the very least, that European institutions are conscious of the fact that they may be led to consider identical or similar situations and that their legal analyses may, as the case may be, complement each other.

This form of circulation of situations from one normative space to another is sure to evolve in the future in view of the adhesion of the European Union to the ECHR (Article 6.2 TEU). For a systematic and detailed analysis of the phenomenon of circulation between the two great European courts in the specific context of institutional crises, see L. Sheeck, 'The Diplomacy of European Judicial Networks in Times of Constitutional Crisis' in F. Snyder and I. Maher (eds), *The Evolution of the European Courts: Institutional Change and Continuity – L'évolution des juridictions européennes: changements et continuité* (Bruylant, 2009), p. 17.

C. The Inter-level Circulation of Cases

The circulation of situations between the different contexts of application of the law encompasses a range of extremely heterogeneous scenarios. Two types of approaches can usefully complement each other: the intervention of courts on different levels (1) or the application of the law on several levels (2).

(i) The intervention of courts on different levels

Considered in relation to the application of the law in different contexts (national, international and European), the first and principal vector of the circulation of situations is the mode of intervention of the international and regional courts that coexist with national courts. The circulation of situations is effectively part of the very process through which access may be gained to the majority of supranational courts, which is dominated by the rule of the prior exercise or exhaustion of domestic remedies. Thus, as one author has observed, in certain cases 'the internal judge and the international judge have been known to rule upon the same complaint'[4] ('le juge interne et le juge international sont réputés connaître de la même reclamation'). The legal situation is successively analysed by courts located at different levels. The phenomenon of circulation may also be observed at European level. The preliminary reference procedure of the CJEU and the right of appeal to the ECtHR allow, according to very different procedures, a legal situation to move from one court to another. Conversely, the phenomenon of circulation between the international and European levels is much rarer.

[4] M. Forteau, 'Le juge CIRDI envisagé du point de vue de son office: juge interne, juge international, ou l'un et l'autre à la fois?', cited *supra*, especially p. 101.

The CJEU jealously defends the principle of its exclusive competence,[5] such that a Member State may not, when the application of European Union law is in question, alternatively summon the ICJ or the CJEU, for example. But cases may exceptionally arise in which one situation is presented successively to a national court, then to the ECtHR and, finally, to the ICJ.

SITUATION – THE CIRCULATION OF SITUATIONS BETWEEN NATIONAL COURTS AND INTERNATIONAL AND EUROPEAN COURTS

Example of circulation between a national court and the International Court of Justice

In order to illustrate the phenomenon of circulation between the national judge and the ICJ, one may envisage the case, for example, of a state that intends to exercise diplomatic protection over one of its citizens after the exhaustion of domestic legal remedies. This diplomatic protection allows a domestic situation (for example, the recourse of the citizen to the authorities of the foreign state which has taken a measure against him) to be elevated to the status of a truly international situation (for example, an interstate dispute brought before the ICJ). In a scenario of this kind, it is useful to speak of circulation, insofar as the legality of the situation may be successively disputed, notably by reference to national law, before a national court and an international court. For an illustration of a case taken before the ICJ relating to the legality of a national measure of expulsion and dispossession: ICJ, 30 November 2010, *Ahmadou Sadio Diallo* case – Republic of Guinea v the Democratic Republic of Congo.

Example of circulation between national courts and the Court of Justice of the European Union or the European Court of Human Rights

This type of circulation of situations is perfectly common in the European context in which situations of domestic law are frequently considered successively by the national judge and then by the European judge. This is the case for the great majority of situations brought before the ECtHR after domestic remedies have been exhausted. The same is also true each time a national judge makes a preliminary reference to the CJEU. In these different scenarios, the application of the law is successively considered by the domestic court and then by the European court, and is sometimes referred back to the national court, as in the

[5] Among other illustrations, see Case C-459/03 *Commission v Ireland* (*MOX*) [2006] ECR I-4635. See more recently: on the compatibility of the envisaged agreement on the European and European Union Patent Court with the European Union Treaties, *Opinion 1/2009* [2011] ECR I-1137.

case of a preliminary reference to the European court or in the case of a re-examination of the situation by a domestic court when such a procedure is exceptionally in place at the national level (see, in criminal matters: Article 626-1 *et seq.* of the French Code of Criminal Procedure relating to the 'reconsideration of a criminal ruling as a result of a decision of the European Court of Human Rights'). The concept of circulation thus helps us to understand that situations may be presented successively before different judges, of national or European rank.

The possibility of circulation can have a strong influence on the work of national judges, who wish to anticipate, at their stage of deliberation, a potential future referral to a European court. It is in this manner that we may read the *Banque Africaine de Développement* case (Cour de cassation, ch. soc., 25 janv 2005, pourvoi n° 04-41012) we presented earlier (see *supra*, p. 100). In this case in which the jurisdictional immunity of an international organisation was disputed, we remember that the French court rejected the claim to immunity and seemingly integrated into its international public order a right of access to justice established by the ECtHR, which did not have jurisdiction over the international organisation. This solution may be criticised from the point of view of public international law theory, notably relating to the resolution of conflicts of conventions (see in particular, the analysis of M. Forteau, 'L'ordre public "transnational" ou "réellement international"' [2011] JDI 17, note 57; on this critique see our discussion *infra*, p. 148). But it may potentially be explained by reference to the concept of the circulation of situations. In integrating a solution of the ECtHR into its international public order, perhaps the French Court of Cassation intended to anticipate an appeal to that court against France for the non-respect, in this case, of the right of access to justice, as protected notably by the ECtHR. In other words, if, formally, the application of the treaty that established the international organisation could not be blocked by the European Convention, the French judges have ensured that at least their decision conforms to the provisions of the European Convention in order to prevent a potential complaint of a violation of the ECHR from coming before the Strasbourg court. This analysis, although we do not know whether or not it precisely reflects the state of mind of the judges of the Court of Cassation in this case, relies on the observation that the situation presented to the French court could later be brought before a European court. When such circulation is not likely to threaten his solution, the national judge may be indifferent to the phenomenon. There is no doubt that this is what motivated the Court of Cassation in a case concerning another international organisation, in which it decided that the right of access to justice was not threatened by the founding treaty of the organisation, such that it was not necessary to raise a conflict with international public order, and went so far as to specify that the organisation had not adhered to the ECHR (Cour de cassation, soc. 11 fév. 2009, pourvoi n° 07-44240, UNESCO).

Example of circulation from national level to European level: a national decision nullifying a European intellectual property right

The case of a national decision nullifying a European intellectual property right provides another example of circulation from national level to European level.

The European Union created the European Union trade mark (Regulation (EC) No. 40/94 of the Council, 20 December 1993 on the community trade mark, replaced by Regulation (EC) No. 207/2009 of the Council of 26 February 2009 and modified by the Regulation (EU) No. 2015/2424 of the 16 December 2015) which constitutes a unique and unitary right to protection in the whole of the European Union. This trade mark is granted by a European agency: the Office for Harmonization in the Internal Market located in Alicante (OHIM). A national court notably has the power to nullify a community trade mark judged to be invalid (arts 95 *et seq.* of Regulation No. 207/2009 cited above). A decision to nullify a trade mark taken by a national court affects the whole of the European Union. It is publicised at a European level. The legal circulation of the national decision is regulated by European law to avoid the delivery of contradictory national decisions on the validity of a European intellectual property right.

Example of circulation between national, European and international courts

A recent decision of the ICJ offers an illustration of the scenario in which a situation has been successively presented to a national court and then, on appeal, to the ECtHR and, finally, to the ICJ, in the context of an interstate conflict. In a case relating to the immunity from jurisdiction and execution enjoyed by Germany, on the subject of actions for compensation and recovery by the next of kin of the victims of massacres perpetrated by the German army in foreign territories during the Second World War, different proceedings were taken at national (actions by the victims' next of kin before Italian, Greek and German courts); European (a case taken to the ECtHR by some of the victims' next of kin whose cases had been rejected by the Greek and German courts on the grounds of the immunity of the German state and which was found inadmissible: App. no. 59021/00 *Kalogeropoulou and others v Greece and Germany* (ECtHR, 12 December 2002); and international levels (a conflict between Italy, plaintiff, and Germany, defendant, with Greece intervening: ICJ 3 February 2012 *Jurisdictional Immunities of the State* – Germany v Italy; Greece (intervening). Even though the situation presented before these three courts (in this case, the massacre of 10 June 1944 which took place in the village of Distomo in Greece, see paragraphs 30–36 of the judgment) was one element among several others of the dispute presented in the case before the ICJ and even though the whole of the proceedings was not considered at the three levels, the fact is that it very much illustrates a phenomenon of circulation between the different levels of application of the law and that the actors in question, notably judges, are becoming increasingly conscious of this. This is why the ICJ decided in this case for the second time in its history to refer to the case law of the ECtHR (for the first case in this sense: ICJ 20 November 2010, the *Ahmadou Sadio Diallo* case – Republic of Guinea v Democratic Republic of the Congo, cited *supra*).

The scenario of the circulation of situations between an alternative method of resolving disputes and a state method must be considered separately. The most remarkable case is that of the relationship between international arbitration and state justice.

SITUATION – THE CIRCULATION OF SITUATIONS BETWEEN INTERNATIONAL ARBITRATION AND STATE JUSTICE

The example of international commercial arbitration

In the international commercial context, arbitration is a form of private justice with its own particular features. It has even been suggested that it constitutes its own legal world (an 'arbitrational legal order' ('ordre juridique arbitral'), to use the expression of one author: E. Gaillard in (notably): *Aspects philosophiques du droit de l'arbitrage international* (Hague Academy of International Law, 2008), p. 60 *et seq.*)). Whether or not one adheres to this theory, the fact is that international arbitration takes place largely outside any state court. This specificity is usually justified by the needs of international commercial law or of the international law of investments which calls for less state intervention in economic activities in the national environment, in this context, than is traditionally the case, whether or not the state is a direct party to the operations.

This international private justice is regularly confronted with state justice. Encounters between these two forms of justice are regulated by rules established notably at national level. In the French context, the Code of Civil Procedure dedicates a whole title to the question (Book IV – Title II: Chapter 1: The international arbitration agreement (Articles 1507–1508) – Chapter II: The court and the arbitration sentence (Articles 1509–1513) – Chapter III: The recognition and the execution of arbitration sentences delivered abroad or in matters of international arbitration (Articles 1514–1517) – Chapter IV: Remedies – Section 1: Sentences delivered in France (Articles 1518–1524) – Section 2: Sentences delivered abroad (Article 1525) – Section 3: Common provisions for sentences delivered in France or abroad (Articles 1526–1527) (author's translation)). The incorporation of sentences of international arbitration into the French legal order is strictly regulated by the Code. This incorporation operates via circulation: the arbitration sentence, exterior to the French legal order, penetrates it via an institutional means and a question may arise as to its recognition by a judge from this national legal order.

(ii) The application of the law on several levels

The jurisdictional and therefore institutionalised method of circulation of situations between national, international and European contexts of application of the law is not the only one that must be envisaged. Other, more diffuse, methods can exist. These methods have a very abstract dimension. They represent the mental process through which lawyers may shift the examination of a case from one national, international or European level to another, without the need for an institutional vector facilitating the move from one level to the other such as those that featured in the previous range of scenarios.

This intellectual shift by lawyers takes place, most often, through the question of how a legal method or solution conceived in one context may be applied at another level. Circulation here is synonymous with application. It refers to the situation in which a law stipulated in one context is implemented at another level. The nature of this situation differs from the phenomena of the application of laws within each level. In order to describe the application of the foreign law, or the relationships of application between international or European norms, lawyers do not need to refer to the figure of circulation, apart from in the concrete cases of circulation we have identified above (see *supra*, p. 111). To the extent that he remains enclosed within one level of the application of law, we have seen, in effect, that his legal environment does not change. It is always a question of applying a law established at one and the same level: national, international or European. The situation is different in those cases of the inter-level application of law which interest us here, where lawyers are led to move from one legal environment to another, or to circulate from one environment to the other.

For the purposes of the presentation, we may distinguish two general types of scenario. The first involves the issues of the application of international or European law in the national context and the second, inversely, involves the issue of the application of national law in the international or European context.

SITUATION – THE CIRCULATION OF LEGAL METHODS AND SOLUTIONS BETWEEN NATIONAL AND INTERNATIONAL OR EUROPEAN LEVELS

The example of the theoretical discussions on the incorporation of international and European law into national legal orders (monism, dualism, pluralism) and the question of whether circulation takes place

The issue of the incorporation of international and European law into national legal orders is perfectly well known and identified. It has been the subject of conflict between two major theories: the monist theory which militates in favour of the immediate incorporation of international and European law into domestic law; and the dualist theory, which requires the formal adoption of a statute at national level allowing for the application of international and European law (for a general background of these two theories, see, for example, J.G. Starke, 'Monism and Dualism in the Theory of International Law' (1936) 17 BYBIL 66).

These two theories coexist in the legal world, including within countries belonging to the same regional legal space such as those we are familiar with in Europe (the European Union or, more modestly, the Council of Europe). The conflict between these two approaches must not be overstated, however (M. Virally, 'Sur un pont aux ânes: les rapports entre droit international et droits internes' in Mélanges Rolin (Pedone, 1964), p. 488; J. Kammerhofer, 'Introduction: The Limited Relevance of Monism and Dualism', in M. Novaković (ed.), *Monism & Dualism* (Faculty of Law, Belgrade, 2013), p. 17) particularly given that it has been demonstrated that neither theory is capable of explaining all the relationships that exist between legal systems (D. Boden, 'Le pluralisme juridique en droit international privé' [2006] 49 *Archives de philosophie du droit* 275).

These discussions are not irrelevant to the theme of circulation. Whatever the method of reasoning adopted, whether monist or dualist (with their numerous variants), lawyers cannot ignore the division between the legal systems in question: one at international or European level, the other at national level. In order to take this division into account, the intellectual concept of circulation is sometimes useful. International and European laws are meant to be applied by the legal systems from which they originate. They remain 'foreign' laws in the national context. The hypothesis of circulation raises the question of whether the application of international and European law in the national context is dependent on its application in the international or European system. If the answer is yes, the concept of circulation is useful. If the answer is no, it is useless (for greater discussion on this theme, see *infra*, Part III).

Examples of circulation from the national level to the international level: the application of a national law evaluated in an international or European law context

Circulation does not take place in only one direction. Although it has not been presented from this angle much before, circulation may be observed from the national level towards the international or European level. The phenomenon is particularly marked in those areas in which an international or European court is called upon to consider the compatibility between the application of a domestic law and the solutions of international and European law. In this case, we are concerned with the issue of the operation of a national law in a context of international or European law. The judge is then led to examine the manner in which the national law disturbs the solutions established in the international or European legal order.

The area in which this circulation is undoubtedly most visible is that of economic rights. The international legal order has created a vast space of free trade endowed with its own rules and institutions (the WTO Agreements and the dispute resolution body). The same is true *a fortiori* for the legal order of the European Union and its institutions (notably the Commission and the CJEU) which, for more than 60 years, have pushed the principle of integration towards the construction of a European internal market. These two legal spaces each function at their own level. It is possible to consider them in themselves, which is to say leaving aside the issue referred to above of their incorporation into national legal orders. This is not to say that national law does not have a place within them. In effect, each time a national law establishes legal solutions that are potentially incompatible with the international or European levels, an international or European institution may be led to consider the impact of the application of a 'foreign' law at its own level, in this case the national law of a Member State. In order to describe the process at work here, the concept of legal circulation is sometimes useful. The application of the national law is examined in light of the constructs of international and European law in order to determine whether it may be tolerated or, on the contrary, judged incompatible. The question may thus arise whether the application of the national law is a barrier to global or regional exchanges, incompatible with the rules of global commerce or the European internal market. Numerous examples exist. See, for an in-depth study centred on this question of the application of national law in the international or European context: S. Bhuiyan, *National Law in WTO Law – Effectiveness and Good Governance in the World Trading System* (Cambridge University Press, 2007); L. Azoulai (ed.), *L'entrave dans le droit du marché intérieur* (Bruylant, 2011).

Another example: global circulation and contractual models inspired by the practice of international lawyers and their application in different national contexts

An international programme of research, led by Professor G. Cordero-Moss of the University of Oslo, undertook an analysis of the global circulation of model clauses drawn from the practice of international lawyers. The processes employed and, above all, the effects produced by the circulation of these models, notably when they are confronted by European or national courts, were reviewed. These reveal a great range of solutions, thus destabilising the myth that one contractual model, albeit dominant in the world of international business, can have exactly the same effect in different legal environments (notably in Common Law and Romano-Germanic systems). For the published result of this research: G. Cordero-Moss (ed.), *Boilerplate Clauses, International Commercial Contracts and the Applicable Law: Common Law Contract Models and Commercial Transactions Subject to Civilian Governing Laws* (Cambridge University Press, 2011).

The second scenario, more recently studied by lawyers, is that of circulation between the international and European levels. We have already remarked several times that the methods and solutions of international law are increasingly penetrating the European level of the application of law. The reverse is less common.

SITUATION – THE CIRCULATION OF LEGAL METHODS AND SOLUTIONS BETWEEN INTERNATIONAL AND EUROPEAN LEVELS

Examples of legal circulation from the international level to the European level: the phenomena of overlap and mimicry

Two major phenomena, already invoked and to which we will return, characterise the propensity of the methods and solutions of international law to circulate in the European context (European Union and Council of Europe). The first is the phenomenon of overlap between the different sources of law. The second relates to the case of the mimicry of the methods and solutions present.

These two phenomena interest us insofar as they illustrate well the concept of legal circulation. Overlapping implies, as we have seen (*supra*, p. 99), that a law formulated at one level is associated in its implementation with a law formulated at another level to produce a potentially different effect to that which pre-existed on each level. As for cases of mimicry, these reveal a very strong porosity between the different laws and, in particular, the aptitude for European law to be applied with reference to the tools and interpretations of international law by which it has largely been inspired. The relationship between the two legal systems is often complex, as European law willingly marks its independence from international law (on the increasing autonomy of European law understood as a form of prioritisation, see *infra,* Part III). But the influence exerted by international law on European law is no less real, thus illustrating a form of circulation between normative spaces.

The activity of the two great European courts yields examples. Focusing only on decisions made between 2007 and 2009 by the CJEU and ECtHR, we observe that cases of the legal circulation of international law in the European law context proliferate (list extracted from the *Chronique* on the interactions of international and European law [2009] JDI 903). See, for example, regarding UN law (App. no. 71412/01 *Behrami and Behrami v France* and App. no. 78166/01 *Saramati v France, Germany and Norway* (ECtHR, 31 May 2007) and Cases C-402/05 and C-415/05 *Kadi and Al Barakaat* [2008] ECR I-6351); WTO law (App. no. 8112/02 *de Luca v France* (ECtHR, 2 August 2006) and Case C-120/06 P and C-121/06 *P FIAMM* [2008] ECR I-6513): UNESCO law (App. no. 57325/00 *D. H. and others v the Czech Republic* (ECtHR, 13 Nov. 2007) and Case C-222/07 *UTECA* [2009] ECR I-1407); the law of the ILO (App. no. 34503/97 *Demir and Baykara v Turquie* (ECtHR, 12 Nov. 2008) and Case C-438/05 *Viking* [2007] ECR I-10779 and Case C-341/05 *Laval* [2007] ECR I-11767); or the law of the WIPO (App. no. 73049/01 *Anheuser-Busch v Portugal* (ECtHR, 11 Jan. 2007) and Case C-456/06 *Peek & Cloppenburg* [2008] ECR I-2731).

For a comprehensive approach to the phenomenon, see notably: L. Gautron and L. Grard (eds), *Droit international et droit communautaire: perspectives actuelles* (Pedone, 2000); J. Wouters, A. Nollkaemper and E. de Wet (eds), *The Europeanisation of International Law* (TMC Asser Press, 2008); M. Delmas-Marty, *Les forces imaginantes du droit, T2. Le pluralisme ordonné* (translated into English by N. Norberg: *Ordering Pluralism: A Conceptual Framework for Understanding the Transnational Legal World* (Hart, 2009)); L. Burgorgue-Larsen,

E. Dubout, A. Maitrot de la Motte and S. Touzé (eds), *Les interactions normatives: droit de l'UE et droit international* (Pedone, 2012); M. Benlolo-Carabot, E. Cujo and U. Candas (eds), *Union européenne et droit international* (Pedone, coll. CEDIN, 2012).

The opposite scenario of the application of European law in the international context remains exceptional. International law resists the incorporation of European law, which is doubly marked by its regional and Western dimensions, into the general and global legal space it governs. But sometimes cases arise. We will give an example.

SITUATION – THE CIRCULATION OF LEGAL METHODS AND SOLUTIONS BETWEEN INTERNATIONAL AND EUROPEAN LEVELS

The example of legal circulation from the European level to the international level: the participation of the European Union in the work of the United Nations

The General Assembly of the United Nations adopted resolution 65/276 on the 'Participation of the European Union in the work of the United Nations' on 10 May 2011. This resolution takes cognisance of the modifications brought about by the Treaty of Lisbon of 13 December 2007 to the European treaties in force regarding, notably, the external representation of the European Union (Article 21 *et seq.* of the Treaty on European Union). Although we cannot speak of the 'international transposition of a European provision', the idea that motivated the UN General Assembly was to allow for a certain implementation of the institutional modifications brought about at European level in the international framework of the United Nations. The concept of circulation may again be mobilised to explain this type of intellectual approach. European law is foreign to UN law but this does not prevent the latter from considering the institutional presence of a European Union, which presents itself – which is to say circulates – in its international legal space.

2. THE EXISTENCE OF A CONSTRAINT ON CIRCULATION: THE ENFORCEABLE NON-APPLICABLE LAWS

The search for all relevant legal resources is rarely undertaken in a purely voluntary manner, free from legal constraints.[6] The lawyer, whether he is a judge or a barrister, for example, is not totally free to do as he pleases in a globalised legal context. He is in effect subject to a number of constraints;[7] among these constraints, there is one that requires him to conduct a deliberately open search for the 'legal framework of reference':[8] the circulation of legal situations. Each time a lawyer situated in one context of application of the law knows that the situation he has to deal with has the potential to move to another context (either it originated in another context or has migrated to another context), he must take into account the law applying in these different legal environments. Notably, the definition of a legal framework of reference is part of this process.

In order to highlight this restraining relationship between the definition of the legal framework of reference and the circulation of legal situations, it is necessary to understand those, doubtlessly exceptional, situations in which a law that originated in one legal system may be invoked in another legal system even though it is not applicable there. This distortion between the applicability of a norm and its enforceability[9] demonstrates that the legal circulation of a situation from one system to another may be experienced by lawyers as a strong constraint that requires them to take into account the effects produced by a foreign national, international or European law which does not have any right to be applied in the receiving legal system.

---

6 For a critical analysis of this type of method, see in the US the opinion of Supreme Court Justice Antonin Scalia who considered that foreign law can never be relevant to the meaning of the US Constitution (see, for example: <http://www.law360.com/articles/661690/scalia-sears-supreme-court-for-foreign-law-references>). Compare in France: P. Brunet, 'L'articulation des normes – Analyse critique du pluralisme ordonné', in J.-B. Auby, *L'influence du droit européen sur les catégories du droit public* (Dalloz, 2010), p. 194.

7 M. Troper, V. Champeil-Desplats and Ch. Grzegorczyk (eds), *Théorie des contraintes juridiques* (Bruylant – LGDJ, 2005).

8 On this concept, see our explanations *supra*, pp. 109.

9 On these two concepts considered separately, see *supra*, p. 23, the elements of definition and illustration presented in Part I.

This very peculiar form of legal circulation exists at national level. It is thus that one may interpret, for example, the legal mechanism of recognition or the question of the effect produced by foreign police laws.

SITUATION – LEGAL CIRCULATION AT NATIONAL LEVEL AND DISTORTION BETWEEN LAWS THAT ARE APPLICABLE AND THOSE THAT ARE ENFORCEABLE

The example of recognition (again)

The mechanism of the recognition of foreign judicial or extrajudicial public decisions and instruments, the extension of which to legal situations originating abroad is sometimes recommended (see notably, *supra*, p. 113 the references to the work of P. Lagarde), originates in a certain manner from a dissociation between the law that is applicable and the law that is enforceable. Assuming that it exists, recognition allows, in effect, the legal effects of a decision, a legal instrument or a situation to be invoked in state B, regardless of the law that was applied to it in state A. Now, it may be that the rules applied in state A are not those which would have been applied to decisions, legal instruments or situations of the same type in state B. For example, state B agrees to give legal effect to a divorce decision delivered in state A according to a law of that country that would not have applied in state B. In another example, state B agrees to give legal effect to the legal instrument establishing a body corporate registered in state A, even though the rules in force in state B do not allow the creation of a body corporate of this type. The interest of the mechanism of recognition is that it allows the legal effects produced by the application of a law in state A to be enforceable in state B, even though the law in question is not applicable in state B. This enforceability is not the result of a purely voluntary or whimsical process. It is made possible and binding because the law establishes a rule according to which the legal circulation of certain legal decisions and instruments must take place between state A and state B. This rule of circulation, which applies incontestably in state B, takes the form of a rule of recognition and allows the benefit of a law to be invoked in state B without the need for its applicability in that state to be verified.

The example of the effects produced by foreign police laws

A notable decision by the French Court of Cassation fuelled academic discussion on the possibility for a foreign police law to be applied and enforced by a national court (Com., 16 mars 2010, pourvoi n° 08-21511; on the decision delivered by the lower court after the case was referred back to it by the Court of Cassation, see Ph. Delebecque, RTDCom 2012, 217). In this case, the question raised was whether the French court ought to take into account an embargo placed by Ghana on French beef when deciding on the validity of the transportation contract pertaining to merchandise of this type. The Court of Cassation struck down the decision of the appeal court which had decided:

> that the embargo decreed unilaterally by the State of Ghana on French beef was not binding (…), that in view of the applicable law the purpose of the transportation contracts did not fulfil any of the conditions established by Article 1133 of the French Civil Code and that it was therefore wrong for the sea transporter to maintain that, due to the embargo, the purpose of these contracts was illegal ('que l'embargo décrété unilatéralement par l'Etat du Ghana sur la viande bovine d'origine française n'a pas de force obligatoire (…), qu'au regard de la loi applicable la cause des contrats de transport ne remplit aucune des conditions énoncées par l'article 1133 du code civil français et qu'en conséquence c'est à tort que le transporteur maritime soutient qu'en raison de l'embargo, la cause de ces contrats n'est pas licite') for the reason that it was for the Court of Appeal 'to determine (…) the effect that could be given to the Ghanaian law invoked before it' ('de déterminer (…) l'effet pouvant être donné à la loi ghanéenne invoquée devant elle').

This reasoning is interesting, insofar as it leaves open the discussion on the manner in which a court should 'give effect' to a foreign police law. As one author notably commented (see, with the numerous references cited, the explanations of P. Deumier, 'La loi de police étrangère: une possibilité que le juge a l'obligation d'envisager' [2010] RDC 1385), this expression refers potentially to two possibilities: that of the pure and simple 'application' of the foreign police law and that of the 'taking into consideration' of the police law at the time of the application of the French law governing the transportation contract. This taking into consideration of the foreign police law illustrates the case of a norm, which may be enforced in a contractual relationship without being applicable to that relationship. This enforceability without applicability was notably discussed on the occasion of the implementation of the European rules of international private law (Article 7(1) of Convention 80/934/CEE on the law applicable to contractual obligations of 19 June 1980 and, in a more restrictive formulation, Article 9(3) of Regulation (EC) No. 593/2008 of the European Parliament and of the Council of 17 June 2008 on the law applicable to contractual obligations; compare Article 17 of Regulation (EC) No. 864/2007 of the European Parliament and of the Council of 11 July 2007 on the law applicable to non-contractual obligations, 'Rome II'; Article 10 of Regulation (EU) No. 1259/2010 of the Council of 20 December 2010 implementing enhanced cooperation in the area of the law applicable to divorce and legal separation, 'Rome III').

But this scenario is of most interest to us in the European and international context. One legal situation may use different vectors to circulate from one international or European system to another. Enforceability is one of the vectors allowing a law to be taken into account even though it is not applicable.

Let us consider, to begin, the European level, in which the phenomenon is the most developed.

SITUATION – LEGAL CIRCULATION AT EUROPEAN LEVEL AND DISTORTION BETWEEN LAWS THAT ARE APPLICABLE AND THOSE THAT MAY BE INVOKED

A historical example: the enforceability of the ECHR before the Court of Justice of the European Communities

The ECHR, which occupies a prominent position in the current Treaty on European Union (art. 6 TEU), had long been totally absent from the provisions of the treaties relating to the different European Communities (before the Single European Act of 1986 (preamble) and above all, before the Treaty of Maastricht of 1992 (art. 6 TEU)). This did not prevent parties from invoking the Convention very early before the Court of Justice, which has considered, since 1976, that 'international treaties for the protection of human rights, on which the member states have collaborated or of which they are signatories, can supply guidelines which should be followed within the framework of community law': Case 4/73 *Nold* [1974] ECR 491. This 'taking into account' of the ECHR despite the fact that it did not bind the European Communities in any sense was progressively reinforced from the moment that all the Member States were bound by this Convention: Case C-260/89 *ERT* [1991] ECR I-2925. The Convention became, with subsequent cases, an essential model for the human rights of the European Union (for example, Case C-23/93 *TV10* [1994] ECR I-4795).

This case law illustrates the increasing enforceability of the ECHR even though the Convention was not to become objectively applicable within the European Union until the day the latter effectively signed the Convention (this signature of the Convention was provided for by the Treaty of Lisbon, which entered into force on 1 December 2009 and which is currently rejected by the CJEU: *Opinion 2/13* [2014] ECLI:EU:C:2014:2454). Enforceability was used as a tool to allow the circulation of a legal situation internal to the legal order of the Community in national normative spaces (those of Member States) subject to a European Convention which remains, for the time being, foreign to the system of the European Union. This circulation is very useful. It anticipates, as we shall see, another process of circulation: the impact of the decisions of the Court of Justice on national legal orders that wish to subject the European structure to a requirement for the protection of fundamental rights.

More recent examples: the enforceability of foreign multilateral or bilateral international legal instruments before European courts

The case law of the CJEU offers more recent illustrations in which international multilateral or bilateral instruments have been enforced by the court despite the fact that they are not formally or materially binding on the European Union or, before its existence, on the European Communities. Different examples exist.

A first example, cited twice in this work, relates to the law of transportation. The *Bogiatzi* decision (Case C-301/08 [2009] ECR I-10185) illustrates, in effect, a case in which the Court of Justice considered that a Community regulation had to be applied in view of the provisions of an international convention which did not, however, form part of the legal order of the European Union (on this judgment, see our discussions *supra*, p. 55). The court therefore accepted that the international convention could be invoked before it with a view to producing legal effects even though the law itself was not objectively applicable. This distortion between the non-applicability of the convention and its enforceability is evidence of the existence of a constraint that judges must take into account. This constraint may be described in the following manner: the international convention forms part of the legal framework of reference of the transportation contract in question in the case, as the European regulation relied upon this legal framework in developing its own solutions, it must be applied in light of the international convention.

A second example concerns the law of social protection. In the important *Gottardo* decision (Case C-55/00 [2002] ECR I-413), the Court of Justice had to consider the question of whether European law, notably the principle of equality (current art. 18 TFEU), authorised a French citizen to invoke the benefit of a bilateral agreement concluded between Switzerland and Italy, allowing the citizens of these two countries to cumulate the contributions paid to both countries in order to assert their right to a pension. Responding that:

> the competent social security authorities of one Member State [Italy] are required, pursuant to their Community obligations (...) to take account, for purposes of acquiring the right to old-age benefits, of periods of insurance completed in a non-member country [Switzerland] by a national of a second Member State [France] in circumstances where, under identical conditions of contribution, those competent authorities will take into account such periods where they have been completed by nationals of the first Member State pursuant to a bilateral international convention concluded between that Member State and the non-member country,

the Court of Justice enforced a bilateral agreement between a Member State and a non-Member State, even though there was no doubt that the convention was not applicable within the legal system of the European Union. This tandem of non-applicability/enforceability allows us to take into account here again the national and international legal framework of reference in which the preliminary reference submitted to the Court of Justice was situated, regardless of whether this framework extended beyond the borders of European law.

A third series of examples relates to the law of intellectual property which has been the subject of a large number of important international conventions, many of which do not bind the European Union, either because the European Union was not party to them, or because the European Union is not considered to be the successor to its Member States in cases in which the latter are party to all of the instruments in question. Several decisions of the Court of Justice illustrate the ability of European law to take into account international legal instruments, which form part of the legal framework of reference of the case. For a demonstration in this sense in industrial intellectual property law, see V. K. Ben Dahmen, *Interactions du droit international et du droit de l'Union européenne: expression d'un pluralisme juridique rénové en matière de protection de la propriété industrielle* (L'Harmattan, 2012). For an illustration in the neighbouring area of copyright, see Case C-135/10 *SCF* [2012] ECLI:EU:C:2012:140, in which an Italian court consulted the Court of Justice, in effect, on the difficulties of interpretation that arose in a case between a company responsible for collecting royalties on behalf of record producers and a dental practitioner who had refused to pay licence fees relating to the playing of ambient music in her dental practice. The case, which raised a question of principle relating to the identification of the holder of these rights similar to copyright and thus capable of falling under the law, involved the application of various legal texts. As in previous cases, it was for the Court of Justice to determine the 'legal framework' of reference in which, in addition to relevant European law (essentially Directive 2006/115/EC of the European Parliament and of the Council, of 12 December 2006, on rental right and lending right and on certain rights related to copyright in the field of intellectual property, which amended and codified Directive 92/100 and, secondarily, Directive 2001/29/EC of the European Parliament and of the Council of 22 May 2001 on the harmonisation of certain aspects of copyright and related rights in the information society) and the national law applicable to the situation in question, figured different international legal texts relating to the protection of certain intellectual property rights. On this last aspect, which interests us here only in the interactions it has with European law, different questions were posed by the national court, notably:

> (1) Are the Rome Convention for the Protection of Performers, Producers of Phonograms and Broadcasting Organisations of 26 October 1961, the TRIPs Agreement (Agreement on Trade Related Aspects of Intellectual Property Rights) and the WIPO Treaty on Performances and Phonograms (WPPT) directly applicable within the Community legal order?
>
> (2) Are the abovementioned sources of uniform international law also directly effective within the context of private-law relationships?
>
> (3) Do the concepts of 'communication to the public' contained in the abovementioned treaty-law texts mirror the Community concepts contained in Directives 92/100 and 2001/29 and, if not, which source should take precedence? (judgment, para. 35).

Responding to this series of questions, the Court of Justice decided that 'the provisions of the TRIPS Agreement and the WPPT are applicable in the legal order of the European Union', that 'as the Rome Convention does not form part of the legal order of the European Union it is not applicable there; however, it has indirect effects within the European Union; individuals may not rely directly either on that convention or on the TRIPS Agreement or the WPPT' and that:

> the concept of 'communication to the public' must be interpreted in the light of the equivalent concepts contained in the Rome Convention, the TRIPS Agreement and the WPPT and in such a way that it is compatible with those agreements, taking account of the context in which those concepts are found and the purpose of the relevant provisions of the agreements as regards intellectual property (judgment, para. 56).

In order to understand this reasoning and the recourse to the notion of 'indirect effect', it is necessary to consider the international regulatory context in which the European secondary law in question was situated. The European Union and, before it, the European Communities, was not party to all the international legal instruments relating to intellectual property, notably including the Convention of

Rome. The Member States of the European Union were not all party to the aforementioned instruments such that the theory of succession effect that the CJEU applied to the GATT Agreement in the famous *International Fruit Company* case (Joint cases 21–24/72 [1972] ECR 1219), could not apply here. It had the result that certain international instruments of intellectual property law were not binding within the legal system of the European Union. Not being applicable, they should not, logically, have been enforceable. Now, the Court of Justice states in this case that, in spite of all, they produced an 'indirect effect'. In order to establish the nature of this effect, one may reason, as was recently proposed, in terms of opposability (K. Ben Dahmen, cited *supra*). An international treaty that does not formally bind the European Union is part of a regulatory whole to which European secondary law voluntarily refers, such that it produces an effect of opposability within the European Union, notably where the interpretation of European secondary law in light of existing international treaties is in question. But one may equally propose considering the question in terms of the dissociation between applicability and enforceability. This dissociation is justified by the fact that the situations presented in a preliminary reference are situated in a national regulatory context which is potentially different from that which exists at European level. Insofar as these two contexts are compatible with each other, which is so in the case in question, because European law never intended to set aside the Rome Convention, but on the contrary, has never ceased to rely upon it, the Court of Justice has developed the clever strategy of interpreting European law in such a way as to fully take into account the regulatory context in which it will be implemented by national courts.

But a related phenomenon may from now on be observed at the international level.

SITUATION – LEGAL CIRCULATION AT EUROPEAN LEVEL AND DISTORTION BETWEEN LAWS THAT ARE APPLICABLE AND THOSE THAT ARE ENFORCEABLE

An example: the question of enforceability before international jurisdictions of a regional character

We have already had the occasion to highlight the decision delivered by the ICJ in the *Diallo* case (ICJ, 30 November 2010: compare also ICJ, 19 June 2012, which ruled on the question of compensation in the *Ahmadou Sadio Diallo* case, cited above). We know that, in this case, the ICJ referred to a regional law: the African Charter on Human and Peoples' Rights of 27 June 1981 and, to a lesser extent, the ECHR of 1950 and the American Convention on Human Rights of 1969.

The enforceability of the African Charter on Human and Peoples' Rights of 27 June 1981 may be explained without great difficulty by the fact that it is applicable in the two countries party to the proceedings (in this case, the Republic of Guinea and the Democratic Republic of Congo). More surprising, in contrast, is the reference made immediately afterwards to the ECHR and to the American Convention and to the case law of the two regional courts:

> The Court also notes that the interpretation by the European Court of Human Rights and the Inter-American Court of Human Rights, respectively, of Article 1 of Protocol No. 7 to the (European) Convention for the Protection of Human Rights and Fundamental Freedoms and Article 22, paragraph 6, of the American Convention on Human Rights — the said provisions being close in substance to those of the Covenant and the African Charter which the Court is applying in the present case — is consistent with what has been found in respect of the latter provisions in paragraph 65 above (para. 68 of the first judgment).

This double reference may first be analysed as an operation of comparison (on the theme of comparison, see *supra*, Part I). But one may nonetheless wonder whether, behind this comparison, the ICJ did not wish to encourage the enforceability of regional norms in cases of this nature, insofar as strong circulation takes place between the case law of regional courts ruling in matters of human rights and that the ICJ did not wish the phenomenon to escape it. If such was its wish, we observe that circulation operates once more in these cases limited by a dissociation between applicability and enforceability.

PART III

The prioritisation of national, international and European law

The first two steps of comparison[1] and combination[2] offer a large toolbox allowing lawyers to apply national, international and European law in a global context. In the third step of the prioritisation[3] of laws, lawyers attempt to fight the effects of this pluralism, which may create disruption by favouring the application of one law over another.

The process of the prioritisation of laws does not have only a static value such that it should be considered in a limited manner in a national, international or European context. It also has a dynamic dimension in which the application of the methods and solutions developed by national, international or European law leads to interactions.

In this regard, two scenarios must thus be carefully distinguished. In the first, lawyers appeal to the application of the law at one level, which, in a process of prioritisation, may bring 'a hierarchy of norms' into play (Chapter 7). In the second, lawyers aspire to apply the law at another level upon which 'a prioritised law' is applied (Chapter 8).

---

1 See *supra*, Part I.

2 See *supra*, Part II.

3 In the broad sense of this expression, which covers not only the narrow case of a hierarchy of norms but also every process of the prioritisation of laws following the affirmation of the preference of one legal system from a national, international or European level over another.

7. Prioritisation through the application of the law at one level: the appeal to a hierarchy of norms

In order to solve a case, lawyers are often led to place themselves, if only in order to develop their reasoning, at one level of the application of law rather than another: national (for example, the application of law in the French context), international (for example, the application of law in the context of the World Trade Organization or traditional international arbitration proceedings), or European (for example, the application of law in the context of the European Union). This positioning of lawyers sometimes requires a prioritisation of laws, which has a particular meaning in a context of global legal pluralism (Section 1). It raises, moreover, the question of the freedom of lawyers to choose one level of application of law rather than another (Section 2).

1. THE PARTICULAR MEANING OF THE PRIORITISATION OF LAWS IN A CONTEXT OF GLOBAL LEGAL PLURALISM

In a context of global legal pluralism where many laws may apply to a given situation, the recourse, by the lawyer, to reasoning of the 'prioritisation of laws' type operates by reference, sometimes explicitly and sometimes implicitly, to a hierarchy of norms. The latter may be analysed as a tool for a legal system to withdraw into itself (A) although this withdrawal may also take other routes (B).

A. The Hierarchy of Norms as a Tool for a Legal System to Withdraw into Itself

How can one determine, in a precise way, the manner in which the operation of a 'hierarchy of norms' manifests itself in a context of global legal pluralism? The answer to this question remains roughly the same, regardless of the scenario envisaged.

In a context of global legal pluralism, the appeal to a 'hierarchy of norms' allows, in effect, any legal system that may be said to be constructed around a hierarchy, to withdraw into itself. Whether the legal system in question belongs to a national, international or European level, the response is invariably the same. The hierarchy of norms is perceived as an instrument for the preservation of legal systems, whenever they are threatened or, more modestly, disturbed by the presence of other systems interfering on levels other than their own.

The best-known illustration of this phenomenon is drawn from national legal orders, whenever they favour a domestic norm over any other rule developed at the international or European level.

SITUATION – SUPREMACY OF NATIONAL PROVISIONS

The example of French case law

In France, for example, both the ordinary courts and the constitutional court have pronounced on the hierarchical relationship existing between French constitutional norms and international and European law. Using identical formulations, the French Council of State (Cons. d'État, ass., 30 oct. 1998, Sarran et Levacher, Req. nos 200286 and 200287) and the Court of Cassation (Cour de cassation, Ass. plén., 2 juin 2000, Fraisse, pourvoi nos 99-60274) decided that 'the supremacy conferred on international obligations by the Constitution (art. 55) does not apply, in the domestic legal order, to provisions of constitutional value' ('la suprématie conférée aux engagements internationaux par la Constitution (art. 55) ne s'applique pas, dans l'ordre interne, aux dispositions de valeur constitutionnelle'). As for the French Constitutional Council, it notably decided in 2006 (Décision n° 2006-540 DC, 27 juillet 2006, *Loi relative au droit d'auteur et aux droits voisins dans la société de l'information*), following a series of judgments delivered in 2004 (see notably Décision n° 2004-496 DC, 10 juin 2004) that:

> the transposition of a Community directive into domestic law results from a constitutional imperative. Thereafter, it is for the Constitutional Council, seized under the conditions stipulated in Article 61 of the Constitution relating to a law transposing a Community directive into domestic law, to enforce the respect of this requirement. Nevertheless, the power it exercises to this effect is subject to a (...) limit (...). The transposition of a directive must not conflict with a rule or a principle inherent in France's constitutional identity, unless the constituent consents to it ('la transposition en droit interne d'une directive communautaire résulte d'une exigence constitutionnelle. Il appartient par suite au Conseil constitutionnel, saisi dans les conditions prévues par l'article 61 de la Constitution d'une loi ayant pour objet de transposer en droit interne une directive communautaire, de veiller au respect de cette exigence. Toutefois, le contrôle qu'il exerce à cet effet est soumis à une (...) limite (...). La transposition d'une directive ne saurait aller à l'encontre d'une règle ou

d'un principe inhérent à l'identité constitutionnelle de la France, sauf à ce que le constituant y ait consenti').

The supremacy accorded to the national Constitution or, more narrowly defined, to the national constitutional identity, may therefore give rise, in France, to a refusal to apply an international or European law that is incompatible with it. This inapplicability is more theoretical than practical. Procedures or legal techniques allow, in effect, cases of conflict to be prevented (amending the Constitution prior to the ratification of an international or European agreement) or reduced (convergent interpretations by the courts). The tool of the 'hierarchy of norms' is nonetheless available. It allows the French legal system to withdraw into its basic norm – here the norm of a constitutional dimension – whenever it is vulnerable to threats from a law defined at another level, whether international or European.

A comparative overview

In other legal systems, observable solutions differ (see, for a general comparative perspective, D. Shelton (ed.), *International Law and Domestic Legal Systems: Incorporation, Transformation, and Persuasion* (Oxford University Press, 2011)).

Most commonly, an equivalence is, by principle, recognised, between international treaties and national laws (or, more precisely, federal laws in federal states). In practice, this means that contrary to the French solution presented above, or to the Italian and German solutions that share the same logic, a later statute can contradict the prior statute that introduced the international treaty in the domestic legal order. This situation is to be found in Canada, the United States and the United Kingdom.

The hierarchical equivalence between international treaties and domestic statutes shows its limits in relationship with the protection of international customary rules, international human rights (*jus cogens*).

In these various instances, it is generally admitted that international law supersedes domestic law provided international law abides by rules of consitutional level.

But comparable situations may be observed in an international or European environment. The approach is generally as follows. In order to avoid the possibility of a national law threatening established international or European legal structures, the national law is declared legally unenforceable. This unenforceability is characteristic of the withdrawal of the international and European legal systems into themselves. Now, this withdrawal would not be possible in the absence of a tool permitting the identification of that which belongs to the systems of international and European law and that which is foreign to them. In the context of the prioritisation of laws, this tool is none other than a hierarchy of norms.

An analysis of this type may be undertaken in the international context in relation to the unenforceability of national law in the international legal order.

SITUATION – THE UNENFORCEABILITY OF NATIONAL LAW IN THE INTERNATIONAL LEGAL ORDER

The example of the *Treatment of Polish Nationals in Danzig* case law

The Permanent Court of International Justice (PCIJ) declared that '(...) a State cannot adduce as against another State its own Constitution with a view to evading obligations incumbent upon it under international law or treaties in force' (PCIJ, 3 March 1928, Treatment of Polish Nationals and other Persons of Polish Origin or Speech in the Danzig Territory, Series A/B, no. 44).

This solution, regularly reaffirmed in international public law, marks the capacity of international law to withdraw into its own structures, driving out of its legal system anything that has not yet received a legal translation into international law (a treaty or an international custom to put it simply). In order to mark the boundary between that which belongs to the system of international law and that which is foreign to it, the concept of the hierarchy of norms is useful. The binding force accorded 'to international law or treaties in force' (to take up the formulation of the court) in the international legal order cannot be contradicted by a law from a domestic source – albeit constitutional in nature – because the latter, except for in highly exceptional cases (which is to say those in which a unilateral practice by a state is in reality part of the operation of an international customary rule), is foreign to the international legal system and, therefore, to its potentially hierarchical structure.

Unenforceability is also relevant in the European context, even though the relationship between European law and national law is clearly better established.

SITUATION – THE UNENFORCEABILITY OF NATIONAL LAW IN THE EUROPEAN (EU) CONTEXT

The example of the *Internationale Handelsgesellschaft* and *Commission v Grand Duché* case law

In the same manner, the Court of Justice of the European Communities (CJEU) have considered that 'the validity of a Community measure or its effect within a member state cannot be affected by allegations that it runs counter to either fundamental rights as formulated by the constitution of that state or the principles of its constitutional structure' (Case 11/70 *Internationale Handelsgesellschaft* [1970] ECR 1125) or, in a more general manner, that 'recourse to provisions of the domestic legal systems to restrict the scope of the provisions of Community law ... cannot be accepted' (Case C-473/93 *Commission v Grand-Duché* [1996] ECR I-3207). The same solution has also been maintained by the European Court of Human Rights (ECtHR) (see, for example, Apps nos. 14234/88, 14235/88 *Open Door and others v Ireland* (ECtHR (Grand Chamber), 29 October 1993).

This setting aside of national law is easily justified where the validity of a European Union norm is in question. As national law is foreign to the European hierarchy of norms, it cannot be a direct and immediate cause of the invalidation of European secondary law, which is subject only to the requirements of European laws, particularly the instituting treaties and general principles of European law.

But it has even greater implications. In a general sense, the scope of European law, which is to say its effectiveness and, in a hierarchical sense, its superiority, cannot be threatened by national law. This assertion must naturally be qualified. The European Union confers a real role on national law, which sometimes, in spite of all, has the power to limit European law (for example, wherever a margin of appreciation or manoeuvre is accorded to national law). But beyond these cases, the European legal system is able to affirm its hierarchical authority by withdrawing into itself, which is to say by purely and simply setting aside national law on the basis that it is fundamentally foreign to its hierarchy of norms.

To a lesser extent, this phenomenon of withdrawal may also be observed in international law in its relationship with European law.

SITUATION – THE NON-OPPOSABILITY OF EUROPEAN LAW IN THE INTERNATIONAL CONTEXT

The example of the ICSID decision in *AES Summit Generation LTD and others v Hungary*

In this case, we can observe that an arbitration tribunal set aside the application of European law for the reason that it was 'merely a fact' and was thus not capable of justifying the failure of a state to meet its international obligations (ICSID, decision of 23 September 2010, *AES Summit Generation LTD and others v Hungary*, ARB/07/22). Although the arbitration tribunal made no reference to it, this type of consideration may find justification in structures of the 'hierarchy of norms' type. The reasoning may be as follows: the penalisation of companies for disrespecting a European Union competition law rule does not exist in international law for the good and simple reason that the said European rule is foreign to the international legal system; consequently, the international arbitration tribunal does not have to allow respect for European rules to prevail over respect for international rules, as no 'hierarchy of norms' obliges it to do so.

Such an intellectual approach is not enough to convince all those who consider that European law is by nature international law. But European law has continually affirmed its uniqueness. This approach is doubtlessly the reason why international law actors distinguish potentially applicable rules according to whether or not they form part of the international legal ordering. European law is thus set aside, on the grounds that it is foreign to the international legal system.

This practice may also be observed in complex situations in which the question of the legality of European law from an international source is discussed in European Union law.

SITUATION – THE LEGALITY OF EUROPEAN LAW FROM AN INTERNATIONAL SOURCE IN EUROPEAN UNION LAW

The example of the *Kadi* case

The *Kadi* case (Case T-306/01 [2005] ECR II-3533, struck down by Joint Cases C-402/05 and C-415/05 [2008] ECR I-6351) has had a great impact on international and European law. It concerned the validity of European secondary law provisions implementing United Nations resolutions pronouncing individual sanctions in relation to the fight against terrorism. It occupies a place of the first order in the dynamic process of the prioritisation of laws studied in this chapter. What of the hierarchy of norms, understood as a tool for a legal system (here the European Union) to withdraw into itself?

In order to tackle the general question of the validity of a European secondary law which was submitted to it, the Court of Justice (Joint Cases C-402/05 and C-415/05, cited *supra*) raised the technical debate to the most general and theoretical level. For the Court of Justice, effectively, the question was whether:

> as a result of the principles governing the relationship between the international legal order under the United Nations and the Community legal order, any judicial review of the internal lawfulness of the contested regulation in the light of fundamental freedoms is in principle excluded, notwithstanding the fact that (…) such review is a constitutional guarantee forming part of the very foundations of the Community (para. 290).

At the end of a particularly finely crafted decision, the Court considered that:

> (…) the Community judicature must, in accordance with the powers conferred on it by the EC Treaty, ensure the review, in principle the full review, of the lawfulness of all Community acts in the light of the fundamental rights forming an integral part of the general principles of Community law, including review of Community measures which, like the contested regulation, are designed to give effect to the resolutions adopted by the Security Council under Chapter VII of the Charter of the United Nations (para. 326).

Consequently, it struck down the Court of First Instance decisions under challenge for the reason that:

> the Court of First Instance erred in law (...) when it held (...) that it followed from the principles governing the relationship between the international legal order under the United Nations and the Community legal order that the contested regulation, since it is designed to give effect to a resolution adopted by the Security Council under Chapter VII of the Charter of the United Nations affording no latitude in that respect, must enjoy immunity from jurisdiction so far as concerns its internal lawfulness save with regard to its compatibility with the norms of jus cogens (para. 327).

This analysis proceeds from a reaffirmation of the internal hierarchy of norms of the European Union. When a case of conflict between the international legal order and the European legal order came to light, the European court worked to construct an airtight division between the two systems. It considered in the final analysis that the fundamental internal structure of European legal space did not depend on another legal system, even an international one. In reaffirming here the superiority of the general principles of European law over European secondary law, the court, by preference, hierarchised European law in relations within the European space. It thus set aside all considerations drawn from respect for international law, all the while specifying that in its external dimension, the European Union may have to take into account the disrespect of its international obligations, if such an issue were to arise (judgment, para. 288). The European hierarchy of norms serves here to exclude international law and with it any risk of interference.

In each of these scenarios, the hierarchy of norms allowed a system of national, international or European law to withdraw into itself, on the grounds that, among all potentially applicable rules, those that 'found' the system must be distinguished from those that are 'fundamentally' foreign. In a context of the application of law on different levels, the hierarchy of norms is used, sometimes explicitly and sometimes implicitly, as a tool for stigmatising the 'foreign' character of laws formulated on another level.

But the phenomenon of withdrawal may not only be detected by reading a few still famous cases in the annals of national, international or European law. It is, in reality, relatively common and takes routes other than the formal hierarchy of norms. The most remarkable illustrations may be observed in highly structured and centralised legal systems (notably the national and the European).

B. Other Methods for Legal Systems to Withdraw into Themselves

(i) The measure of the phenomenon: differentiation, individualisation, appropriation, division, etc.

When an actor in a legal system, notably an institutional actor (a judge, Government and, potentially, a legislator),[1] shows an unwillingness to apply a legal method or solution from elsewhere for the, more or less explicit, reason that it does not naturally find a place in the structure of the system to which the actor belongs, he contributes, no more and no less, to the withdrawal of the legal system into itself. Multiple techniques are used. One may identify four principle ones (which often overlap): the differential treatment of law foreign to the system; the individualisation of the system in relation to the influences that may come from other laws; the appropriation by a legal system of methods and solutions from elsewhere; and the organisation of a divided system according to whether the legal system has to deal with an internal or external situation.

The practical results of this type of withdrawal may be questioned whenever it constitutes a sort of reflex, consisting of the refusal to apply, *a priori*, and without any necessity, legal methods or solutions foreign to the system. This type of behaviour is probably the result of the now strongly contested dualist and monist theories clouding the analysis of the relationships between legal systems. In dualist theories, the phenomenon of the withdrawal of a legal system into itself is clear, because it is always a matter for lawyers to use the resources present in their system to incorporate (theory of incorporation) law originating from elsewhere. Monism, which aims to meld all systems into one, must also make a choice between conferring primacy on domestic law or on international law. The system, albeit unique, withdraws into its fundamentals, into its fundamental law. Therefore, the same phenomenon of prioritisation is at work.[2]

---

[1] This intellectual figure is often influenced by the works of academics. On the allegory of law 'from elsewhere', see in particular J. Carbonnier (*Droit et passion du droit sous la Ve République* (Flammarion, 1996), especially pp. 44 *et seq*). who exerted a great influence over legal thought in the second half of the twentieth century.

[2] Even though it must be recognised that in the case of the concept of monism, in which primacy is given to international law, the concept of withdrawal is not entirely fitting, as international law is then supposed to encompass all national laws. It remains necessary, in this case, for international law to be defined as an integrated system, capable of conferring a real status on national law. The analysis of positive law demonstrates that except for a very

But these legal techniques that facilitate the withdrawal of a legal system into itself are also very useful. They form part of the panoply of tools that allow lawyers to undertake the task of prioritisation, whenever the need arises to protect a legal system from the disturbances that may result from the coexistence of other legal systems on levels other than its own. Nonetheless, all systems do not offer these possibilities in the same manner. Effectively, only truly organised and centralised systems allow them. This is the case, notably, of the national legal system and of the legal system of the European Union which offer multiple illustrations of the phenomenon of withdrawal.

(ii) Illustrations from the national legal system: the example of the French system

The French legal system has progressively opened itself up to the application of international and European law. This is not to say that the phenomenon of the withdrawal of the French legal system into itself has totally disappeared and, with it, the legal techniques that allowed it to occur. Without claiming to be exhaustive, we offer four main illustrations of this.

The first relates to the work of the interpretation of international conventions binding on France undertaken by national judges.

SITUATION – THE FRENCH INTERPRETATION OF INTERNATIONAL CONVENTIONS TO WHICH FRANCE IS A PARTY

Multiple examples from case law

The role of the ordinary French judge, as we have observed (see *supra*, p. 138), has grown considerably in the area of the interpretation of international treaties. His power of interpretation is not often counterbalanced by another power: the French executive power has lost its earlier role in this area and authentic interpretations emanating from international courts (such as, for example, the International Court of Justice) remain rare.

The position of privileged interpreter places the French administrative and ordinary courts in a position to impose their interpretations of the international conventions to which France is party. As these interpretations are potentially imbued by the legal culture of national judges, one may claim without any great

---

particular islet of international law (for example, the court system put in place by the International Criminal Court) this development has not begun, nor is it even anticipated.

risk of shock or surprise that a French jurisprudential doctrine of the interpretation of a given instrument exists.

Pioneering work has been done on this subject. See for example, D. Simon, *L'interprétation judiciaire des traités d'organisations internationales: Morphologie des conventions et fonction juridictionnelle* (Pedone, 1981).

Specialist works or chronicles on a given instrument are regularly published. We give the example of a doctoral thesis (K. Parrot, *L'interprétation des conventions de droit international privé* (Dalloz, 2006)). In it, the author, relying on case law, develops a particularistic view of the interpretive work of these conventions by national judges, thus clearly challenging the myth of uniform interpretation. But even if one does not necessarily share this pessimistic view of the development of uniform international law (a vision which one may, moreover, extend without great difficulty to all the myths of uniform interpretation, including on a strictly national or even local level) nor the lessons the author draws from it in terms of a resolutely dualist approach to the relationships between legal systems, the fact is that it is difficult to deny the existence of divergent interpretations in different state parties of the same instrument of uniform law. These interpretations are a tool for the withdrawal of national legal systems into themselves. This withdrawal may be conscious (the desire to develop a national exceptionalism). But more often it is unconscious (as the lawyer continues to apply, without question, the solutions that he knows in the national context).

Several other works exist on this theme, regarding one particular convention or another. See, for example, the panorama of case law gathered annually by Cl. Witz on the uniform law of the international sale of goods ((2012) D., 1114.) which indicates, in a footnote, the existing measures for collecting decisions: CISG-online (University of Basel), http://www.cisg-online.ch; The Pace University Database (State of New York), http://www.cisg.law.pace.edu; The Unilex Database (Rome), http://www.unilex.info. These three databases gather together all decisions regardless of their origins. French case law is gathered into the CISG-France database (Saarland University), http://Witz.jura.uni-sb.de/CISG/; see, as examples of other national databases: CISG-Belgium, http://www.law.kuleuven.ac.be/ and CISG-Spain, http://www.uc3m.es/cisg/; see the full list by country on http://Witz.jura.uni-sb.de/CISG/cisglinks.htm; a collection of jurisprudential references will also usefully guide the reader: M.R. Will, *Twenty Years of International Sales Law Under the CISG, International Bibliography and Case Law Digest (1980–2000)* (Kluwer Law International, 2000). See also the already indicated works relating to the interpretation of the New York Convention on the Rights of the Child by the French courts (1990, see *supra*, p. 40), etc.

The second illustration concerns the incorporation of European law into French law.

SITUATION – THE INCORPORATION OF EUROPEAN LAW INTO FRENCH LAW (EU OR ECHR)

A few examples from case law

European law, whether European Union law or the law of the European Convention of Human Rights (ECHR), is marked by the presence of two jurisdictions – the Court of Justice of the European Union (CJEU) and the European Court of Human Rights – (ECtHR) which fully assume their role as authentic interpreters. The work done by these two European courts in terms of the uniform interpretation of the law is considerable. There is no equivalent in international law, but despite this imposing institutional architecture, we cannot assume that the incorporation of European law into national law cannot be an opportunity for the French legal system to withdraw into itself.

We think, first of all, of cases in which European law and European courts accord a wide margin of appreciation to Member States, which occur more frequently than one often believes (absence of a uniform or autonomous definition given by the European court, national appreciation of the conditions of the implementation of a European legal rule in the name of subsidiarity, etc.). In these situations, the expert lawyer often must deploy a treasury of intelligence to measure the respective places occupied by the European legal order and the domestic legal order. Now, the perimeter of each order cannot be defined other than through experimentation, interrogation and, sometimes, provocation. A power struggle may result from this freedom preserved at the national level, involving greater or lesser attempts by the French legal system to withdraw into itself, whenever it seeks to impose a legal method or solution belonging to it (for a dynamic presentation of the phenomenon, on the subject of the incorporation of the case law of the ECtHR into French law, see M. Guyomar, 'Le dialogue des jurisprudences entre le Conseil d'Etat et la Cour de Strasbourg: appropriation, anticipation, émancipation', in Mélanges J.-P. Costa (Dalloz, 2011), p. 311).

But above all there are cases in which the incorporation of European law into national law gives rise to explicit demonstrations of rejection. In this context, the withdrawal of the French legal system into itself is obvious. It participates in a breakaway approach, in a power struggle that is even more violent than that which may have been observed in previous cases. Let us take a situation that has remained famous in the annals of French case law: the refusal of the Council of State to allow European directives to replace an individual administrative act (*Cohn-Bendit* case – Conseil d'Etat Ass., 22 déc. 1978, Rec. Lebon, 524 – which was overturned by the decision in the *Perreux* case – Conseil d'Etat Ass., 30 oct. 2009, Req. n° 298348). The position taken by the French administrative court in this case went against the interpretation given by the Court of Justice (for a comprehensive presentation, see R. Kovar, *Le Conseil d'État et l'effet direct des directives: la fin d'une longue marche*, Europe janv. 2010, Etude n° 1). This line of case law was maintained in France for 31 years, during which a solution from French law would be favoured over a solution of European law through a refusal to apply the latter. Even though this situation could be considered to be abnormal from the point of view of European law, it was undeniably the result of the desire of the French legal system to withdraw into itself which cannot be ignored by lawyers in practice.

The third illustration concerns the appropriation of concepts of international or European law by domestic law.

SITUATION – THE APPROPRIATION BY DOMESTIC LAW OF NOTIONS OF INTERNATIONAL AND EUROPEAN LAW

The example of public order: returning to the *Banque Africaine de Développement* case

We have twice referred to a case entitled *Banque Africaine de Développement* (Cour de cassation, ch. soc., 25 janv 2005, pourvoi n° 04-41012, see *supra*, p. 100). In this case in which the jurisdictional immunity of an international organisation was challenged, we remember that the French court rejected the supposed immunity by incorporating into its international public order a right of access to justice established by the ECHR, even though the Convention was not binding on the international organisation. This solution has been criticised by a specialist of international and European law (M. Forteau, 'L'ordre public "transnational" ou "réellement international"' (JDI, 2011), especially p. 17, note 57:

> In the *Banque Africaine de Développement* case, the French courts were for example confronted by the application of two contradictory conventions (the ECHR and the headquarters agreement of the bank) which was impossible to articulate with the help of the classical principles of conflicts of law (lex specialis, lex posterior) because each bound distinct parties and was thus res inter alios acta in relation to the other. By directly integrating the right of access to justice into French international public policy instead of invoking Article 6 of the ECHR, which could not, formally, prevail over the immunity established by the headquarters agreement, the Court of Cassation adroitly sidestepped the difficulty (...). Legally, the solution is not at all convincing because a domestic legal norm (international public order) cannot trump a conventional norm (the immunity). Moreover, immunity is distinct from competence. The trick in this case consisted of displacing the debate from the realm of international public law (unresolvable conflict of conventions) to the realm of international private law (reasoning in terms of international public policy) in order to better avoid (but then by disguising) the problem ('Dans l'affaire de la Banque africaine de développement, les juridictions françaises ont été confrontées par exemple à l'application de deux conventions contradictoires (la CEDH et l'accord de siège de la Banque) qu'il était impossible d'articuler à l'aide des principes classiques de conflits de normes (lex specialis, lex posterior) car chacune liait des parties distinctes et était donc res inter alios acta à l'égard de l'autre. En intégrant directement le droit à un juge dans l'ordre public international français au lieu d'invoquer l'article 6 de la CEDH qui ne pouvait prévaloir, formellement, sur l'immunité prévue par

l'accord de siège, la Cour de cassation a adroitement contourné la difficulté (...). La solution n'est, juridiquement, guère convaincante car une norme interne (l'ordre public international) ne peut écarter une norme conventionnelle (l'immunité). Par ailleurs, l'immunité se distingue de la compétence. L'astuce en l'occurrence a consisté à déplacer le débat du plan du droit international public (conflit insoluble de conventions) au plan du droit international privé (raisonnement en termes d'ordre public international) pour mieux esquiver (mais alors en le travestissant) le problème').

This criticism is interesting. It simply denounces the appropriation by the French legal order of a principle of public policy originating from international or European law. But it does not offer any tool for preventing the phenomenon. In other words, although one may regret the appropriation by a national court of an inapplicable solution of international law, one may not prevent it from nationalising it.

The example of general legal principles: the *KPMG* case

The French Council of State, ruling in the famous *KPMG* case (Conseil d'Etat, 'Ass., 24 mars 2006, n° 288460) had adopted a more extensive concept of legal security than that adopted by the Court of Justice (P. Brunet and O. Dubos, 'Approche critique du vocabulaire juridique européen: la pratique des juges' Chronique du CEJEC, LPA, 2008, n° 164–165, 7; see also more generally on the phenomenon of national appropriation: J. Sirinelli, 'Les transformations du droit administratif par le droit de l'Union européenne – Une contribution à l'étude du droit administratif européen' ed. (LGDJ, 2011)). By so proceeding, the administrative court equipped itself with an autonomous concept, liberated from the European principle of legitimate expectations, a principle that it could always say in future was only applicable in the field of European law.

The fourth illustration highlights the withdrawal of the French legal system into itself using procedural routes.

SITUATION – THE PROCEDURAL ROUTES FOR THE WITHDRAWAL OF THE FRENCH LEGAL SYSTEM INTO ITSELF

The example of the 'priority' character of questions of constitutionality in France

Let us recall that the French institutional law (*Loi organique n° 2009-1523 du 10 décembre 2009 relative à l'application de l'article 61-1 de la Constitution)*, which defined the procedural rules for the priority question of constitutionality ('la question prioritaire de constitutionalité'), introduced a double reference to France's 'international obligations'. Thus one may read in Articles 23-2 (applicable to courts of first instance) and 23-5 (applicable to superior courts) of

Ordonnance n° 58-1067 du 7 novembre 1958 portant loi organique sur le Conseil constitutionnel, as modified by the institutional law of 2009 (cited *supra*):

> In all cases, the court must, when presented with arguments contesting the conformity of a legislative provision with, first, the rights and freedoms guaranteed by the Constitution and, second, France's international obligations, first pronounce on the transmission of the priority question of constitutionality to the Council of State or the Court of Cassation (art. 23-2);
>
> In all cases, the Council of State or the Court of Cassation must, when presented with arguments contesting the conformity of a legislative provision with, first, the rights and freedoms guaranteed by the Constitution and, second, France's international obligations, first pronounce on the referral of the priority question of constitutionality to the Constitutional Council (art. 23-5).
>
> ('En tout état de cause, la juridiction doit, lorsqu'elle est saisie de moyens contestant la conformité d'une disposition législative, d'une part, aux droits et libertés garantis par la Constitution et, d'autre part, aux engagements internationaux de la France, se prononcer par priorité sur la transmission de la question de constitutionnalité au Conseil d'Etat ou à la Cour de cassation' (art. 23-2);
>
> En tout état de cause, le Conseil d'Etat ou la Cour de cassation doit, lorsqu'il est saisi de moyens contestant la conformité d'une disposition législative, d'une part, aux droits et libertés garantis par la Constitution et, d'autre part, aux engagements internationaux de la France, se prononcer par priorité sur le renvoi de la question de constitutionnalité au Conseil constitutionnel' (art. 23-5).)

This double provision is intended to express the fact that rulings on constitutionality have priority over rulings on conformity with an international convention. Whether it is a question of examining the conformity of the French law in force with international law or European law, the ordinary judge must, 'in any case (...) first pronounce on (...)' the transmission or the referral of the issue. It results from this French domestic procedural rule that the consideration of the conformity of a law with an international convention is secondary to the consideration of the constitutionality of a law, which has priority.

This procedural prioritisation clearly expresses a desire to prioritise a domestic preliminary ruling, concerning national law (the Constitution) over any question arising from international or European law that may involve referring the law to the Court of Justice of the European Union. It is a form of the temporary withdrawal of the French legal system into itself.

The example of the absence of a preliminary reference

Another illustration of withdrawal arises whenever a national court refrains from requesting a preliminary ruling from the CJEU even though a case poses a potential difficulty of interpretation of European law. Although this refusal may have serious consequences in terms of the liability of the state, the fact is that a multitude of situations exist in which the opportuneness of a preliminary reference is discussed before French courts that result in the conclusion that there is no question to resolve. These situations may be motivated by contingent considerations where the national court and/or the parties object to the suspension of proceedings (three months for an urgent preliminary reference and 16 months for a classic preliminary reference). But they sometimes have a deeper meaning. Making a preliminary reference to the Court of Justice means taking the risk that national actors, particularly judges, will lose their power to interpret the law. In these circumstances, the refusal to make a preliminary reference must clearly be understood as a procedural tool allowing the French legal system to withdraw into itself.

(iii) Illustrations from the legal system of the European Union

In order to illustrate the withdrawal of the legal system of the European Union into itself, it is most interesting to study the relationship between European law and international law. The European Union, in effect, gives an important place to international legal sources. This is why it sought very early on to protect itself from this 'external' influence. There are multiple manifestations of this withdrawal. For the most part, we have already encountered them. Here we will revisit four main illustrations.

The first concerns the phenomenon of the individualisation of European law, including in cases in which its formulation is identical or close to that employed by international law.

SITUATION – THE INDIVIDUALISATION OF A EUROPEAN LAW INSPIRED BY INTERNATIONAL LAW

Examples from the early days of today's European structure

The phenomenon of the individualisation of European law, whenever it borrows methods and solutions from international law, is quite simply historical (CJCE, 5 févr. 1963, Case 26/62 *Van Gend en Loos* [1963] ECR 3, see *supra* p. 52). Multiple illustrations exist, notably in the case law of the Court of Justice. Thus, for example, the articulation, by the European court, of European principles with the support, notably, of international customary rules, has sometimes allowed it to free itself from existing definitions (Case T-115/94 *Opel Austria* [1997] ECR II-39; see nonetheless, on the contrary, firmly condemning this position: Case C-162/96 *Racke* [1998] ECR I-3655). This attitude may also prevail for the written sources of international law. The assertion that a European norm, formulated identically to an international source, may receive an autonomous interpretation, potentially different to that given to it by the international legal order, is another example of individualisation-appropriation (see, for example, the case of EU-third-party state association agreements, the contents of which are identical to the TFEU on a given point but which are nonetheless subject to a different interpretation, taking into account the objectives of the European Union legal order: Case 270/80 *Polydor* [1982] ECR 329; nevertheless, counter-examples do exist: see notably Case C-438/00 *Deutscher Handballbund* [2003] ECR I-4135). The practice is all the more developed in that European institutions, whenever they have an interest in doing so, try to reproduce the international norm in a secondary law, as the interpretation of the latter may be more easily managed (examples are notably very numerous in transportation law and environmental law).

The second illustration concerns a practice of European institutions which consists in 'pre-empting' international law by 'pre-empting' the competence of Member States.

SITUATION – THE PRE-EMPTION OF INTERNATIONAL LAW BY EUROPEAN LAW

The example of the Hague Protocol on the Law Applicable to Maintenance Obligations (2007)

Regulation (EC) No. 4/2009/EC of 18 December 2008 on jurisdiction, applicable law, recognition and enforcement of decisions and cooperation in matters relating to maintenance obligations notably provides that: 'The law applicable to maintenance obligations shall be determined in accordance with the Hague Protocol of 23 November 2007 on the law applicable to maintenance obligations (…) in the Member States bound by that instrument' (art. 15). In defining all the available solutions for conflicts of law, the European secondary law thus trusts to the application of an international legal instrument binding on Member States, as the case may be, where it describes its own rules belonging to conflict of jurisdictions lato sensu (competences of courts, recognition and execution of decisions). The nature of the conditional combination of a European law with an international protocol radically changed following the adoption of Council Decision 2009/941/EC of 30 November 2009 on the conclusion by the European Community of the Hague Protocol of 23 November 2007 on the Law Applicable to Maintenance Obligations. The Council considered, in effect, that the European Community 'has exclusive competence over all matters governed by the Protocol', such that it could adhere to it, which it in fact did. Except for those states not bound by Regulation 4/2009/EC (today, only Denmark remains, as the European Commission has noted the desire of the United Kingdom to opt into the regulation: Commission decision 2009/451/EC of 8 June 2009), the combination of the European regulation and the Hague Protocol was to become effectively binding on the day that the latter entered into force. This in any case was the wish expressed by the Council of the European Union in the decision referred to. The change is important and, to be honest, spectacular. Although the Council Regulation seemed to make the application of the Hague Protocol subject to the will of Member States, a literal reading of the Council decision implies that the aforementioned states would henceforth be bound by the Hague instrument without even having to ratify it (which none of them have done to this day). The

European Union purely and simply pre-empted the competence of Member States in their freedom to decide whether or not to sign up to the Protocol. This approach is clearly part of a process of prioritisation. By considering that the European Community (now the European Union) had exclusive competence to adopt The Hague Protocol on the Law Applicable to Maintenance Obligations, the Council of the European Union clearly expressed its wish to incorporate the international legal text into European law. With this decision, the international Convention became a source of European law in its own right. The European legal system thus withdraws into itself and integrates into its own hierarchical structure a law from elsewhere.

The third illustration is drawn from the manner in which the Court of Justice has sometimes refused to recognise the direct effect of international conventions binding on the European Union in order to prevent them from encouraging European litigation on the legality of secondary law texts or the tortious liability of the European Union.

SITUATION – THE WITHHOLDING OF DIRECT EFFECT FROM INTERNATIONAL LEGAL NORMS LIKELY TO INTERFERE WITH EUROPEAN UNION LAW

Examples of WTO Agreements, the Kyoto Protocol and the Montego Bay Convention

The example of the agreements concluded under the auspices of the World Trade Organization (WTO – 1994) is famous. The Court of Justice, manifestly, does not wish for the rules of world trade to interfere systematically with the legality of European secondary law texts nor encourage actions in tort against the European Union (see for example, openly refusing to appreciate the legality of a directive in light of an agreement concluded under the auspices of the WTO, Case C-491/01 *BAT and others* [2002] ECR I-11453; more recently, in the famous banana case: Case C-377/02 *Van Parys* [2005] ECR I-1465; compare in the context of an action in tort against the EU: Joint Cases C-120 and 121/06 *FIAMM* [2008] ECR I-6513). Similar discussions took place on the lack of direct enforceability of the Kyoto Protocol (1997) to the United Nations Framework Convention on Climate Change (1995). See, for an example concerning litigation on the legality of European secondary law texts, Case C-366/10 *ATAA* [2011] ECR I-13755. Compare, in relation to the United Nations Convention on the Law of the Sea (Montego Bay – 1982): Case C-308/06 *Intertanko* [1988] ECR I-4057.

A final example concerns the manner in which the European Union militates in favour of the insertion of disconnection clauses in international conventions despite the fact it had participated in their negotiation.

SITUATION – THE SPLITTING OF INTERNATIONAL AND EUROPEAN LAW

The example of disconnection clauses

'Disconnection clauses' are those clauses inserted into international conventions negotiated by the European Union that stipulate that all or part of the international convention does not apply to the internal relations of the European Union wherever a specific European regulation, potentially a derogation, exists – or may exist – in this domain. Examples are known in broadcasting (European Convention on Transfrontier Television of 1989), international bankruptcy (Council of Europe Istanbul Convention 1990) and the protection of cultural goods (Unidroit Convention of 1995). Other older illustrations exist but do not carry the name of this clause. We refer, notably, to the possibilities offered by the GATT Agreement (1947, revised in 1994) for creating systems of regional integration, potentially derogating from the rules governing world trade.

These convention provisions give rise to two distinct legal regimes. One regime internal to the European area from a European source and an international regime applying to external relations with third-party states or third-party international organisations. Depending on whether it concerns an internal or external relationship, the content of the law applying within the legal system of the European Union is not the same: priority is given to the European norm in internal relations; priority is given to the international norm in external relations.

All these examples show that the law of the European Union has developed a variety of tools allowing it both to integrate international law into its legal system and to protect itself from it. The situation is not fundamentally different from the one we are familiar with in French law, in its relations with international law and, to a lesser extent, with European law.

2. THE CHOICE OF ONE LEVEL OF APPLICATION OF LAW OVER ANOTHER

The fact that lawyers place themselves at one national, international or European level of the application of law rather than another to deal with a particular case raises the question of their freedom of choice. In a strongly internationalised and regionalised context, this freedom is sometimes presented in the rather frightening form of the spectre of global forum shopping (A). The reality is much more complex and nuanced, as numerous limits are placed on the lawyer's freedom of choice (B).

A. The spectre of global forum shopping

The expression 'forum shopping' refers to situations in which a plaintiff makes use of his freedom to choose one court over another, in the hope that this choice will have an influence on the outcome of the case. The use of this strategy is well known to international private lawyers: by choosing a court in state A, the plaintiff hopes that the law that this court will apply will be more favourable to him than that which would have been applied by a different court in state B. Understood in this somewhat simplified and exaggerated form, forum shopping becomes law shopping. By seeking to reach one court rather than another, the plaintiff seeks to place himself under the application of one law rather than another.

Returning to the case under consideration here in which a lawyer intends to place himself on one national, international or European level of the application of law rather than another, is the concept of 'forum shopping' capable of describing a practice of global dimensions?

If we try, to begin, to respond to this question in the affirmative, we may say that the theme of forum shopping occupies a more and more visible place in the handling of international and regional litigation. We may give a few significant examples.

Practices of forum shopping have been noted in the area of international and regional human rights protection.

SITUATION – INTERNATIONAL AND REGIONAL HUMAN RIGHTS LITIGATION AND CHOICE OF FORUM

The example of the *Georgia v Russia* case

Rosalyne Higgins, then president of the International Court of Justice, made a speech before the European Court of Human Rights in 2009. In it, she evoked a case between Georgia and Russia which was pending at the time (the ICJ has since declared itself not to be competent to decide the case, in a decision delivered on 1 April 2011), before the international court. The terms used by the President deserve to be presented here as they describe well the manner in which an international judge may experience the phenomenon of forum shopping. Here they are:

The *Georgia v Russia* case is significant for another reason – it is an example of the contemporary phenomenon of the same or similar legal questions surfacing in diverse fora. This is a consequence of the dispersal of responsibility for interpreting international law – especially human rights law – among different judicial and quasi-judicial bodies. In addition to the International Court of Justice and the three major regional systems for the protection of human rights in Europe, the Americas and Africa, there are the treaty bodies responsible for monitoring implementation of the provisions of international human rights treaties dealing with the two Covenants, the elimination of racial discrimination, discrimination against women, torture, the rights of the child, and the rights of migrant workers. Moreover, in the last fifteen years, following the mass atrocities in the former Yugoslavia and Rwanda, we have seen the creation of ad hoc international tribunals with jurisdiction to try the individuals responsible for such crimes as well as the establishment of a permanent International Criminal Court. The dispute between Georgia and Russia over the events of August 2008 came before the ICJ as a contentious proceeding regarding the application of the Convention on the Elimination of All Forms of Racial Discrimination. In its order, the International Court noted that the matter might also properly be brought to the attention of the Committee on the Elimination of Racial Discrimination. Around the same time, Georgia lodged an inter-state application with the European Court of Human Rights alleging violations of Articles 2 (right to life) and 3 (prohibition of inhuman and degrading treatment) of the European Convention on Human Rights and Article 1 (protection of property) of Protocol No. 1 to the Convention. The European Court ordered provisional measures calling on both parties to comply with their obligations under the Convention, particularly Articles 2 and 3. In addition, the European Court has since received thousands of applications against Georgia concerning hostilities which broke out in South Ossetia in August 2008. Meanwhile, the Prosecutor of the International Criminal Court has stated that the situation in Georgia is under analysis by his Office. We saw this same phenomenon of reformulated claims, on essentially the same subject matter, at the time of the 1999 air strikes by NATO against the Federal Republic of Yugoslavia. Here, too, the International Court of Justice and the European Court of Human Rights were both engaged. The plethora of judicial and quasi-judicial bodies operating in the field of human rights does pose the risk of divergent jurisprudence (ECtHR, Annual Report 2009, Council of Europe 2010, p. 45).

For a systematic study of the treatment of parallel proceedings in the human rights area, see J.-F. Flauss and S. Touzé (eds), *Contentieux international des droits de l'homme et choix d'un forum: les instances internationales de contrôle face au forum shopping* (Bruylant-Némésis, 2012). Compare, S. Joseph, *Corporations and Transnational Human Rights Litigation* (Hart, 2004); C. Scott (ed.), *Torture as Tort: Comparative Perspectives on the Development of Transnational Human Rights Litigation* (Hart, 2001).

Forum shopping has also been studied in the area of criminal law.

SITUATION – MULTIPLE NATIONAL AND INTERNATIONAL JUDGES IN CRIMINAL MATTERS

The judicial repartition of the penal field and choice of court

Criminal lawyers have long reflected on situations in which competition arises between national and international judges (see, the pioneering work in this area by M. Delmas-Marty, a criminal lawyer by training, on global legal pluralism, cited in the bibliography at the end of this work).

Among other recent works on the subject, we point out one study (A. Gogorza, 'CPI, TPI, tribunaux internationalisés, juridictions nationales: quel juge pour quelle infraction internationale?' in V. Malabat (ed.), *Juge national, européen et international et droit pénal* (Cujas, 2012), p. 61) in which the author tries to draw a 'judicial repartition of the penal field'. In order to do so, the author studied different criteria (criteria drawn from the nature of the offence and criteria drawn from the offender) which contributed to a division of competence between the different national and international criminal courts. The objective was to clearly avoid any competition between the international, regional and national courts working towards globalised criminal justice. The use of these criteria is not homogenous, however, depending on the legal context in question. The criteria themselves are not stable and their manipulation in a subject governed by broad principles (principle of the speciality of international jurisdictions, principle of complementarity (on this, see *supra*, p. 76) inherent in international criminal justice, etc.) means that the 'choice of criminal judge' remains a reality in an ever-more internationalised context.

Scenarios of global forum shopping exist in other domains. We have thus had the occasion to imagine a case of a multi-front strategy in intellectual property matters.[3] But this is true for all economic law subjects, particularly when the ends justify such an abundance of means.

SITUATION – THE DEVELOPMENT OF MULTILEVEL PROCEDURES IN ECONOMIC AND ENVIRONMENTAL LAW

Returning to multiple-front strategies

In economic and environment law, the development of parallel legal proceedings before national, international and European courts is nothing unusual. Whenever, for example, a state or a regional authority regulates an activity, it exposes itself to a discussion being opened on several jurisdictional fronts at the same time: national (respect for general principles), European (EU) or international (DRB).

[3] See *supra*, p. 130.

Highly specialised lawyers have thus developed the capacity to manage the challenges presented by these multiple-front strategies which are all the more necessary given that they concern a conflict between a public authority (for example a state) and a private operator, with the latter seeking to alter the positions of the former in a power struggle that could last for years. On the management of these multiple-front strategies in general, see, for example, S. McCaffrey and Th. Main, *Transnational Litigation in Comparative Perspective: Theory and Application* (Oxford Univeristy Press, 2009). For a specific perspective in environment law, see, for example, H. Osofsky and J. Peel, 'The Role of Litigation in Multilevel Climate Change Governance: Possibilities for a Lower Carbon Future?' (2013) 30 *Environmental and Planning Law Journal* 303.

Analyses drawing upon a certain number of famous cases concerning competition between international or regional courts and conflicts of proceedings have also been offered.

SITUATION – COMPETITION BETWEEN INTERNATIONAL OR REGIONAL JURISDICTIONS AND CONFLICTS OF PROCEEDINGS

Returning to the *Mox Factory, Iron Rhine Railway* and *Bosphorus* cases

Two studies have been published that aim to examine the phenomenon of competition between international or regional courts and conflicts of proceedings: N. Lavranos, *Jurisdictional Competition–Selected Cases in International and European Law* (Europa Law, 2009); Y. Kerbrat (ed.) *Forum Shopping et concurrence des procédures contentieuses internationales* (Bruylant, 2011). The first is presented as a case study, preceded by an introduction and followed by various proposals for resolving conflicts. The second envisages competition between proceedings in the main branches of international law in a systematic manner (investment law, world trade, human rights, criminal law and environmental law).

Among the different cases presented, we find, notably, the *Mox Factory* (Case C-459/03 *Commission v Ireland* [2006] ECR I-4635), *Iron Rhine Railway* (CPA, 24 May PCA 2005) and *Bosphorus* cases (App. 45036/98 *Bosphorus v Ireland* (ECtHR, 30 June 2005)). What all these cases have in common is that they bring together a plurality of international or European courts, which have dealt with, or more modestly, may potentially have to deal with an identical or similar situation. Thus, in the *Mox Factory* case, two arbitration tribunals, the International Tribunal for the Law of the Sea and the Court of Justice of the European Communities, were both seized of all or part of the dossier, the Court of Justice deciding to brutally reaffirm its exclusive competence for resolving the dispute between the UK and Ireland. In the *Iron Rhine Railway* case, the Permanent Court of Arbitration took particular care to verify that its work in applying European Union law did not overlap with the power of interpretation via preliminary ruling conferred on the CJEU by the TFEU. In the *Bosphorus* case, the ECtHR established a simple presumption of the conformity of European Union law with the ECHR, a presumption which found its justification in part in the presence in the European Union of a court (the CJEU) able to guarantee the protection of fundamental rights and to verify the legality of European secondary law.

These doubtlessly somewhat exceptional examples demonstrate that in different contexts, international and European courts are becoming more conscious of their coexistence/rivalry. This consciousness is demonstrated in decisions either through expressions of rejection (as in the *Mox Factory* case) or of empathy (as in the *Iron Rhine Railway* and *Bosphorus* cases). This situation is likely to cause lawyers to consider that several jurisdictions are open to them in the international and European context and that they must make a choice guided notably by a comparative analysis of the decision-making practices of the different actors present (on multilevel comparison, see *supra*, our discussions in Part I, p. 57).

Even though it may be observed, the phenomenon of forum shopping nonetheless presents important specificities in a global context, specificities that concern the presence of important limits on freedom of choice.

B. The Limits on Freedom of Choice

(i) The presence of diversely specialised courts on different levels

As we noted at the beginning of this paragraph, the expression 'forum shopping' was originally developed in the context of state justice, in which the courts of various countries in the world were potentially open to strategic plaintiffs. It cannot be used in a wider context, including international and European courts, without some modifications. As is often the case, a concept developed at one level, here the national level, does not necessarily have the same meaning and the same scope at other levels, in this case the international and European levels, and *a fortiori*, in relations between these different levels.

In the present case, we may say that forum shopping is often impeded by too-wide differences between the justices that may be delivered at the national, international and European level. If the plaintiff knows that the result he seeks cannot be attained except for on one level, in the absence of comparable traits in the justice exercised at another level, he cannot exercise his freedom of choice. The situation is therefore paradoxical: if the hope for different solutions contributes to forum shopping, these differences must not be too great, as otherwise all possibility of choice will be annihilated. In order to illustrate this point, we will distinguish between two types of situation.

The first group of situations concern procedural considerations.

SITUATION – DIFFERENCES BETWEEN THE PROCEDURAL RULES GOVERNING DIFFERENT JURISDICTIONS AT DIFFERENT LEVELS

Examples of procedural rules limiting the freedom for plaintiffs to choose a court

There are numerous situations in which a plaintiff, who would like to choose a particular national, international or European court, finds his choices severely limited by procedural rules. Let us take a few examples: the lack of direct access, or very limited direct access, for ordinary parties to an international or European court (the ICJ or DRB and, in a great number of cases, the CJEU, for example); the subsidiary character of international or European justice which requires the exhaustion of domestic legal remedies (before the ECtHR, for example); the purely voluntary character of the submission of a plaintiff to certain forms of international justice (arbitration or international legal justice), etc.

These general considerations must sometimes be qualified in certain contexts. For example, international and European human rights litigation, international penal litigation or litigation concerning international investment offers forms of national, international or European justice that tend to resemble each other. It is not a coincidence that forum-shopping practices are most obvious in these matters. See, previously cited, Lavranos, *Jurisdictional Competition*; Kerbrat (ed.), *Forum Shopping* (cited *supra*).

A particular case: actions for annulment

The action for annulment is a good example of restricted access to a court. Let us take as a working hypothesis the situation of a plaintiff who wishes to declare a legal norm to be void due to its non-conformity with a superior norm. According to whether this norm is the product of a national, international or European legal system, the plaintiff will have to direct himself to one court rather than another according to whether or not he has access to an annulment procedure there. In principle, only an international court may annul an international norm and only a national court may annul a national norm. The action for annulment – like many other actions – literally changes its subject according to whether it is considered at one level of application of the law rather than another. The plaintiff can, in the absolute, choose to demand the annulation of a national norm rather than a European or international one. But for each of these norms, there will in principle be no freedom to choose a court, except in very exceptional cases.

Other situations of difference concern the material law that may be applied by different courts on different levels.

SITUATION – DIFFERENCES BETWEEN THE MATERIAL LAW THAT MAY BE APPLIED BY DIFFERENT COURTS AT DIFFERENT LEVELS

Practical examples of differences in applicable material law limiting the freedom for a plaintiff to choose a court

A simple consideration consists of observing that courts present at different levels – national, international or European – do not necessarily apply the same laws for the good and simple reason that their legal cultures are not the same. A limitation on economic freedom, for example, is not understood in the same manner, according to the same reasoning and the same justifications, by a national court that is protective of individual freedoms, an international court in charge of commercial disputes between states and a European court ruling in the context of regional integration. If a company believes that its economic freedom has been infringed by a public authority, it is not faced with a choice between three different courts all able to decide upon the same question. It is faced with three profoundly different legal questions, each of which may be decided in its own way by a different court. The national judge may annul or declare a national norm unenforceable due to its unconstitutional nature. The international judge will note a violation of a free trade agreement and invite the parties to negotiate an end to the conflict or face retaliatory measures. A European judge will only have eyes for a principle of freedom of movement and will eventually identify an infringement and seek any justifications for it.

This illustration – a little exaggerated – should not let us forget that differences in applicable material law often have a greater impact than one may think. Lawyers are sometimes tempted to consider that, because the problem is objectively the same in the beginning (in our example: a public authority that puts limits on an economic freedom), its treatment at national, international and European level is, or should necessarily be, the same. This vision is often contradicted by reality. Judges present a degree of specialisation which means that they do not apply the same law to situations of a common origin. The differences in the solutions that result from this are more the result of a global legal pluralism that lawyers must learn to master than an expression of incoherence or even a simple contradiction. The comparison of national, international and European law can highlight some of these differences (see *supra*, Part I, the numerous illustrations given). Lawyers must keep them in mind when they are presented with the choice of one national, international or European court rather than another. According to the objective they wish to pursue, it may be that they simply will not have a choice, as one court on a given level (national, international or European) is the only one qualified to consider it.

Theoretical approach: comparing the methods of international public law and international private law for designating the applicable law

The practical considerations above do not exclude a more theoretical approach in which the question posed is whether the methods used by international public law to designate the applicable law and those used by international private law are becoming increasingly similar. The question may generally be posed in these terms. For a long time, it was considered that on the (very particular) subject of the search for the applicable law, the difference between an international judge and a national judge, both faced with an international situation, was that the first could only apply his own law (international law) whereas the second could apply a foreign law (designated by a rule governing conflict of laws). The dissociation between a competent judge and an applicable law was inconceivable in international public law but appeared to be possible in international private law.

This split between the two disciplines is increasingly subject to challenge (see in particular on this theme, the analysis offered by M. Forteau, 'Forum shopping et fragmentation du droit applicable aux relations internationales – le regard de l'internationaliste publiciste', in *La fragmentation du droit applicable aux relations internationales – Regards croisés des internationalistes privatistes et publicistes*, scientific editor M. Forteau; coord. J.-S. Bergé, M. Forteau, M.-L. Niboyet and J.-M. Thouvenin (Editions Pedone, 2011), p. 143). It is becoming more frequent for an international court to apply a national or even a regional law. Arbitration is often given as an example: the 1965 Washington Convention establishing the ICSID provides for this possibility:

> The Tribunal shall decide a dispute in accordance with such rules of law as may be agreed by the parties. In the absence of such agreement, the Tribunal shall apply the law of the Contracting State party to the dispute (including its rules on the conflict of laws) and such rules of international law as may be applicable (art. 42.1).

Arbitration decisions are distinguished by their capacity to directly apply several laws, developed on different levels (PCA, partial decision of 30 January 2007 in the Eurotunnel v France and United Kingdom case, articulating different national, international and European laws around the question of the legal regime applicable to relations between the parties to a concession contract). As for the court of the European Union, there are examples of cases in which it could alternatively apply, in addition to European law, national law and international law (the most significant example is that of actions in liability, drawing on national law in contractual matters and international law in matters of tort).

This convergence, although it does not really concern methods for designating the applicable law but rather the law that may be applied by judges (on the importance of this reference to the law applied, see our discussions *infra*, p. 165) undeniably reduces the differences that may be observed between national, international and European justice. It even favours, as we have already seen, the circulation of legal methods and solutions (see *supra*, Part II, p. 107). But lawyers must remain vigilant. Case-by-case analysis of the law effectively applied by different courts shows that important differences remain. For a demonstration in this sense, in the sensitive area of investment arbitration in which forum shopping practices are developing, see F.-X. Train, 'Forum shopping et fragmentation du droit applicable aux relations internationales – le regard de l'internationaliste privatiste', in *La fragmentation du droit applicable aux relations internationales – Regards croisés des internationalistes privatistes et publicistes*, cited *supra*, pp. 138 *et seq*. Compare K. Yannaca-Small 'Parallel Proceedings' in P. Muchlinski, F. Ortino, and Ch. Schreuer (eds), *The Oxford Handbook of International Investment Law* (Oxford Univeristy Press, 2016).

(ii) The presence of integrated systems

The freedom of the plaintiff to choose which national, international or European court will decide his case is also limited by the presence of integrated legal systems. For a French lawyer, it is clear that the role of the national judge cannot be conceived with total indifference for the legal system of the European Union and notably for the place that another court – the Court of Justice – occupies in it.

SITUATION – DE LEGE LATA: THE CJEU AND MEMBER STATE COURTS

The example of the constraints weighing on European courts and national courts respectively

The choice for a plaintiff to summon a national court or a European court as a tool for the national or European system to withdraw into itself (see *supra*, p. 137, the examples offered) is greatly limited by legal integration. In an integrated system, such as that which exists within the European Union, numerous legal tools can restrict attempts by legal systems to withdraw into themselves.

In the context of national legal systems, we know, for example, that if a court refuses to make a preliminary reference to the CJEU in order to favour a national interpretation over an autonomous interpretation of the European norm, there are three ways to avoid this obstacle: the plaintiff, if his case has not been definitively decided, can try to convince a superior judge of the necessity of making a preliminary reference; if he does not succeed, he can, under certain conditions, take legal action against his state for the fault committed by the public legal service (Case C-224/01 *Köbler* [2003] ECR I-10239; the French Court of Cassation recognised this possibility in 11 judgments delivered on the same day: 1ère civ., 26 octobre 2011, 10-24250-10-24261); he can also invite the European Commission to open infringement proceedings against the state in question (arts 258 *et seq.* TFEU); finally, if the plaintiff's case is repeated, which is the case in recurrent actions, there will always be time for him to convince different national judges, in new proceedings, who may finally concede and make a preliminary reference, albeit against the position of a higher court (this occurred in the *Cofidis* case (Case C-473/00 [2002] ECR I-10875) in which a French court of first instance (Vienne) had the audacity to make a preliminary reference to the CJEU when the Court of Cassation had previously refused to do so; this, in an even more obvious manner, also happened in the *Köbler* case (cited *supra*) in which a local court raised the question of the liability of the Austrian state for the refusal of its superior court to make a preliminary reference to the same Court of Justice).

In the context of the European legal system, safeguards also exist. Member States occupy a place in an integrated European structure which cannot ignore the Court of Justice, guardian of the European Treaties. The *Solange* case is the most striking illustration of this (on this case, see *infra*, p. 186). In a more general sense, the place accorded to national legal traditions, the margin of appreciation left to states and to national courts, the direct role played by states in the application of the principles of subsidiarity and of proportionality (Protocol 2 annexed to TEU and TFEU; the so-called 'yellow card' procedure was used for the first time in May 2012 by 12 national parliaments regarding a proposal for a Council Regulation on the exercise of the right to take collective action within the context of the freedom of establishment and the freedom to provide services, COM(2012)130 final) are all tools at the service of a legal integration that we too often forget works both ways.

In the uncertain future, another form of integration must be taken into account, once the European Union has adhered to the European Convention of Human Rights. In effect, relations between the Court of Justice and the European Court of Human Rights will be deeply altered.

8. Prioritisation through the application of the law at another level: the appeal to a prioritised law

In order to solve a case with the help of proritisation of norms, lawyers have made the more or less free choice to place themselves on one level of the application of law rather than another. This positioning is confronted with the reality of a global legal pluralism that demands that other methods and solutions operate at other levels. Now, these methods and solutions may also participate in a process of the prioritisation of laws. Lawyers must therefore master the passageways from one prioritisation established at one level to another prioritisation established at another level (Section 1) which sometimes necessarily require reference to a 'prioritised law'(Section 2).

1. THE PASSAGEWAYS FROM ONE PRIORITISATION ESTABLISHED AT ONE LEVEL TO ANOTHER PRIORITISATION ESTABLISHED AT ANOTHER LEVEL

The identification of the passageways from one prioritisation established at one level to another prioritisation established at another level borrows from the theme of the circulation of situations which was tackled in the phase of the combination of laws (see *supra*, Chapter 6, p. 107). In the configuration that principally interests us in this work, which is to say the circulation of situations between the national, international or European levels, three scenarios may be envisaged: the passageways between the national and international levels (A), between the national and European levels (B) and between the international and European levels (C).

A. The Passageways between the National and International Levels

Movement from a national level to an international level and vice versa may operate through different passageways.

SITUATION – MOVEMENT FROM A NATIONAL INSTITUTION TO AN INTERNATIONAL INSTITUTION AND VICE VERSA

The example of a conflict between a state and a foreign citizen, elevated to the status of an interstate conflict: returning to the *Diallo* case

In order to illustrate the phenomenon of circulation between national courts and the International Court of Justice (ICJ), we have taken the example of the *Diallo* case (ICJ 30 November 2010, *Ahmadou Sadio Diallo* – Republic of Guinea v Democratic Republic of Congo; on this case see our discussion *supra* p. 73). This decision illustrates the case in which a state exercises diplomatic protection over one of its citizens, after the exhaustion of domestic legal remedies. Let us recall that this diplomatic protection allows a national situation (here the recourse by the citizen to the authorities of the foreign state which had taken measures of dispossession and expulsion against him) to be elevated to the international level (an interstate conflict brought before the ICJ).

In a case of this kind, the hierarchical structures of national law that allow the legality of the dispossession and expulsion measure to be evaluated, in the national context, determine in the international legal order whether a state has violated an obligation of international law by adopting the dispossession and expulsion measure in question. The hierarchical structures established at national level thus find a certain echo at international level.

The example of international arbitration proceedings incorporated into a national legal order: the case of an arbitration decision confronted by a national international public policy

Say that an international arbitration tribunal has delivered a decision. The question may arise of how this decision will be incorporated into the legal order of a state (recognition or an action for annulment), for example the national legal order. Pursuant to this incorporation, the domestic judge may examine whether the decision is 'manifestly contrary to international public policy'. This international public policy is national (for an illustration in France, in a case of the disrespect by an international arbiter of the principle of the suspension of individual bankruptcy proceedings notably stipulated at French level, Cour de cassation, 1ère civ., 8 mars 1988, pourvoi n° 86-12015). Even though this public policy is meant to be specific to international relations, it proceeds from a prioritisation that is potentially unique to the national legal system. This prioritisation may not be the same as that which the arbiter may have considered in international public policy ('truly international public policy'). It may be, therefore, that two prioritisations coexist and interact, as the case may be, with each other.

But this type of institutional movement is not always possible or cannot be fully achieved. In such cases, it is the movement from the application of the law in the national context to the application of the law in the international context and vice versa that allows us to understand movement from one prioritisation established at one level to another prioritisation established at another level.

SITUATION – MOVEMENT FROM AN APPLICATION OF THE LAW IN THE NATIONAL CONTEXT TO AN APPLICATION OF THE LAW IN THE INTERNATIONAL CONTEXT AND VICE VERSA

The example of a national law solution evaluated in an international context: returning to the handling of a complaint by the DRB

The handling of violations of the rules of international trade established by the WTO by the legislation of state parties to the organisation constitutes, as we have seen, a case of circulation (see *supra*, p. 122). A law formulated in a national context is evaluated, through the making of a complaint, in an international context. This confrontation generally takes an abstract form. The WTO tribunals confront the national regulation and seek to confirm or disprove a conflict with the terms of one of the WTO Agreements (see in this sense, S. Bhuiyan, *National Law in WTO Law – Effectiveness and Good Governance in the World Trading System* (Cambridge University Press, 2007), especially p. 37; for an illustration in matters of intellectual property: China — Measures Affecting the Protection and Enforcement of Intellectual Property Rights, WTO, Report of the Panel, 26 January 2009, *United States v China*, WT/DS362). This abstract approach sometimes gives way to a more concrete analysis. This is the case, for example, in situations in which it is the absence of effective implementation of the national law that constitutes a violation of international obligations (for an example, from a conflict between Argentina and the European Communities, WTO, Report of the Panel, 29 September 2006, *Argentina v EC*, WT/DS293, see the explanations below, p. 75). In both cases, we cannot exclude, for example, a discussion on what type of domestic dysfunction reveals the disrespect of international obligations by the defendant state. Potential dysfunctions may include, for example, a failure to apply a domestic prioritisation of norms: a national administrative practice that conflicts with national legislative prescriptions, a conflict that therefore constitutes a violation of the international agreement on free trade.

B. The Passageways between National and European Levels

The institutional passageways that allow us to pass from the national level to the European level and vice versa are well known. They illustrate the potential movement from a prioritisation established on one level to a prioritisation established on another level.

SITUATION – MOVEMENT FROM A NATIONAL INSTITUTION TO A EUROPEAN INSTITUTION AND VICE VERSA

The example of the preliminary reference made to the CJEU and then received by a national court

The bouncing back and forth that results from preliminary reference procedures between national courts and the European court often leads to convergence between national and European legal solutions. But sometimes, it is used in the pursuit of another goal altogether, notably when it concerns the opposition between the hierarchical structures of domestic law and the hierarchical structures of European law.

The French *Melki* case is a remarkable illustration of this. In domestic proceedings, a French court of first instance submitted a priority question of constitutionality to the Court of Cassation with a view to its eventual transmission to the Constitutional Council, which derived its competence from the new Article 61-1 of the French Constitution. The question formulated by the judge challenged the compatibility of a French legal provision (Code of Criminal Procedure, Article 78-2, para. 4) with 'the rights and freedoms guaranteed by the Constitution of the French Republic'. Refusing to adhere strictly to the terms of the question posed by the court of first instance, the Court of Cassation relied on the submissions of the plaintiff to displace the discussion from the domain of the constitutionality of the French law to that of its conformity with European legal provisions (Cour de cassation, QPC, 16 avr. 2010, n° 10-40002). In order to do so, the higher court took two successive leaps in its reasoning. First, it examined the compatibility of the rule of criminal procedure with an article of the Treaty on the Functioning of the European Union relating to the free movement of persons in the area of freedom, security and justice (TFEU, art. 67). Then, moving up a rung into general issues, it examined the sensitive question of the compatibility of certain procedural rules regarding the priority question of constitutionality (Ord. 7 Nov. 1958, Art. 23-2 and 23-5, modified by the institutional law of 10 December 2009) with the provisions of the European Treaty on the preliminary reference procedure (TFEU, art. 267). The reasoning followed by the Court of Cassation, without any hesitation, is part of a process of prioritisation. The Court of Cassation appeals to the primacy of European law to determine whether the French institutional laws that govern the relationship between the verification of the constitutionality of a law and that of its conformity with a treaty are compatible with European Union law. The approach of the French court deserves further explanation. We may, in effect, ask why the Court of Cassation made the deliberate choice to view the relationship between French law and European law through the prism of conflict of norms? The court could have itself found the means for reconciling French rules and European rules by considering that the national procedure of the priority question of constitutionality did not prevent, in a second stage, the examination of the conformity of French law with a treaty, albeit following the preliminary reference procedure (for an analysis in this sense, see Constitutional Counsel, 12 May 2010, n° 2010-605 DC, notably point 15, in which the court formulates its own analysis of the preliminary reference posed by the Court of Cassation to the Court of Justice). Instead, the Court of Cassation refused to submit the priority question of constitutionality to the Constitutional Council and found itself obliged to make a preliminary reference to the Court of Justice. The explanation for this attitude must, it seems to us, be sought in French law. Whatever interpretation we seek to give to Articles 23-2 and 23-5 of the *ordonnance* of 7 November 1958 cited above, as modified by the institutional law of 10 December 2009, it seems difficult to avoid seeing in it a desire to proritise the order of the examination of questions of constitutionality and that of questions of conformity with a treaty when they are submitted to the French ordinary or administrative courts (on this point, see our discussions *supra*, p. 138). Naturally, this order is only procedural in nature. Nonetheless, it signals a preference for the formulation in time of domestic legal solutions (the review of constitutionality) over solutions of international or European law (the review of conformity with a treaty). The chronology that the French legislature wanted to impose regulates nothing in a context of global legal pluralism in which a prioritisation established on one level (here national) may be misused at another level by another hierarchical structure. This is what the French Court of Cassation wished to evoke in seeking, through the application of the provisions of the TFEU that offered it that possibility, the Court of Justice's interpretation of European Union law.

The Court of Justice delivered its decision in an effort to clear the way for reconciliation between the domestic constitutionality proceedings and the demands of European law limiting the institutional and procedural autonomy of the Member States (Cases C-188/10 and C-189/10 *Aziz Melki and Sélim Abdeli* [2010] ECR I-5667:

> Article 267 TFEU precludes Member State legislation which establishes an interlocutory procedure for the review of the constitutionality of national laws, in so far as the priority nature of that procedure prevents – both before the submission of a question on constitutionality to the national court responsible for reviewing the constitutionality of laws and, as the case may be, after the decision of that court on that question – all the other national courts or tribunals from exercising their right or fulfilling their obligation to refer questions to the Court of Justice for a preliminary ruling. On the other hand, Article 267 TFEU does not preclude such national legislation, in so far as the other national courts or tribunals remain free: to refer to the Court of Justice for a preliminary ruling, at whatever stage of the proceedings they consider appropriate, even at the end of the interlocutory procedure for the review of constitutionality, any question which they consider necessary, to adopt any measure necessary to ensure provisional judicial protection of the rights conferred under the European Union legal order, and to disapply, at the end of such an interlocutory procedure, the national legislative provision at issue if they consider it to be contrary to European Union law. It is for the referring

court to ascertain whether the national legislation at issue in the main proceedings can be interpreted in accordance with those requirements of European Union law (para. 57).

Proceedings resumed before the Court of Cassation, which persisted and:

Held that the national judge responsible for applying, within the limits of his competence, provisions of Union law, is obliged to ensure the full effect of these norms by disapplying where necessary, of his own motion, any contrary national legislative provision, even posterior, without having to request or wait for the prior elimination of the latter by legislative means or by any other constitutional procedure; Held that, in the special case in which the judge is simultaneously seized of a question concerning the constitutionality of a legislative provision and its conformity with a treaty, he is obliged to implement, where necessary, any provisional or conservatory measures capable of ensuring the jurisdictional protection of the rights conferred by the European legal order; that in cases in which it is impossible to satisfy this requirement, as is the case of the Court of Cassation, proceedings before which prohibit recourse to such measures, the judge must pronounce on the conformity of the provision under challenge with the law of the Union thus disapplying the provisions of the modified Ordonnance of 7 November 1958 providing for the priority examination of questions of constitutionality (Court of Cassation, QPC, 29 June 2010, n° 10-40002).

('Attendu que le juge national chargé d'appliquer, dans le cadre de sa compétence, les dispositions du droit de l'Union, a l'obligation d'assurer le plein effet de ces normes en laissant au besoin inappliquée, de sa propre autorité, toute disposition contraire de la législation nationale, même postérieure, sans qu'il ait à demander ou à attendre l'élimination préalable de celle-ci par voie législative ou par tout autre procédé constitutionnel; Attendu que, dans l'hypothèse particulière où le juge est saisi d'une question portant à la fois sur la constitutionnalité et la conventionnalité d'une disposition législative, il lui appartient de mettre en œuvre, le cas échéant, les mesures provisoires ou conservatoires propres à assurer la protection juridictionnelle des droits conférés par l'ordre juridique européen; qu'en cas d'impossibilité de satisfaire à cette exigence, comme c'est le cas de la Cour de cassation, devant laquelle la procédure ne permet pas de recourir à de telles mesures, le juge doit se prononcer sur la conformité de la disposition critiquée au regard du droit de l'Union en laissant alors inappliquées les dispositions de l'ordonnance du 7 novembre 1958 modifiée prévoyant une priorité d'examen de la question de constitutionnalité').

The deliberate choice by the Court of Cassation not to refer the priority question of constitutionality to the Constitutional Council illustrates quite remarkably the manner in which the lawyer, in this case a judge, can manipulate several legal systems and their respective prioritisation procedures. In the context of this case, two formal prioritisations were at work. One prioritisation established by French law required priority to be given to the procedural treatment of the question of constitutionality over the question of conformity with a treaty (Articles 23-2 and 23-5 of the Ordonnance of 7 November 1958 as modified by the institutional law of 10 December 2009, cited above). Another prioritisation established by the Treaty on European Union obliged national supreme courts to defer their decisions and to make a preliminary reference to the Court of Justice in cases of difficulties in interpreting European law (art. 267, TFEU). In order to escape from the restrictions inherent in the first hierarchical rule, the French judge deliberately placed himself under the thumb of the second hierarchical rule. The legal situation submitted to the Court of Cassation in this case is literally outsourced. It passes from the national level to European level.

As objectionable as this may seem (see, among other analyses, with the numerous works cited: D. Simon, 'Les juges et la *priorité* de la question prioritaire de constitutionnalité: discordance provisoire ou cacophonie durable?' (RCDIP, 2011), p. 1; see for a contrary view, the approach of P. Puig (notably in relation to the institutional law), *La question de constitutionnalité: prioritaire mais pas première* ... (RTDCiv., 2010), p. 66), this attitude is a logical consequence of the existence of a plurality of legal systems. A major institutional actor demonstrates here his capacity to use all of the tools put at his disposal by the different systems to choose to place himself, at one time or another, under one prioritisation rather than another. But this choice was only possible due to the fact that the domestic French judge disposed of a procedural tool allowing him to solicit, during proceedings, an authentic interpretation of European law. This is not always the case, indeed often it is far from it.

The example of the application made to the ECtHR after the exhaustion of domestic legal remedies: the case of the examination of conformity with a convention following a priority question of constitutionality

The situation described above of a national court of first instance refusing to submit a priority question of constitutionality and preferring to have a question of the interpretation of European law examined beforehand is doubtlessly exceptional. Much more frequent, conversely, is the strategy of the plaintiff who, not having (totally) won his case following a priority question of constitutionality procedure (either because the question was not transmitted to the Constitutional Council, or because the response of the Constitutional Council did not completely satisfy the plaintiff) decides, in the same case or in a similar one, to bring the question to the European Court of Human Rights (ECtHR) after exhausting domestic remedies. In situations such as these, two successive prioritisation procedures are put to the test: the constitutionality of French law and its conformity with the demands of the European Convention for the Protection of Human Rights and Fundamental Freedoms (ECHR). This double review inevitably leads to comparative exercises which will not fail to inform the plaintiffs of the best strategy to follow between the two prioritisation procedures. In this manner, the passageways from one hierarchy to another are clearly marked. See on this question, P. Popelier, C. Van De Heyning and P. Van Nuffel, *Human Rights Protection in the European Legal Order: The Interaction Between the European and the National Courts* (Intersentia, 2011), G. Janneke and J. Fleuren (eds.), *Implementation of the European Convention on Human Rights and of the Judgments of the ECtHR in National Case Law. A Comparative Analysis* (Intersentia, 2014).

Before even considering making a preliminary reference to the CJEU or making an application to the ECtHR, a lawyer may anticipate movement from one hierarchy defined on one level to another hierarchy defined on another level by comparing the application of the law in the national context with its application in the European context.

SITUATION – MOVEMENT FROM AN APPLICATION OF THE LAW IN THE NATIONAL CONTEXT TO AN APPLICATION OF THE LAW IN THE EUROPEAN CONTEXT AND VICE VERSA

The example of a solution of national law evaluated in a European context: the interpretation of a decision of the Constitutional Court in conformity with a decision of the ECtHR

The working hypothesis is as follows. Following the priority question of constitutionality procedure, the Constitutional Council pronounces on the conformity of a law with the constitution. It is for a national lower court to draw the consequences from this decision of the Constitutional Court. A question arises concerning the interpretation of the exact meaning of the decision of the Constitutional Court. Rather than contemplating posing a second priority question of constitutionality, the ordinary court may be tempted to read the French decision as having been implicitly or explicitly inspired by a decision of the ECtHR. The result of this move by the lower court is the coexistence of two prioritisation processes for one situation: the first participates in a review of the constitutionality of the national law and the second undertakes a review of the conformity of the law with the European Convention with reference to the analysis undertaken at the European level by a European court. For an illustration of this scenario, in a case of merely implicit reference to the case law of the ECtHR, see the analysis offered by N. Maziau, Constitutionnalité et conventionnalité au regard des motifs de la décision n° 2010-2 QPC du Conseil constitutionnel (à propos d'un arrêt rendu par la Cour de cassation, 1re ch. civ, le 15 décembre 2011 sur dispositif transitoire de la législation 'anti-Perruche'), D. 2012, 297.

The example of a solution of European law evaluated in a national context

A decision delivered by the French Council of State in the *Conseil national des barreaux (CNB)* case illustrates the manner in which national judges arrange, in their reasoning, potential routes for the hierarchisation of laws at national level and the prioritisation of laws at European level with or without recourse to preliminary reference-type institutional procedures (Conseil d'Etat, 10 avril 2008, Req. n° 296845):

Considering that the plaintiffs maintain that the directive of 4 December 2001 and the law of 11 February 2004 that transposed it violated Articles 6 and 8 of the European Convention for the Protection of Human Rights and Fundamental Freedoms as well as the general principles of Community law; Considering, first, that it results as much from Article 6 § 2 of the Treaty on European Union [current Article 6(3) TEU] as from the case law of the Court of Justice of the European Communities, notably from its decision of 12 December 2002, that, in the legal order of the Community, the fundamental rights guaranteed by the European Convention for the Protection of Human Rights and Fundamental Freedoms are protected as general principles of Community law; that consequently it is for the administrative judge, presented with an argument founded on the violation by a directive of the stipulations of the European Convention for the Protection of Human Rights and Fundamental Freedoms, to review whether the directive is compatible with the fundamental rights guaranteed by these provisions; that it is for him, in the absence of serious difficulties, to set aside the argument, or, in the contrary case, to make a preliminary reference to the Court of Justice of the European Communities, under the conditions specified by Article 234 of the Treaty Establishing the European Community [current Article 267 TFEU]; Considering, secondly, that when an administrative court is presented with an argument that the law transposing a directive is itself incompatible with a fundamental right guaranteed by the European Convention for the Protection of Human Rights and Fundamental Freedoms and protected as a general principle of Community law, it is for the administrative court to satisfy itself that the law transposed the provisions of the directive exactly; that if such is the case, the argument founded on the violation of this fundamental right by the law transposing the directive cannot be considered other than according to the procedure for the review of the directive itself described above.

('Considérant que les requérants soutiennent que la directive du 4 décembre 2001 et la loi du 11 février 2004 prise pour sa transposition méconnaîtraient les articles 6 et 8 de la convention européenne de sauvegarde des droits de l'homme et des libertés fondamentales ainsi que des principes généraux du droit communautaire; Considérant, en premier lieu, qu'il résulte tant de l'article 6 § 2 du Traité sur l'Union européenne [actuel article 6.§ 3 TUE] que de la jurisprudence de la Cour de justice des Communautés européennes, notamment de son arrêt du 15 octobre 2002, que, dans l'ordre juridique communautaire, les droits fondamentaux garantis par la convention européenne de sauvegarde des droits de l'homme et des libertés fondamentales sont protégés en tant que principes généraux du droit communautaire; qu'il appartient en conséquence au juge administratif, saisi d'un moyen tiré de la méconnaissance par une directive des stipulations de la convention européenne de sauvegarde des droits de l'homme et des libertés fondamentales, de rechercher si la directive est compatible avec les droits fondamentaux garantis par ces stipulations; qu'il lui revient, en l'absence de difficulté sérieuse, d'écarter le moyen invoqué, ou, dans le cas contraire, de saisir la Cour de justice des Communautés européennes d'une question préjudicielle, dans les conditions prévues par l'article 234 du Traité instituant la Communauté européenne [actuel article 267 TFUE]; Considérant, en second lieu, que lorsqu'est invoqué devant le juge administratif un moyen tiré de ce qu'une loi transposant une directive serait elle-même incompatible avec un droit fondamental garanti par la convention européenne de sauvegarde des droits de l'homme et des libertés fondamentales et protégé en tant que principe général du droit communautaire, il appartient au juge administratif de s'assurer d'abord que la loi procède à une exacte transposition des dispositions de la directive; que si tel est le cas, le moyen tiré de la méconnaissance de ce droit fondamental par la loi de transposition ne peut être apprécié que selon la procédure de contrôle de la directive elle-même décrite ci-dessus').

In order to explain the difference between cases in which a preliminary reference to the CJEU is required and those in which it is not, French courts distinguish between questions that fall under domestic prioritisation processes (no preliminary reference) and those that fall under European processes (compulsory preliminary reference).

C. The Passageways between International and European Levels

Cases of circulation between international and European levels and their translation in terms of the prioritisation of laws are doubtlessly more difficult to identify. There are two main reasons for this. First, international law is, as we have seen, a weakly proritised law, such that the case of movement from a European legal prioritisation to a purported international legal prioritisation appears to be purely academic. Second, cases of conflict between international and European law are so few that recourse to a prioritisation, conceived as a tool for resolving conflicts, is seldom useful.

Nonetheless, a few cases do exist.

SITUATION – MOVEMENT FROM AN INTERNATIONAL INSTITUTION TO A EUROPEAN INSTITUTION AND VICE VERSA

The example of a situation successively submitted to an international institution and a European institution and vice versa: returning to the *Kadi* case

The *Kadi* case (Case T-306/01 [2005] ECR II-3533, struck down by Joint Cases C-402/05 and C-415/05 [2008] ECR I-6351) illustrates, to the highest degree, the review of the legality of a European secondary law text that finds its source in a United Nations resolution introducing individual sanctions (notably the freezing of assets) against individuals suspected of being in league with terrorist movements (see *supra*, p. 142). But if we consider the situation in its totality, we observe that it circulates through different decision-makers ('legislator', 'executive' and 'judiciary' understood in the broad sense) from the international to the European level. This institutional movement from one level to another can bring together different processes of the prioritisation of laws: an international process, at the centre of which a place would be, for example, occupied by *jus cogens*, and a European process, which notably rests on the affirmation of a community of law and the protection of fundamental rights. In *Kadi*, the European Court of First Instance (CFI) was tempted, as we have indicated, to refer to an international process of the prioritisation of law presented as a rival to the European process (Case T-306/01 [2005], paras 334 *et seq.*). The Court of Justice firmly closed off this route (Joint Cases C-402/05 and C-415/05 [2008]: notably paras 290 and 327). The CFI clearly did not (fully) hear it (Case T-85/09 [2010], ECR II-5177:

> the institutions and intervening governments have, moreover, forcefully reiterated in these proceedings the concerns – already expressed by them in the case culminating in the judgment of the Court of Justice in *Kadi* – regarding the risk that the system of sanctions put in place by the United Nations in the context of the fight against international terrorism would be disrupted if judicial review of the kind advocated by the applicant in the light of the judgment of the Court of Justice in *Kadi* were instituted at national or regional level. It is true that, once it is accepted that the Security Council has inherent competence to adopt sanctions targeted at individuals rather than at States or their governments (smart sanctions), such judicial review is liable to encroach on the Security Council's prerogatives, in particular with regard to determining who or what constitutes a threat to international peace or security, to finding that such a threat exists and to determining the measures necessary to put an end to it. More fundamentally, certain doubts may have been voiced in legal circles as to whether the judgment of the Court of Justice in *Kadi* is wholly consistent with, on the one hand, international law and, more particularly, Articles 25 and 103 of the Charter of the United Nations and, on the other hand, the EC and European Union Treaties, and more particularly Article 177(3) EC, Articles 297 EC and 307 EC, Article 11(1) European Union and Article 19(2) European Union (see, also Article 3(5) TEU and Article 21(1) and (2) TEU, as well as declaration No 13 of the Conference of the Representatives of the Governments of the Member States concerning the common foreign and security policy annexed to the Treaty of Lisbon, which stresses that 'the [EU] and its Member States will remain bound by the provisions of the Charter of the United Nations and, in particular, by the primary responsibility of the Security Council and of its members for the maintenance of international peace and security'. In that regard, it has in particular been asserted that, even though the Court of Justice stated, at paragraph 287 of *Kadi*, that it was not for the Community judicature, under the exclusive jurisdiction provided for by Article 220 EC, to review the legality of a resolution adopted by the Security Council under Chapter VII of the Charter of the United Nations, the fact remains that a review of the legality of a Community act which merely implements, at Community level, a resolution affording no latitude in that respect necessarily amounts to a review, in the light of the rules and principles of the Community

legal order, of the legality of the resolution thereby implemented. etc., paras 113 *et seq.*).

This particularly convoluted reasoning by the CFI reveals difficulties for judges in organising a prioritisation process that operates in parallel on two different levels – here international and European – although in the final analysis, it is the European process of the prioritisation of laws that is preferred by the European judge. The passageways between one prioritisation and another have not been mastered here. We will see how it is possible to remedy this type of difficulty (see *infra*, p. 165).

It is also possible to envisage a further case.

SITUATION – MOVEMENT FROM AN APPLICATION OF THE LAW IN AN INTERNATIONAL CONTEXT TO AN APPLICATION OF THE LAW IN THE EUROPEAN CONTEXT AND VICE VERSA

The example of the international arbitration decision confronted with a European legal order: the example of the *Eco Swiss* and *Poupardine* cases

International arbitration law could not remain indifferent to the emergence of European law, particularly in its public policy dimension. Thus, in one still famous case: Case C-126/97 *Eco Swiss* [1999] ECR I-3055, the Court of Justice notably declared:

> a national court to which application is made for annulment of an arbitration award must grant that application if it considers that the award in question is in fact contrary to Article 85 of the Treaty [now Article 101 TFEU], where its domestic rules of procedure require it to grant an application for annulment founded on failure to observe national rules of public policy (para. 41).

Having regard to the consequences flowing from the disrespect of a European police law, the international arbiter, if he does not wish his decision to be annulled by a national judge in a European Union Member State, is invited to incorporate into his reasoning the prioritising structures of European law. The difficult question of the method of this integration is therefore posed.

It is this difficulty that is illustrated by the recent *Poupardine* case (French Court of cassation, 1ère ch. civ., 29 June 2011, pourvoi n° 10-16680; for an understanding of the judgment (that cannot be gleaned solely by reading it), see notably the note by P. Mayer, RA 2012, 76). In this case, the Court of Cassation, in less than explicit terms:

> But held that, on one hand, having found that the aim of the dispute submitted to the arbiters was the evaluation of the validity of the unilateral breach of contract by Poupardine, the Court of Appeal, judge of the

annulment, which did not have the power to alter the initial decision, could deduce from it that the arbiters, by, albeit falsely, declaring themselves non-competent for so ruling on the conformity of the agreement refusal decision of Smeg with Community law, taken by the ONIC in applying the national regulations then in force only on the legality of Article L. 211-16 of the Rural Code in relation to Community rules, and by declaring the breach to be legitimate, conformed with their task

('Mais attendu, d'une part, qu'ayant relevé que le litige soumis aux arbitres avait pour objet l'appréciation du bien-fondé de la rupture unilatérale du contrat par la société Poupardine, la cour d'appel, juge de l'annulation, qui n'avait pas le pouvoir de réviser la décision au fond, a pu en déduire que les arbitres, en se déclarant, fût-ce à tort, incompétents pour statuer tant sur la conformité au droit communautaire de la décision de refus d'agrément de la société Smeg, prise par l'ONIC en application de la réglementation nationale alors en vigueur que sur la légalité de l'article L. 211- 16 du code rural au regard des règles communautaires, et en déclarant la résiliation fondée, s'étaient conformés à leur mission')

denounced, without punishment, the excuse of 'non-competence' advanced by the arbiters for not examining the conformity of a decision taken by a French public institution with European Union law. In other words, the Court of Cassation recalled that the arbiters were indeed competent to apply European law, in this case relating to public policy, albeit it was another matter to examine whether, in this case, the violation of the European rule could change the outcome of the dispute.

The example of a solution of European law (EU) evaluated in an international context: returning to the handling of a complaint submitted to the DRB

As the European Union, along with its Member States, is a party to the WTO, European regulation may be evaluated in light of the demands of international trade rules before the DRB. Incidentally, this scenario is common. The European Union has thus participated, as a defendant, in more than 70 sets of proceedings. That which has already been said in relation to national law (see *supra*, p. 166) may also be true for European law. For an illustration, concerning a moratorium practice that consisted, by the admission of the European administration, in refusing, for more than five years, to approve new biotechnical products 'without scientific or legal justification' (sic), see Report of the Panel, 29 September 2006, *Argentina v EC*, WT/DS293.

2. THE REFERENCE TO A PRIORITISED LAW

It is one thing to proceed to the prioritisation of laws at one level, it is another to consider the place that this prioritised law occupies at another level. Two questions arise in this regard: in which cases is this reference to a prioritised law useful, or even necessary (A) and how can we determine the content and, without doubt, the nature of this prioritised law (B)?

A. The Situations in which Reference to a Prioritised Law is Useful and Necessary

It is probably a truism but it deserves explanation: in order for lawyers to trouble themselves to consider a prioritised law at a level other than that upon which they approach their case, it must be useful to the legal reasoning. Independently of the questions we will consider below (see *infra*, Section B), this legal utility relates to a simple reality that is nonetheless rarely considered as such: prioritised law is useful because it has been, because it is being or because it will be applied to the case in question.

SITUATION – PRIORITISED LAW AND APPLIED LAW

Examples in which prioritised law has been, is being or will be applied to a case

Whether the application of prioritised law is considered in the past, present or future (as lawyers may place themselves at one moment or another in their analysis, according to whether they are dealing with a past, present or future situation), the fact is that it does not interest lawyers unless it is likely to affect the case to be dealt with.

Having regard to the different scenarios envisaged previously (see *supra*, Section 1), one could say that the application of a prioritised law is envisaged by lawyers whenever the operation of the law in one context is evaluated, in terms of compatibility, in another context.

Thus, the compatibility of the law applied in a national context, according to the prioritising structures defined at national level, may be measured in an international context (in the framework of proceedings before the ICJ or the DRB, for example) and in a European context (EU or ECHR). More rarely, we may envisage the inverse case in which the compatibility of a law applied in an international context (for example, international arbitration) or a European context (EU or ECHR) is evaluated in a national context (for example, on the occasion of the adoption of a rule or a national decision of execution). In certain specific cases, the compatibility of the law applied in a European context may be evaluated in an international context (proceedings before the DRB against the EU) or in another European context (EU-ECHR). In very rare cases, finally, the compatibility of the law applied in an international context (for example, UN, international arbitration) may be judged, at least indirectly, in a European context (EU or ECHR).

Of the different situations highlighted by the pathways from one prioritisation to another, some clearly give a more important place to prioritised laws than others.

The situations in which reference to a prioritised law may be seen by lawyers to be a necessity intersect with those in which a limitation on circulation exists. This limitation on circulation, which we have already encountered in relation to the combination of laws (see *supra*, Part II), intervenes from time to time in the process of the prioritisation of laws. When this limit exists, lawyers are prompted, more than in all other situations, to refer to a prioritised law.

SITUATION – PRIORITISED LAW AND LIMITATIONS ON CIRCULATION

Examples in which a prioritised law is subject to a limitation on circulation

Among the different situations envisaged on the subject of movement from one prioritisation to another (see *supra*, Section 1), some reveal a limitation on circulation. Three main scenarios may be distinguished.

The first scenario concerns situations in which the examination of the manner in which the law is applied is a condition of the review of a case of international tortious liability. A notable example is the state conflict raised to the status of an interstate conflict before the ICJ or, more rarely, of the handling of a complaint against a state or the European Union brought before the DRB.

The second scenario relates to cases in which an institutional procedure allows a factual relationship to be successively reviewed at national level and then at European level and vice versa. Examples of this are preliminary references to the CJEU or applications to the ECtHR after all domestic legal remedies have been exhausted and their repercussions for national legal orders. In time, when the European Union has signed the European Convention of Human Rights, it will be necessary to add the case of movement from one European level (EU) to another (ECtHR).

The third scenario concerns those cases in which a rule or decision of international law is confronted with a national or European legal order at the stage of its recognition or execution. An example of this is the case of an international arbitration decision confronted with a national legal order (the French, for example) or an integrated legal order (EU or ECtHR). Another example is a decision of the UN Security Council executed within the European Union.

Beyond these cases, the phenomenon of circulation we observed in the previous section (see *supra*, p. 165) does not give rise to such restrictions that reference to a hierarchised law is justified. Thus, the application of the law at different levels without recourse to an institutional vector or the propensity for a legal system to withdraw into its own prioritising structures, without any reference to the structures of another legal order, are not to be envisaged in the earlier discussions.

B. The Determination of the Content and Nature of the Prioritised Law

The question of the content and nature of that which we call here 'the prioritised law' is essentially envisaged by international private law scholarship in rather specific situations. What these situations have in common is that they all feature a judge (from a state court or from an arbitration body) responsible for applying a foreign law that is usually applicable. In these precise cases, the question is whether reference to the hierarchy of norms applied in a foreign legal system is possible and what its terms are.

There are three possible scenarios.

In the first scenario, the question of the constitutionality of the usually applicable foreign law is raised before a state judge.

SITUATION – THE UNCONSTITUTIONALITY OF THE FOREIGN LAW THAT USUALLY APPLIES

Provisional answer and theoretical and practical difficulties

The scenario of a foreign *lex causae* found to be unconstitutional in the state from which it originated calls for a provisional answer, largely tempered by practical considerations. When a national judge, for example, applies a foreign law, the provisional answer dictates that he should not simply apply the law, understood in a narrow sense, implying a mere reference to a legal text (for example, an article of a foreign statute law), but also the law of a foreign legal system, which is to say all the legislative and judicial sources of the law, domestic, international or European, applied in the foreign state. If a conflict arises between these sources, the judge must normally apply the solutions to the conflict developed by the foreign state. If the latter adopts structures of the 'hierarchy of norms' type, the foreign prioritisation of norms serves as a reference and in no case does the French prioritisation of norms apply. In our working hypothesis, if it is argued that the foreign law is unconstitutional, it is obvious that the issue must be considered by reference to the constitutional law of the foreign country in question. No one would consider arguing, in such circumstances, that the foreign law was not valid due to its incompatibility with the national Constitution. This analysis merely expresses the relativity of any structure of the hierarchy of norms type, which authorises, at most, the examination of the validity of norms within the legal system under consideration, in this case in the foreign system (see on this theme, the general study of G. Ferraz de Campos Monaco, *Controle de Constitucionalidade de la Lei Estrangeira* (Quartier Latin, São Paulo, 2013).

This provisional answer nonetheless encounters theoretical and practical difficulties. From a theoretical point of view, it is the legal nature of the foreign law and therefore, indirectly, the legal nature of the prioritisation of norms it contains, that is disputed. Considered for a long time to be a simple fact, a foreign law cannot have the same force as a national law. Thus, the consideration that the foreign law is unconstitutional in its country of origin would have no more weight than any other fact that may influence the decision of the judge. This theoretical obstacle is outmoded. It does not take into account the efforts of lawyers to give foreign law a true legal status, if not equal to that of the *lex fori*, at least approaching it.

These are, in reality, the practical considerations that, still today, hamper judicial review of the unconstitutionality of the applicable foreign law. The authority of the national judge, when he applies a foreign law, cannot be the same as the authority of a foreign judge when he applies his own law. The 'external' position of the national judge when he applies a foreign law means that he is not able to operate all the legal tools that allow the foreign law to be applied in the foreign legal system it comes from. The national judge may encounter obstacles of two orders: an obstacle of legitimacy, regardless of the importance of the means, notably of information, made available to him by the institution or by the parties to the proceedings, the national judge is always less legitimate than the foreign judge when applying foreign law, such that his role can only be more modest; a procedural obstacle, whenever the national judge does not have access to a foreign procedure that allows a foreign law to be applied in whole and in full. This is so in the case of the examination of the constitutionality of a foreign law. If a procedure similar to a preliminary reference to a constitutional judge is in place abroad, the national judge will be excluded from it, unless the foreign law provides otherwise. In any case, the foreign judges, no more than arbiters from elsewhere, do not have access to the French priority constitutional question procedure (cited above).

As fragile as it may be, the situation in which a foreign law is argued to be unconstitutional allows us to lay the foundations for the distinction that interests us here between the application of a prioritisation of norms and the reference to a prioritised law. Faced with the difficulties that a national judge may encounter in operating a foreign hierarchy of norms, his role may be restricted to the application of a foreign hierarchised law. Being unable to mobilise all the resources, notably procedural, of the foreign legal system, the national judge will seek the manifestations, in that system, of a prioritised law, which is to say of a law applied by, notably institutional, foreign actors. Thus, for example, the national judge may come across a decision by a foreign constitutional judge, invalidating the foreign law that usually applies. This decision is a manifestation of that which we call here a 'prioritised law'. The national judge does not directly operate a foreign prioritisation of norms. He refers to a prioritised law, such as it was applied in the foreign legal system by an official actor.

In the second scenario, it may be claimed before a national state judge that the foreign law is in breach of an international convention.

SITUATION – FOREIGN LAW CLAIMED TO BE IN BREACH OF AN INTERNATIONAL CONVENTION BEFORE A STATE JUDGE

Preliminary answer and theoretical and practical difficulties

The same preliminary answer elaborated for the case of the constitutionality of a law is valid in the case of the conformity of a law with an international convention. For example, a French judge applying the law of the State of New York must apply a treaty between the United States and Switzerland, insofar as the situation in question is covered by its scope of application (in this example in which the French judge of first instance considered nonetheless that the treaty in question only concerned relations between 'Swiss citizens and citizens of the United States of America' and not French nationals: Cour de cassation, 1ère ch. civ., 1er février 1972, Rougeron, pourvoi n° 70-11911). This reference to a 'foreign' international treaty (in the decision cited above, the Court of Cassation indicated, directly, that the 'treaty ought to be considered as a foreign law') implies that, in case of conflict with the applicable foreign law, it is the foreign legal system that will deliver the means for resolving the conflict. It is notably for the foreign Constitution and/or case law to say, for example, whether the international treaty is superior to domestic law, even where the treaty preceded it in time. This response naturally encounters the same practical difficulties as those described above in relation to the unconstitutionality of a foreign law. The national judge applying an international treaty in a foreign legal context is not in the same position as if he had to apply an international treaty binding on a national country in the national context. As for the application of the foreign law, his role is different and the review led by the Court of Cassation, for example, would not be exactly equivalent to that which governs the application of national laws or treaties ratified by the country.

This rather general response may nonetheless come up against theoretical as well as practical difficulties. It may be the case, effectively, that the international or European convention that is applicable in the foreign country in question is also applicable in the national context. This has even become a frequent occurrence with the development of European law, whenever the law of another Member State (EU – COE) is declared inapplicable. In this situation, what must the national judge do if, by some extraordinary circumstance, the international or European convention operates in a different prioritising manner abroad than in the national context? Three radically different solutions may be envisaged. The first consists in imposing upon the judge the concept of 'role splitting' (*dédoublement fonctionnel*) developed by Georges Scelle to describe the relationship between the international legal order and the national judge (Précis de droit des gens. Principes et systématique, Sirey (2 t.), 1932, spec. vol. 2, p. 317 *et seq.*) by projecting it upon the case of the relationship between two national legal orders: the national judge who applies an international or European legal text in a foreign context taking into account only the prioritising rules of application provided by the law of the foreign country. This solution follows the *Hocke* case law (Cour de cassation, Com., 4 mars 1963, JDI 1964, p. 806 note B. Goldman and P. Lagarde, *Les interprétations différentes d'une loi uniforme donnent-elles lieu à un conflit de lois?*: (RCDIP, 1964), p. 235): the conflict of interpretations of an international convention introducing uniform law is treated as an ordinary conflict of laws. A second solution is to favour the national prioritising legal structure over the foreign one. This results in the, at least partial, ousting of the foreign law in favour of national law (for the part of the legal solution that depends on the international or European legal text), for a reason to be determined (we think, for example, of a public policy defence at the domestic level that integrates a public policy imperative developed at an international level, e.g., an international or a European (EU or ECtHR) convention; on the phenomenon of the Europeanisation of public policy, see Jerca Kramberger Skerl, 'European Public Policy' (2011) 7(3) *Journal of Private International Law* 461–90, see also M.-N. Jobard-Bachellier and F.-X. Train, 'Juris-classeur de droit international, Ordre public international' Fasc. 534-1, n° 16 *et seq.*; Fasc. 534-2, spéc. n° 64 *et seq.*). A third and final solution would be to have recourse, where possible, to a technique of uniform interpretation, either where the interpretation has already been delivered by an authentic interpreter, or that it may be solicited. We think, naturally, in the European context, of reference to a decision of the ECtHR (already delivered) or of the CJEU (already delivered or delivered following a preliminary reference).

In the first branch of this alternative, the national judge who is obliged to resolve the issue of the conformity of an applicable foreign law with an international convention does not operate a foreign hierarchy of norms. He refers to a foreign hierarchised law, which is to say to the manner in which this foreign hierarchy of norms has been operated abroad by, notably institutional, actors better qualified than him so to do. This quest becomes useless whenever the judge decides to prioritise a reference to his own legal structures (a public policy exception) or defers to an authentic interpretation, or to an international or European court.

A third scenario concerns the position of the international arbiter responsible for applying a national law who considers the impact of the hierarchy of norms as it is applied in the national context in question.

SITUATION – THE INTERNATIONAL ARBITER CALLED UPON TO APPLY A NATIONAL LAW AND THE HIERARCHY OF NORMS

A proposed distinction between conflicts between superior and inferior norms that have been noted, those that may be noted and those that have not yet been noted

One author (P. Mayer, *L'arbitrage international et la hiérarchie des normes* (RA 2011), p. 361) has demonstrated that the international arbiter, when he is obliged to apply a national law, cannot mobilise the hierarchy of norms established by the national legal system in which the law is applied on his own. He must rely on how the law may be applied in the system under consideration. The analysis is summarised in the following terms:

> the duty of the arbiter is not to enforce the hierarchy of norms that is in force in the country in which the law is applicable. This hierarchy is not relevant for him except insofar as it influences the content of the rules effectively in force (p.15, § 22 *in fine*).
>
> ('la mission de l'arbitre n'est pas de faire respecter la hiérarchie des normes en vigueur dans le pays dont la loi est applicable. Cette hiérarchie n'est pertinente pour lui que dans la mesure où elle influe sur le contenu des règles effectivement en vigueur').

Although the author justifies this situation by reference to considerations belonging to international arbitration and a marked preference, in this context, for realistic conceptions of the hierarchical conflict of norms over the normativist conceptions that had been chosen as the point of departure for the analysis (P. Mayer responding on this point to the work of J. Paulsson, 'Unlawful Laws and the Authority of International Tribunals' (2008) 23(2) *ICSID Review Foreign Investment Law Journal* 215; one may wonder whether it would not have been more simple to renounce, at the outset, from a formal approach in order to prioritise a material approach), it seems particularly interesting to us to incorporate his analysis into our own consideration of the application of prioritised law at different levels.

Thus, we willingly take up the three series of cases outlined in this study (cited *supra*, p. 178): (1) the 'situations in which the conflict between the inferior and superior norms does not lead to the inapplicability of the inferior norm' (cases in which the conformity of the inferior norm does not lead, in the country under consideration, to an *a posteriori* review of validity; this was long the case in France in matters of the review of the constitutionality of a law before the introduction of the priority question of constitutionality procedure was introduced in 2009); (2) the 'situations in which the conflict between the inferior and superior norms usually leads the judges in the country in question to declare the inferior norm to be inapplicable' (three possibilities in which the conflict between the inferior and superior norms has already been noted by an authority, has not yet been noted but is obvious, has not yet been noted but is not obvious; in these different situations great attention is paid by the author to the solutions already noted either in the national legal system or in the system that integrates it (EU or ECHR); and (3) finally, those 'situations in which the conflict between the inferior and superior norms can only be pronounced by a special authority in the country in question, and it has not yet been so pronounced' (two possibilities in which the arbiter may or may not make a preliminary reference to a constitutional authority that has the sole prerogative to make such an pronouncement). And the author concludes that, depending on the situation and according to the case, the arbiter is more or less inclined to refer to a law applied according to the hierarchical methods established in the national context of the law he is called upon to apply (see in particular, the systematisation proposed in conclusion).

The position of the arbiter is not wholly different from that of a state judge external to the legal system of which he must apply the solutions. Doubtlessly the arbiter is not subject to his own prioritised legal order and his freedom to act is all the greater for this fact (P. Mayer, article (cited *supra*), para. 7). Nonetheless, it is not certain that the restrictions weighing on the arbiter wishing to operate a law effectively applied in a legal system that is foreign to him (here the national system in which the law is applicable), if only to avoid the invalidation of the arbitration decision by a state judge, are radically different from those that may be observed in different contexts. The scenarios envisaged in the context of an international arbiter applying a state law may usefully contribute, it seems to us, to a more general reflection encompassing the national, international and European jurisdictions responsible for applying a law defined at another level than their own.

Even though it is not referred to as such in these three situations, it is nonetheless the existence of a 'prioritised law' that is truly being discussed here. The lawyer, acting under the auspices of state justice or international arbitration, considers, at the stage of the operation of the national law declared to be applicable, the possibility, the usefulness and, as the case may be, the necessity of referring to a prioritised law, which is to say a law applied in the sense in which we have begun to understand it.

It is therefore necessary to broaden our perspective and to consider it as a whole when a constraint on circulation exists and an international or European judge may encounter hierarchised law.

This perspective encompasses three situations.

The first situation is that in which the compatibility of a national law is appreciated by an international or European judge.

SITUATION – NATIONAL PRIORITISED LAW BEFORE AN INTERNATIONAL OR EUROPEAN JUDGE

The state pleading the content of its prioritised national law

Whether we are concerned with a state conflict elevated to the status of an interstate conflict before the ICJ (as was the case in *Diallo*, cited above), a complaint against a state brought before the DRB (as was the case in the *United States v China*, cited above), an appeal to the ECtHR (several examples have been given), an application to the CJEU (idem), in all these situations the state party to the proceedings may be put to proof of the content of its national law. Whenever the question is posed, more or less, in terms of the compatibility of the national law with an applicable international or European law, the debate is often the occasion for a discussion of the substance of the national law and, as the case may be (but more and more frequently), on the manner in which it has been, is, or, as the case may be, will be applied.

This potential reference to an applied law may integrate considerations drawn from the manner in which the hierarchy of norms has been, is, or will eventually be put in motion at national level. The content of this applied prioritised law naturally depends on what national positive law provides. A discussion may take place on its meaning and impact. But what matters most is the value that will be given to this national prioritised law at international or European level.

In responding to this question, the temptation to reduce national law to a mere fact is strong (on this practice of avoidance, see our discussion *supra*, p. 140). Without being false, naturally, the assertion is a little short, if not to say frustrating. It does not take into account the process through which this fact materialises. Now, if in the national context, this process is legal and, notably, if it implicates a structure of the 'hierarchy of norms' type, lawyers placed on another level, international or European, must be able to consider it as such, that is to say to see a discussion open before him, a debate on the manner in which national law is legally made, structured and applied.

The result of this investigation may have consequences at another level. We will take three examples in which the reference to a national prioritised law has an impact at international or European level.

The first example is drawn from the *Diallo* case (cited above). The disrespect by the defendant state of its internal decision-making processes, notably the violation of the law or of the Constitution by the executive power, characterises the existence in the international legal order of an illegal act capable of giving rise to tortious liability on behalf of the state.

The second example concerns proceedings before the DRB (for example China – Measures Affecting the Protection and Enforcement of Intellectual Property Rights, WTO, Report of the Panel, 26 January 2009, *United States v China*, WT/DS362, cited above). In such a case, the problem may be grasped in two main ways. The first consists of verifying whether the content of the national law conforms to the international agreements ratified by the state in question (this was the choice made by the United States in this case). But the debate may also revolve around the manner in which the law of the defending entity was (badly) implemented (this was the case in WTO, Report of the Panel, 29 September 2006, *Argentina v EC*, WT/DS293, see below). The orientation of the debate is important. It allows us to precisely identify the nature of the dysfunction at the source of the violation of the international obligations concerned and, consequently, the nature of the remedial measures that may be taken by the defendant. Now, this dysfunction may result, at national level, from disregard for a domestic hierarchy of norms (disregard by the law for an international treaty or the disregard by an administration for a law implementing an international treaty).

A third example concerns the exchanges between national and European jurisdictions (CJEU – ECtHR). The most spectacular example is found in the impact of German case law on the decision-making practices of the Court of Justice in matters of the protection of fundamental rights. We know, effectively, that German constitutional case law aided the development of the case law of the Court of Justice in this field. Refusing, at first, to give full effect to European law on the grounds that it did not fully guarantee fundamental rights (decision known by the name of *Solange I*, delivered by the German constitutional court in 1974 (BVERFGE 37, 271)), the German constitutional court provoked an abundant case law from the Court of Justice protective of fundamental rights and relying, notably, upon the famous European Convention for the Protection of Human Rights and Fundamental Freedoms. This European case law is clearly an example of the taking into account at European level of a hierarchical structure established at national level, as a reaction to a European hierarchical provision that was then incomplete. Moreover, one author has suggested that this famous case serves as a general method for resolving conflicts of procedures brought before judges belonging to different levels (N. Lavranos, *Jurisdictional Competition Selected Cases in International and European Law* (Europa Law, 2009), especially pp. 72 *et seq.*).

The second situation is that in which the compatibility of a European law is examined by an international judge.

SITUATION – EUROPEAN PRIORITISED LAW BEFORE A NATIONAL, INTERNATIONAL OR (BY EXTENSION) ANOTHER EUROPEAN JUDGE

The European Union as a guarantor of the content of European prioritised law

Let us take three examples to illustrate the manner in which European Union law can present itself as a prioritised law before a national, international or even, by extension, another European judge. Before the national judge, the question of the validity of a European secondary law text, for example, may be posed in relation to the European instituting treaties, the Charter of Fundamental Rights of the EU, the general principles of European Union law or the rules of international law applicable within the European Union. In this situation, the national judge is not authorised to mobilise the hierarchy of norms belonging to the European legal system himself. He will therefore inquire as to the existence of a European prioritised law, which is to say the existence, within the European Union, of legal instruments or decisions capable of advising him on the manner in which the prioritisation of norms is there applied. This may consist of a decision delivered by the CJEU deciding whether or not the secondary law in question is valid. We may also envisage the case of a secondary law resulting from an incompatibility between two European laws (an amendment provision). If this prioritised law has not yet materialised, the national judge, if a Member State court is concerned (which is not the case for an arbiter, or an administrative authority not exercising a judicial function, or a judge from a non-EU state), may make a preliminary reference to the CJEU on the question of the validity of the secondary law text (art. 267 TFEU). We have already encountered this scenario. See as an illustration, Case C-366/10 *ATAA* [2011] ECR I-13755, *supra*, p. 46. See, also, on the articulation of this procedure with the examination of conformity with an international convention undertaken by the ordinary French judge: Conseil d'Etat, 10 avril 2008, CNB, Req. n° 296845, *supra*, p. 172).

Before the DRB, the defence position of the European Union is no different from that of a state (see our explanations *supra*, p. 186). For example, in the European Communities — 'Measures Affecting the Approval and Marketing of Biotech Products' case (*Argentina v EC*, cited above), the community institutions of the time had to recognise that a *de facto* moratorium had been applied in the European zone. Concretely this meant that a European administration had knowingly refused to apply a European regulation establishing an approval procedure for biotech products. This refusal constituted a violation of a prioritisation of norms within the European zone. At the international level, before the DRB, it constituted a 'wrongful act', characteristic of a violation of international obligations (The WTO Agreement on the Application of Sanitary and Phytosanitary Measures (SPS) notably).

By extension, the situation of the European Union before the ECtHR will be no different in future (once the European Union has ratified the ECHR). Whether or not it is upheld (see on this point, our analysis p. 158), the *Bosphorus* case (App. 45036/98, cited above) saw the European Union trying to prove, before the ECtHR, the existence of a prioritised European Union law that offers sufficient guarantees in terms of respect for fundamental rights.

In any case, the law of the European Union is presented, in another context, in the guise of a prioritised law that is the fruit of a legal system capable of implementing its own hierarchy of norms and to bear the consequences. The use that may be made of this prioritised law varies widely from one context to another. But in every case, an applied prioritisation of norms is in question. This applied law is most often regarded as a fact – a legal fact – from which the actors, at another level, draw legal consequences from their own system of solutions.

Finally, the last situation is that in which the compatibility of an international law is evaluated by a national or European judge.

SITUATION – POTENTIALLY HIERARCHISED INTERNATIONAL LAW BEFORE A NATIONAL AND EUROPEAN JUDGE

Respect for truly international public policy or *jus cogens* before a national or European court

International law is, as we have seen, weakly prioritised. It may happen, nonetheless, that the elements of the prioritisation of international law are discussed at another level, national or European.

For the national level, the scenario is that in which an international arbitration decision applies a transnational or truly international public policy principle and that this application is incorporated into a state legal order at the stage of the recognition (*lato sensu*) of the decision in the domestic legal order. We have thus offered the example of several celebrated cases involving the incorporation, into the domestic legal order, of a truly international public policy. This operation may be interpreted as an expression of the existence of a truly international public policy of international public law common to all actors in international society. But it may also be analysed as the incorporation, at the domestic level, of a prioritising structure of international law, a structure that is capable of influencing the review of the compatibility of the arbitration decision with the international public policy of the court seized of the matter. The latter, through mimicry, aligns its international public order with that which has been or that which should have been applied by the arbiter on the international level.

For the European level, we must consider afresh the first *Kadi* case in the manner in which it was understood by the European Court of First Instance (Case T-306/01 [2005] ECR II-3533, struck down by Joint Cases C-402/05 and C-415/05 [2008] ECR I-6351, see *supra*, p. 174). In this case the Court of First Instance thought fit to hold that:

> It must therefore be considered that the resolutions of the Security Council at issue fall, in principle, outside the ambit of the Court's judicial review and that the Court has no authority to call in question, even indirectly, their lawfulness in the light of Community law. On the contrary, the Court is bound, so far as possible, to interpret and apply that law in a manner compatible with the obligations of the Member States under the Charter of the United Nations. None the less, the Court is empowered to check, indirectly, the lawfulness of the resolutions of the Security Council in question with regard to jus cogens, understood as a body of higher rules of public international law binding on all subjects of international law, including the bodies of the United Nations, and from which no derogation is possible (judgment, paras 276 and 277).

This analysis was criticised by the Court of Justice for the reasons we have already noted (Joint Cases C-402/05 and C-415/05, cited above). In order to justify this criticism, we may offer an explanation in terms of hierarchised law. If the Court of First Instance contradicts itself when it affirms that it cannot invalidate UN resolutions but that, at the same time, it must 'indirectly' verify that these resolutions conform to the highest norm in the international legal order (*jus cogens*), it is because it confuses two very different things. The first part of the phrase refers to a formal hierarchy of norms that commands that a European judge cannot strike down a piece of international law (just like a European judge cannot strike down a domestic legal norm). The second part of the phrase evokes the existence of a prioritised law that, at the moment when the decision was delivered, simply did not exist. In effect, at the time of the first *Kadi* case, we know that no provision existed within the UN allowing persons suspected of being in league with terrorist movements to defend themselves and notably to be heard before the pronouncement of a sanction by the Security Council. By striking down the judgment of the Court of First Instance, the Court of Justice punished the failure to apply a prioritised law to which the lower court thought it had the power to refer.

This case demonstrates that reference to a prioritised law can be perceived to be a requirement of applied global legal pluralism. Now, this prioritised law can only exist if it is applied.

9. Conclusion

Lawyers cannot do what they like when they like in a global context. But they may – and often they must when their own liability is in the balance – learn to explore the mysteries of a plurality of laws: several national, international and European laws applying to the same situation, and several national, international and European contexts in which these laws may be implemented.

In order to attempt to present and to illustrate the many ways in which the law operates, it is necessary to look at it from a different perspective. Rather than considering this operation upstream, through the structure of the methods and solutions capable of grasping global legal pluralism, we must tackle, downstream of these methods and solutions, the resolution of the numerous difficulties with which lawyers are confronted when they are called upon to apply the law. As was said in the introduction, it is less the definition of the law that is at the heart of this work and more the explanation of the work of lawyers in a context of global legal pluralism.

This change of perspective has important implications. In order to compare and, as the case may be, combine and prioritise the laws present and the contexts in which they are implemented, it is necessary to break out of the existing categories. The methods and solutions of national law, of international law and of European law (which may be articulated, notably, around the public-private distinction and numerous legal specialties) are no longer understood separately. They are envisaged together, on a single plane, having regard to the effects they are capable of producing when they are found to coexist on the occasion of the treatment of a situation.

But the objective is not to abuse them. National law, international law (transnational, public and private) and European law (EU and ECHR), notably, expand through this operation, insofar as they all potentially occupy a place in the process of the application of law in the national, international and European context.

This open process of the treatment of legal cases and situations, of which lawyers must be conscious, in passing from one context – national, international or European – to another, exerts in spite of all an influence on the uses of the law and, sometimes, on its content.

Five main operations have thus successively been undertaken in this work which culminate in the affirmation of an applied and hierarchised law: (1) a multilevel comparison in which the search for applied legal methods and solutions takes place in a national, international and European context; (2) the definition of a legal frame of reference allowing, for a given case, the whole of the legal methods and solutions applied on different levels to be identified; (3) the search for complementary relationships, particularly of implementation, capable of characterising the relationship between these methods and solutions; (4) the identification of restrictions on circulation which demand that a situation pass from one level to another and, finally; (5) the materialisation of a law applied on another level, which is to say, in its most complete form, the affirmation of a prioritised law.

The goal of these operations and, definitively, of this applied global legal pluralism is to clarify and orientate the analysis of lawyers whenever the legal case or situation they have to resolve involves several laws applied in the national, international and European context.

Analytical table of situations and examples used

SITUATION – NATIONAL, INTERNATIONAL OR EUROPEAN CLASSIFICATIONS

An example concerning goods: the case of medicines

An example concerning contracts: the distinction between the sale of goods and the provision of services

An example concerning persons: the definition of a child

An example concerning legal situations: the distinction between domestic situations and international or European situations

SITUATION – UNIVERSAL CLASSIFICATIONS AND PARTICULAR CLASSIFICATIONS

An example concerning persons: returning to the definition of a child

SITUATION – AUTONOMOUS CLASSIFICATIONS AND DEPENDENT CLASSIFICATIONS

An example concerning contracts: returning to the distinction between the contract for sale of goods and the contract for services

SITUATION – SUPPLEMENTARY CLASSIFICATIONS AND IMPERATIVE CLASSIFICATIONS

Two examples concerning arbitration and the contract for sale of goods

SITUATION – THE LOCATION OF CASES IN SPACE

Examples of the criteria used to locate a case in space

SITUATION – THE EXISTENCE OF RULES OF GEOGRAPHIC APPLICABILITY

A few examples from national, international and European law

SITUATION – THE SCOPE OF APPLICABILITY OF INSTITUTIONAL LAWS

Examples concerning national, international or European courts

SITUATION – THE APPLICABILITY IN SPACE OF MATERIAL RULES AND RULES OF CONFLICTS OF LAWS AND JURISDICTIONS

Examples of solutions in national, international and European law

SITUATION – ON THE SUBJECT OF SO-CALLED UNIVERSAL AND SELF-LIMITED APPLICABILITY

Examples of solutions in national, international and European law

SITUATION – OPTIONAL OR MANDATORY APPLICABILITY

Examples of solutions in contract law

SITUATION – THE QUESTION OF THE NON-RETROACTIVITY OF LAWS

Examples of solutions from national, international and European law

SITUATION – THE TEMPORAL SCOPE OF APPLICATION OF NATIONAL, INTERNATIONAL AND EUROPEAN LAW

Examples of provisions on the date of entry into force and transitional law

SITUATION – THE TEMPORAL EFFECT OF THE OVERTURNING OF NATIONAL, INTERNATIONAL OR EUROPEAN CASE LAW

An example of a comparative analysis in national and European law

SITUATION – THE ENFORCEABILITY OF INTERNATIONAL LAW BY A NATIONAL COURT

The example of the enforceability of the New York Convention on the Rights of the Child in the national context

SITUATION – THE ENFORCEABILITY OF NATIONAL LAW BY AN INTERNATIONAL COURT

The example of national law as a measure of the execution of an international obligation

The example of a national law invoked before an international court to demonstrate the existence of a rule of international customary law

SITUATION – THE ENFORCEABILITY OF EUROPEAN LAW BEFORE NATIONAL COURTS

The example of European Union directives that have not been transposed or have been incorrectly transposed invoked before a national court

SITUATION – THE ENFORCEABILITY OF NATIONAL LAW BY A EUROPEAN COURT

The example of national legal traditions invoked before the CJEU and the ECtHR

SITUATION – THE ENFORCEABILITY OF INTERNATIONAL LAW BY A EUROPEAN COURT

The example of the enforceability of WTO Agreements and the decisions of the DSB by European Union courts

The example of the enforceability of international customary law and international agreements concerning transport by air and environmental protection by the CJEU

SITUATION – THE ENFORCEABILITY OF EUROPEAN LAW BEFORE AN INTERNATIONAL COURT

The example of the enforceability of European law by the WTO dispute resolution body

The example of European law invoked before the International Court of Justice

SITUATION –VERTICAL ENFORCEABILITY

The example of a national public institution confronted with the requirements of international or European law

SITUATION – HORIZONTAL ENFORCEABILITY

The example of the horizontality of human rights and economic freedom of movement

SITUATION – DIRECT EFFECT, SELF-EXECUTING CHARACTER OR IMMEDIACY AND THE DIFFERENT FORMS OF ENFORCEABILITY

Examples drawn from the enforceability of international or European law

SITUATION – THE FACTUAL EFFECT, THE MANDATORY EFFECT AND THE OPPOSABLE EFFECT

Examples regarding the 'factual effect' in national, international and European law

Examples relating to the distinction between 'mandatory effect' and 'opposable effect' in international and European law

SITUATION – BASIC PRINCIPLES GOVERNING THE INTERPRETATION OF CONTRACTS

Examples from French, English and international law

SITUATION – PRINCIPLES OF INTERPRETATION DEVELOPED IN EUROPEAN UNION LAW

Example of the theory of 'useful effect'

SITUATION – INSTRUMENTS WITH INTERPRETIVE VALUE

Examples from national, international and European law

SITUATION – THE PRESENCE OF PRIVILEGED INTERPRETERS

Examples from national, international and European law

SITUATION – THE USE OF THE SAME LEGAL TERM IN THE NATIONAL, INTERNATIONAL AND EUROPEAN CONTEXT

The example of the term 'constitution'

The example of the term 'codification'

SITUATION – EUROPEAN LAW OUT OF ITS USUAL CONTEXT

The example of European food law projected on national private law constructs

The example of the European internal market compared with international rules on free trade

SITUATION – NATIONAL LAW OUT OF ITS USUAL CONTEXT

The example of the interpretation of national law in the context of European human rights protections

SITUATION – INTERNATIONAL LAW OUT OF ITS USUAL CONTEXT

The example of international public order

SITUATION – THE APPLICATION OF A LAW ORIGINATING FROM ANOTHER CONTEXT BY NATIONAL, INTERNATIONAL OR EUROPEAN INSTITUTIONS

The example of the application of international and/or European law by national institutions

The example of the application of a national law by an international or European institution

The example of the application of international law by a European institution

The example of the application of European law by an international institution

SITUATION – INSTITUTIONAL COMPLEMENTARITY ESTABLISHED AS A PRINCIPLE

The example of the relations between the International Court of Justice and the judges of Member States

SITUATION – INSTITUTIONAL COMPLEMENTARITY GOVERNED BY COORDINATING RULES

The example of the relationship between international arbitration and state justice

SITUATION – THE RARE CASE OF THE COMBINATION OF NATIONAL LAWS

An example from national case law

SITUATION – THE MOST COMMON CASES OF THE COMBINATION OF NATIONAL AND INTERNATIONAL LAW

The historical example of the *Boll* decision of the International Court of Justice

SITUATION – OTHER CASES OF THE COMBINATION OF NATIONAL, INTERNATIONAL AND EUROPEAN LAW

An example of the combination of national, international and European law in relation to transportation

An example of the combination of national, international and European law in the area of the protection of cultural objects

An example of the combination of national, international and European law in the area of the protection of fundamental rights

SITUATION – THE EXECUTION OF INTERNATIONAL OR EUROPEAN LAW BY NATIONAL INSTITUTIONS

The execution of international law: the example of the incorporation of international treaties into the national legal order

The execution of European law: examples of the recognition of institutional or procedural autonomy of European Union Member States and the transposition of directives

SITUATION – THE EXECUTION OF INTERNATIONAL LAW BY EUROPEAN INSTITUTIONS

The execution of international law: the example of the implementation of international law by the European Union institutions

SITUATION – THE EXECUTION OF INTERNATIONAL LAW BY EUROPEAN AND NATIONAL INSTITUTIONS

The execution of international law: the example of the organisation of the relationships between national and European institutions in cases of mixed agreements

SITUATION – COOPERATION BETWEEN NATIONAL, INTERNATIONAL AND EUROPEAN INSTITUTIONS

An example of cooperation between national, international and European institutions in the area of trademark law

An example of cooperation between national, international and European institutions in relation to the fight against terrorism

SITUATION – INTERNATIONAL JUDICIAL COOPERATION IN CIVIL AND CRIMINAL MATTERS

Example drawn from the application of the European right to due process in the context of the European Union law of judicial cooperation in civil matters

An example drawn from the application of the European right to due process in the context of the European Union law of judicial cooperation in criminal matters

SITUATION – EUROPEAN FREEDOM OF MOVEMENT

Example drawn from the application of national law by European Union law on freedom of movement

SITUATION – THE SEARCH FOR AN EQUIVALENT EFFECT

The example of the identification of an international custom having regard to the solutions applied on the national and European levels

The example of the formulation of general principles of European law from national legal traditions and the principles of international law

The example of the equivalent interpretation of the ECHR and the CFREU

SITUATION – THE SEARCH FOR A DIFFERENT EFFECT

The example (again) of the development of general legal principles

SITUATION – THE SEARCH FOR A GLOBAL EFFECT

Examples of the taking into account the application of domestic law in the international or European context

Examples of international law taken into account in the European context

Examples of taking into account in the international context of European law

Examples of taking into account in the national context of international and European law

SITUATION – THE SEARCH FOR A LIMITED EFFECT

Examples of judicial subsidiarity, notably in relation to the principle of proportionality in European case law

Examples drawn from the reading of the principle of speciality by the International Court of Justice

Examples drawn from national case law elaborated in a strongly internationalised context

SITUATION – EARLY APPROACHES TO THE CIRCULATION OF SITUATIONS

Examples of the circulation of legal situations

SITUATION – THE DEFINITION OF A LEGAL FRAMEWORK OF REFERENCE BY JUDGES

Examples from European case law

Examples from international and national case law

SITUATION – CIRCULATION BETWEEN NATIONAL SPACES

The case of the mobile conflict

The example of the recognition of foreign judicial or extrajudicial public legal instruments and judgments

The example of the recognition of a factual situation constituted abroad

SITUATION – CIRCULATION IN THE INTERNATIONAL CONTEXT

An example of circulation between international institutions: the relationship between the United Nations and the International Criminal Court

SITUATION – CIRCULATION IN THE EUROPEAN CONTEXT

Examples of circulation between the institutions of the Council of Europe and the European Union

SITUATION – THE CIRCULATION OF SITUATIONS BETWEEN NATIONAL COURTS AND INTERNATIONAL AND EUROPEAN COURTS

Example of circulation between a national court and the International Court of Justice

Example of circulation between national courts and the Court of Justice of the European Union or the European Court of Human Rights

Example of circulation from national level to European level: a national decision nullifying a European intellectual property right

Example of circulation between national, European and international courts

SITUATION – THE CIRCULATION OF SITUATIONS BETWEEN BETWEEN INTERNATIONAL ARBITRATION AND STATE JUSTICE

The example of international commercial arbitration

SITUATION – THE CIRCULATION OF LEGAL METHODS AND SOLUTIONS BETWEEN NATIONAL AND INTERNATIONAL OR EUROPEAN LEVELS

The example of the theoretical discussions on the incorporation of international and European law into national legal orders (monism, dualism, pluralism) and the question of whether circulation takes place

Examples of circulation from the national level to the international level: the application of a national law evaluated in an international or European law context

Another example: global circulation and contractual models inspired by the practice of international lawyers and their application in different national contexts

SITUATION – THE CIRCULATION OF LEGAL METHODS AND SOLUTIONS BETWEEN INTERNATIONAL AND EUROPEAN LEVELS

Examples of legal circulation from the international level to the European level: the phenomena of overlap and mimicry

SITUATION – THE CIRCULATION OF LEGAL METHODS AND SOLUTIONS BETWEEN INTERNATIONAL AND EUROPEAN LEVELS

The example of legal circulation from the European level to the international level: the participation of the European Union in the work of the United Nations

SITUATION – LEGAL CIRCULATION AT NATIONAL LEVEL AND DISTORTION BETWEEN LAWS THAT ARE APPLICABLE AND THOSE THAT ARE ENFORCEABLE

The example of recognition (again)

The example of the effects produced by foreign police laws

SITUATION – LEGAL CIRCULATION AT EUROPEAN LEVEL AND DISTORTION BETWEEN LAWS THAT ARE APPLICABLE AND THOSE THAT MAY BE INVOKED

A historical example: the enforceability of the ECHR before the Court of Justice of the European Communities

More recent examples: the enforceability of foreign multilateral or bilateral international legal instruments before European courts

SITUATION – LEGAL CIRCULATION AT EUROPEAN LEVEL AND DISTORTION BETWEEN LAWS THAT ARE APPLICABLE AND THOSE THAT ARE ENFORCEABLE

An example: the question of enforceability before international jurisdictions of a regional character

SITUATION – SUPREMACY OF NATIONAL PROVISIONS

The example of French case law

A comparative overview

SITUATION – THE UNENFORCEABILITY OF NATIONAL LAW IN THE INTERNATIONAL LEGAL ORDER

The example of the *Treatment of Polish Nationals in Danzig* case law

SITUATION – THE UNENFORCEABILITY OF NATIONAL LAW IN THE EUROPEAN (EU) CONTEXT

The example of the *Internationale Handelsgesellschaft* and *Commission v Grand Duché* case law

SITUATION – THE NON-OPPOSABILITY OF EUROPEAN LAW IN THE INTERNATIONAL CONTEXT

The example of the ICSID decision in *AES Summit Generation LTD and others v Hungary*

SITUATION – THE LEGALITY OF EUROPEAN LAW FROM AN INTERNATIONAL SOURCE IN EUROPEAN UNION LAW

The example of the *Kadi* case

SITUATION – THE FRENCH INTERPRETATION OF INTERNATIONAL CONVENTIONS TO WHICH FRANCE IS A PARTY

Multiple examples from case law

SITUATION – THE INCORPORATION OF EUROPEAN LAW INTO FRENCH LAW (EU OR ECHR)

A few examples from case law

SITUATION – THE APPROPRIATION BY DOMESTIC LAW OF NOTIONS OF INTERNATIONAL AND EUROPEAN LAW

The example of public order: returning to the *Banque Africaine de Développement* case

The example of general legal principles: the *KPMG* case

SITUATION – THE PROCEDURAL ROUTES FOR THE WITHDRAWAL OF THE FRENCH LEGAL SYSTEM INTO ITSELF

The example of the 'priority' character of questions of constitutionality in France

The example of the absence of a preliminary reference

SITUATION – THE INDIVIDUALISATION OF A EUROPEAN LAW INSPIRED BY INTERNATIONAL LAW

Examples from the early days of today's European structure

SITUATION – THE PRE-EMPTION OF INTERNATIONAL LAW BY EUROPEAN LAW

The example of the Hague Protocol on the Law Applicable to Maintenance Obligations (2007)

SITUATION – THE WITHHOLDING OF DIRECT EFFECT FROM INTERNATIONAL LEGAL NORMS LIKELY TO INTERFERE WITH EUROPEAN UNION LAW

Examples of WTO Agreements, the Kyoto Protocol and the Montego Bay Convention

SITUATION – THE SPLITTING OF INTERNATIONAL AND EUROPEAN LAW

The example of disconnection clauses

SITUATION – INTERNATIONAL AND REGIONAL HUMAN RIGHTS LITIGATION AND CHOICE OF FORUM

The example of the *Georgia v Russia* case

SITUATION – MULTIPLE NATIONAL AND INTERNATIONAL JUDGES IN CRIMINAL MATTERS

The judicial repartition of the penal field and choice of court

SITUATION – THE DEVELOPMENT OF MULTILEVEL PROCEDURES IN ECONOMIC AND ENVIRONMENTAL LAW

Returning to multiple-front strategies

SITUATION – COMPETITION BETWEEN INTERNATIONAL OR REGIONAL JURISDICTIONS AND CONFLICTS OF PROCEEDINGS

Returning to the *Mox Factory, Iron Rhine Railway* and *Bosphorus* cases

SITUATION – DIFFERENCES BETWEEN THE PROCEDURAL RULES GOVERNING DIFFERENT JURISDICTIONS AT DIFFERENT LEVELS

Examples of procedural rules limiting the freedom for plaintiffs to choose a court

A particular case: actions for annulment

SITUATION – DIFFERENCES BETWEEN THE MATERIAL LAW THAT MAY BE APPLIED BY DIFFERENT COURTS AT DIFFERENT LEVELS

Practical examples of differences in applicable material law limiting the freedom for a plaintiff to choose a court

Theoretical approach: comparing the methods of international public law and international private law for designating the applicable law

SITUATION – DE LEGE LATA: THE CJEU AND MEMBER STATE COURTS

The example of the constraints weighing on European courts and national courts respectively

SITUATION – MOVEMENT FROM A NATIONAL INSTITUTION TO AN INTERNATIONAL INSTITUTION AND VICE VERSA

The example of a conflict between a state and a foreign citizen, elevated to the status of an interstate conflict: returning to the *Diallo* case

The example of international arbitration proceedings incorporated into a national legal order: the case of an arbitration decision confronted by a national international public policy

SITUATION – MOVEMENT FROM AN APPLICATION OF THE LAW IN THE NATIONAL CONTEXT TO AN APPLICATION OF THE LAW IN THE INTERNATIONAL CONTEXT AND VICE VERSA

The example of a national law solution evaluated in an international context: returning to the handling of a complaint by the DRB

SITUATION – MOVEMENT FROM A NATIONAL INSTITUTION TO A EUROPEAN INSTITUTION AND VICE VERSA

The example of the preliminary reference made to the CJEU and then received by a national court

The example of the application made to the ECtHR after the exhaustion of domestic legal remedies: the case of the examination of conformity with a convention following a priority question of constitutionality

SITUATION – MOVEMENT FROM AN APPLICATION OF THE LAW IN THE NATIONAL CONTEXT TO AN APPLICATION OF THE LAW IN THE EUROPEAN CONTEXT AND VICE VERSA

The example of a solution of national law evaluated in a European context: the interpretation of a decision of the Constitutional Court in conformity with a decision of the ECtHR

The example of a solution of European law evaluated in a national context

SITUATION – MOVEMENT FROM AN INTERNATIONAL INSTITUTION TO A EUROPEAN INSTITUTION AND VICE VERSA

The example of a situation successively submitted to an international institution and a European institution and vice versa: returning to the *Kadi* case

SITUATION – MOVEMENT FROM AN APPLICATION OF THE LAW IN AN INTERNATIONAL CONTEXT TO AN APPLICATION OF THE LAW IN THE EUROPEAN CONTEXT AND VICE VERSA

The example of the international arbitration decision confronted with a European legal order: the example of the *Eco Swiss* and *Poupardine* cases

The example of a solution of European law (EU) evaluated in an international context: returning to the handling of a complaint submitted to the DRB

SITUATION – PRIORITISED LAW AND APPLIED LAW

Examples in which prioritised law has been, is being or will be applied to a case

SITUATION – PRIORITISED LAW AND LIMITATIONS ON CIRCULATION

Examples in which a prioritised law is subject to a limitation on circulation

SITUATION – THE UNCONSTITUTIONALITY OF THE FOREIGN LAW THAT USUALLY APPLIES

Provisional answer and theoretical and practical difficulties

SITUATION – FOREIGN LAW CLAIMED TO BE IN BREACH OF AN INTERNATIONAL CONVENTION BEFORE A STATE JUDGE

Preliminary answer and theoretical and practical difficulties

SITUATION – THE INTERNATIONAL ARBITER CALLED UPON TO APPLY A NATIONAL LAW AND THE HIERARCHY OF NORMS

A proposed distinction between conflicts between superior and inferior norms that have been noted, those that may be noted and those that have not yet been noted

SITUATION – NATIONAL PRIORITISED LAW BEFORE AN INTERNATIONAL OR EUROPEAN JUDGE

The state pleading the content of its prioritised national law

SITUATION – EUROPEAN PRIORITISED LAW BEFORE A NATIONAL, INTERNATIONAL OR (BY EXTENSION) ANOTHER EUROPEAN JUDGE

The European Union as a guarantor of the content of European prioritised law

SITUATION – POTENTIALLY HIERARCHISED INTERNATIONAL LAW BEFORE A NATIONAL AND EUROPEAN JUDGE

Respect for truly international public policy or *jus cogens* before a national or European court

Selected bibliography (monographs and edited books)

Abraham, R., Droit international, droit communautaire et droit français: Hachette supérieur, 1989.

Allard, J. and A. Garapon, Les juges dans la mondialisation: Paris, Seuil, 2005.

Anagnostou, D., *Rights and Courts in Pursuit of Social Change*: Hart, 2014.

Andenaes, M. and E. Bjorge, *A Farewell to Fragmentation: Reassertion and Convergence in International Law*: Cambridge University Press, 2015.

Auby, J.-B., La globalisation, le droit et l'État: Montchrestien, 2nd edn, 2010.

Basedow, J. and T. Kono (eds), *Legal Aspects of Globalization*: Kluwer Law International, 2000.

Basedow, J., *The Law of Open Societies – Private Ordering and Public Regulation in the Conflict of Laws*: Brill, 2015.

Benlolo-Carabot, M., E. Cujo and U. Candas (dir.), Union européenne et droit international: Pedone, s. CEDIN, 2012.

Bergé, J.-S. and M.-L. Niboyet (dir.), La réception du droit communautaire en droit privé des États membres: Bruylant, 2003.

Bergé, J.-S., S. Francq and M. Gardeñes Santiago (eds), *Boundaries of European Private International Law*: Bruylant, 2015.

Bergé, J.-S., Les ordres juridiques: Dalloz, 2015.

Bergel, J.-L. (dir.), Le plurijuridisme. Actes du 8ème congrès de l'Association internationale de méthodologie juridique: PUAM, 2005.

Berman, P.S., *Global Legal Pluralism. A Jurispudence of Law Beyond Borders*: Cambridge University Press, 2012.

Bhandari, S., *Global Constitutionalism and the Path of International Law: Transformation of Law and State in the Globalized World*: Leiden; Boston, Brill Nijhoff, 2016.

Bhuiyan, S., *National Law in WTO Law – Effectiveness and Good Governance in the World Trading System*: Cambridge University Press, 2007.

Bonnet J.-B. (dir.), Traité des rapports entre ordres juridiques: LGDJ, 2016.

Boulouis, L. (en hommage à), Droits nationaux, droit communautaire: influences croisées: La Documentation Française, 2000.

Burgorgue-Larsen, L., E. Dubout, A. Maitrot de la Motte and S. Touzé (dir.), Les interactions normatives: droit de l'UE et droit international: Pedone, 2012.

Callies, G.-P. and P. Zumbansen, *Rough Consensus and Running Code – A Theory of Transnational Private Law*: Hart, 2012.

Carmody, C., F.J. Garcia and J. Linarelli (eds), *Global Justice and International Economic Law: Opportunities and Prospects*: Cambridge University Press, 2012.

Chérot, J.-Y. and B. Frydman (dir.), La science du droit dans la globalisation: Bruylant, 2012.

Collectif, La mondialisation entre illusion et utopie, Archives de Philosophie du Droit: Dalloz, t. 47, 2003.

Collier, J.G., *Conflict of Laws*: Cambridge University Press, 3d edn, 2001.

Darmois, B. and E. Glucksmann (eds), Procédures parallèles et décisions contradictories: Bruylant, 2015.

Delmas-Marty, M., Trois défis pour un droit mondial: Seuil, 1998.

Delmas-Marty, M., Les forces imaginantes du droit, T1. Le relatif et l'universel, T2. Le pluralisme ordonné (traduit en anglais par N. Norberg, *Ordering Pluralism: A Conceptual Framework for Understanding the Transnational Legal World*, Hart, 2009), T3. La refondation des pouvoirs, T4. Vers une communauté de valeurs?: Seuil, 2004, 2006, 2007, 2011.

Delmas-Marty, M. and S. Breyer (dir.), Regards croisés sur l'internationalisation du droit: France – Etats-Unis, SLC, 2009.

Doumbé-Billé, S. (coord.), La régionalisation du droit international public: Bruylant, 2012.

Dubout, E. and S. Touzé (dir.), Les droits fondamentaux: charnières entre ordres et systèmes juridiques: Pedone, 2010.

Dunoff, J.L. and Joel P. Trachtman (eds), *Ruling the World? Constitutionalism, International Law, and Global Governance*: Cambridge University Press, 2009.

Fatima, S., *Using International Law in Domestic Courts*: Hart, 2005.

Fauchald, O.K. and A. Nollkaemper (eds), *The Practice of International and National Courts and the (De-Fragmentation) of International Law*: Hart, 2014.

Forteau, M., J.-S. Bergé, M.-L. Niboyet and J.-M. Thouvenin (dir.), La fragmentation du droit applicable aux relations internationales – Regards croisés des internationalistes privatistes et publicistes: Pedone, 2011.

Frydman, B. and A. van Waeyenberge, Gouverner par les standards et les indicateurs: Bruylant, 2014.
Frydman, B., Petit manuel pratique de droit global: Académie Royale de Belgique, 2015.
Garcia, F.J., *Global Justice and International Economic Law: Three Takes*: Cambridge University Press, 2013.
Gautron, L. and L. Grard (dir.), Droit international et droit communautaire: perspectives actuelles: Pedone, 2000.
Gilissen, J. (dir.), Le pluralisme juridique: Université Libre de Bruxelles, 1972.
Goode, R., H. Kronke and E. McKendrick, *Transnational Commercial Law*: Oxford University Press, 2nd edn, 2015.
Graf Vitzthum, V.W., C. Prieto and R. Mehdi (dir.), Europe et Mondialisation – Europa und die Globalisierung: PUAM, 2006.
Halpérin, J.-L., Profils des mondialisations du droit: Dalloz, 2009.
Hartkamp, A., *European Law and National Private Law*: Kluwer, 2012.
Helfand, M.A. (ed.), *Negotiating State and Non-State Law: The Challenge of Global and Local Legal Pluralism*: Cambridge University Press, 2015.
Hervé, A., L'Union européenne et la juridictionnalisation du système de règlement des différends de l'OMC: Bruylant, 2015.
Higgins, R., 'United Kingdom,' in Francis G. Jacobs and Shelley Roberts (eds), *The Effect of Treaties in Domestic Law*: Sweet and Maxwell, 1987.
Joerges, Ch. and E.-U. Pettersmann (eds), *Constitutionalism, Multilevel Trade Governance and Social Regulation*: Hart, 2006.
Kaddous, Ch., *The European Union in International Organisations and Global Governance*: Hart, 2015.
Kanetake, M. and A. Nollkaemper (eds), *The Rule of Law at the National and International Levels: Contestations and Deference*: Hart, 2016.
Kerbrat, Y. (dir.), Forum Shopping et concurrence des procédures contentieuses internationales: Bruylant, 2011.
Kessedjian, C. and E. Loquin (dir.), La mondialisation du droit: Litec, 2000.
Klabbers, J., A. Peters and G. Ulfstein, *The Constitutionalization of International Law*: Oxford University Press, 2009.
Klabbers, J. and Touko Piiparinen (eds), *Normative Pluralism and International Law: Exploring Global Governance*: Cambridge University Press, 2013.
Klamert, M., Services Liberalization in the EU and the WTO: CUP, 2015.
Ku, Ch., International Law, *International Relations, and Global Governance*: Routledge, 2012.

Lagrange, E., A. Hamann and J.-M. Sorel (dir.), Si proche, si loin: La pratique du droit international en France et en Allemagne: SLC, 2012.
Lavranos, N., *Jurisdictional Competition – Selected Cases in International and European Law*: Europa Law, 2009.
Le Barbier-Le Bris M. (dir.), L'Union européenne et la gouvernance mondiale – Quel apport avec quels acteurs?: Bruylant, 2012.
Lewis, B., R. Maguire, and Ch. Sampford (eds), Shifting Global Powers and International Law: Challenges and Opportunities: Routledge, 2013.
Lhuilier, G., Le droit transnational: Dalloz, 2016.
McLachlan, C., *Foreign Relations Law*: Cambridge University Press, 2014.
McLaughlin Mitchell, S. and E. Justyna Powell, *Domestic Law Goes Global: Legal Traditions and International Courts*: Cambridge University Press, 2011.
Maduro, M., K. Tuori and S. Sankari, *Transnational Law*: Cambridge University Press, 2014.
Marguénaud, J.-P. (dir.), CEDH et droit privé: La documentation Française, 2001.
Menétrey, S. and B. Hess (s-dir.), Les dialogues des juges en Europe: Larcier, 2014.
Mitsilegas, V., P. Alldridge and L. Cheliotis (eds), *Globalisation, Criminal Law and Criminal Justice*: Hart, 2015.
Morand Deviller, J. and J.-C. Bénichot, Mondialisation et globalisation des concepts juridiques: l'exemple du droit de l'environnement: IRJS, 2010.
Muir Watt, H. and D.P. Fernández Arroyo, *Private International Law and Global Governance*: Oxford University Press, 2015.
Olson T. and P. Cassia, Le droit international, le droit européen et la hiérarchie des normes: PUF, 2006.
Ost F. and M. van de Kerchove, De la pyramide au réseau? Pour une théorie dialectique du droit: Bruxelles, 2002.
Paulsson, J., *The Idea of Arbitration*: Oxford University Press, 2014.
Poillot-Peruzzetto, S. and L. Idot (dir.), Internormativité et réseaux d'autorités: l'ordre communautaire et les nouvelles formes de relations entre les ordres juridiques: Petites Affiches, 2004, n° 199 and 200 (numéros spéciaux).
Qazbir, H., L'internationalisation du droit constitutionnel: Dalloz, 2015.
Rigaux, F., Droit public et droit privé dans les relations internationales: Pedone, 1977.
Robin-Olivier, S. and D. Fasquelle (dir.), Les échanges entre les droits, l'expérience communautaire: une lecture des phénomènes de régionalisation et de mondialisation du droit: Bruylant, 2008.

Romano, S., L'ordre juridique, trad. P. Gothot et L. François: Sirey 1975, rééd. Dalloz, 2002.
Ruiz Fabri, H. (dir.), Procès équitable et enchevêtrement des espaces normatifs: SLC, 2003.
Ruiz Fabri, H. and L. Gradoni (eds), La circulation des concepts juridiques: le droit international de l'environnement entre mondialisation et fragmentation: SLC, 2009.
Ruiz Fabri, H. and M. Rosenfeld (eds), Repenser le constitutionnalisme à l'âge de la mondialisation et de la privatisation: SLC, Paris, 2011.
Shelton, D. (ed.), *International Law and Domestic Legal Systems: Incorporation, Transformation, and Persuasion*: Oxford University Press, 2011.
Sloss, D. (ed.), *The Role of Domestic Courts in Treaty Enforcement: A Comparative Study*: Cambridge University Press, 2nd edn, 2014.
Snyder, F., 'Governing Economic Globalization: Global Legal Pluralism and European Union Law', in S.F. Moore (ed.), *Law and Anthropology: A Reader*: Blackwell, 2004.
Supiot, A. (ed.), L'entreprise dans le monde sans frontiers: Dalloz, 2015.
Teubner, G. (ed.), *Global Law without a State*: Dartmouth, 1997.
Thouvenin, J.-M. and Ch. Tomuschat (dir.), Droit international et diversité des cultures juridiques: Pedone, 2008.
Trachtman, Joel P., *The Future of International Law: Global Government*: Cambridge University Press, 2013.
Vanderlinden, J., Les pluralismes juridiques: Bruylant, 2013.
Varella, M.D., *Internationalization of Law: Globalization, International Law and Complexity*: Springer, 2014.
Wouters, J., A. Nollkaemper and E. de Wet (eds), *The Europeanisation of International Law*: TMC Asser Press, 2008.
Young, M. (ed.), *Regime Interaction in International Law – Facing Fragmentation*: Cambridge University Press, 2012.

Index

Introductory Note

References such as '178–9' indicate (not necessarily continuous) discussion of a topic across a range of pages. Wherever possible in the case of topics with many references, these have either been divided into sub-topics or only the most significant discussions of the topic are listed. Because the entire work is about 'operating law', the use of this term (and certain others which occur constantly throughout the book) as an entry point has been restricted. Information will be found under the corresponding detailed topics.